HERE COME THE CLOWNS

HERE COME THE CLOWNS

A Cavalcade of Comedy
from Antiquity to the Present

LOWELL SWORTZELL

Illustrated by
C. WALTER HODGES

THE VIKING PRESS · NEW YORK

Translations and adaptations that appear in quoted passages in
HERE COME THE CLOWNS *have been made by the author from the*
following dramatists and plays: Aristophanes, Menander,
Plautus, "The Farce of the Worthy Master Pierre Patelin,"
"Harlequin and the Hiccups," Molière, Beaumarchais, SHA-
KUNTALA, *and the Kyogen sketch* KUSABIRA. *In their present*
form they are intended for the reading public only, and no
performance, representation, production, recitation, public
reading, or radio broadcasting may be given except by special
arrangement with the publisher.

First Edition
Text Copyright © Lowell Swortzell, 1978
Illustrations Copyright © C. Walter Hodges, 1978
All rights reserved
First published in 1978 by The Viking Press
625 Madison Avenue, New York, N.Y. 10022
Published simultaneously in Canada by
Penguin Books Canada Limited
Printed in U.S.A.
1   2   3   4   5   82   81   80   79   78

Library of Congress Cataloging in Publication Data
Swortzell, Lowell S   Here come the clowns.
Bibliography: p.   Includes index.
Summary: Discusses comedians and the use of
comedy throughout history, from ancient Greek drama,
through traveling shows, to present-day radio
and television.
1. Clowns—Biography. 2. Comedians—
Biography. 3. Comedy. [1. Clowns. 2. Comedians.
3. Comedy] I. Hodges, Cyril Walter, 1909—
II. Title.
GV1811.A1S95   791.3'3'0922   [B]   [920]   77–10115
ISBN 0–670–36874–1

This book is dedicated to my mother, Ora Smith,
for her love,
and to all the clowns whose names appear herein,
for their laughter

CONTENTS

INTRODUCTION

What Is a Clown?

Every family claims its clown. There are clowns in every classroom, every club, and every community; in fact, the impulse to "be funny," to play before an audience is probably buried somewhere inside all of us, however serious we may be on the surface. With most of us, though, once a few secondhand jokes and twice-told tales have exhausted our comic repertory, we begin to appreciate and perhaps even revere the professional entertainer who makes a lifelong career of being funny. It should not surprise us then that in some cultures clowns are considered to be sacred personages who expound the law, explain the order of the cosmos, and may even assume the personalities of the gods themselves. In the past, clowns have enjoyed many of the privileges as well as the enthusiastic patronage of royalty, and today, of course, clowns have gained fame and fortune from their curious talent for making people laugh.

More important than a rubbery face, a fright wig, or a card file full of jokes is a point of view, a way of looking at the world that is different, unexpected, and perhaps even disturbing. This does not mean simply "looking on the lighter side," as we do when we regale our friends with the small comical misfortunes of everyday life. The clown is not particularly interested in making people comfortable; tragicomedy is his real specialty—sharing all his emotions with an audience in a way that often seems childlike and naïve but is really something of an artistic mystery. Clowns themselves, recognizing all the contradictory aspects of their profession, find it just as difficult as anyone to explain how they work, or even precisely what they do.

Oleg Popov, the comic star of the Moscow Circus, devotes an entire chapter of his autobiography to the obvious, and probably unanswerable, question "What is a Clown?" Popov, known as "the sunlit clown," believes that the clown should emphasize the best in the human spirit, and he criticizes the "negative tendencies" on which many of his famous colleagues based their comic personalities. A highly acclaimed trio of French circus clowns, the Fratellini brothers, behaved with such awe-inspiring silliness that they seemed almost to make virtues of absent-mindedness and ineptitude. And clowns have often been cruel and selfish—Mr. Punch of the Punch-and-Judy show is an old example—and, in fact, have displayed "negative tendencies," without being any the less real clowns.

Clowns contain as many contradictions as humanity itself, and as performers they are always at great pains to make those contradictions felt. For to be a clown is to create and to express a total personality. The title of an old play about an Elizabethan jester states it very simply: *When You See Me You Know Me.* A great clown can communicate this comic personality sympathetically and instantaneously, whether he is alone in a spotlight on a stage, or trading gags, insults, and smacks of a slapstick with his fellow clowns, or simply as part of a vast comic landscape, filled with rocketing cars, flying pies, and other perils and pitfalls well known to circus buffs and fans of silent movie comedy.

When Charles Dickens was young he was fascinated with clowns and was constantly asking questions about them. Who were they? Where did they live? Were they born clowns or did they become clowns when they grew up? The answer to the last question, of course, is *both.* The art of clowning, like all comedy, is the expression of an individual, a culture, and of a universal human need.

Even the most original performers are influenced by historical styles and traditions of clowning. A clown's costume and appearance are really only symbols of his comic personality that make his character readily identifiable to an audience, whether he is a modern American circus clown wearing the baggy pants and battered derby of a mournful hobo, or an East Asian clown whose intricate makeup and precisely stylized gestures are part of a tradition many centuries old.

In Japan great clowns are honored by the title "Intangible Cultural Treasure"; but this distinction really belongs to all clowns. As satirists and social critics, their material may be extremely topical, inspired by the latest fad or the morning's newspaper, and just as quickly forgotten; as mimes and physical comedians, their routines may seem to be the spontaneous inspirations of a moment, never to be repeated. But clowns have also been performing many of the same routines (and even telling many of the same jokes) for several thousand years. In the plays of Aristophanes, the great Athenian satirist of the fifth century B.C., or in the comedies of Shakespeare, we find comic observations and situations that still seem fresh and funny. Some of these jokes and classic story lines in fact may be already familiar to us from their latest reappearance in the movies or on television.

Our attempt to answer the simple question "What is a clown?" seems to lead us very quickly into a dense thicket of complexities and contradictions. Clowns are both unique and universal; the art of clowning involves at once spontaneous acts of creation, many years devoted to the expression of an individual comic identity, and many centuries of tradition, imitation, and unbroken cultural continuity. The best way to try to answer this question, then, is to take a closer look at the personalities and performing styles of some of the great clowns themselves, from their origins in the rituals of tribal societies before the dawn of history to the comic stars of the stage, films, and television today.

And so, step right up and get ready to laugh, for here come the clowns!

·1·

ANTIQUITY

Dwarfs, Parasites, Satirists,
Tricky Slaves, and the Clowns
of Aristophanes and Plautus

The comic spirit, in fact the need for comedy, exists in every known
culture. Comedy is probably as old as humanity itself, certainly
older than recorded history. The theater is believed to have originated
in religious ceremonies, and most present-day tribal peoples do not
seem to feel, as we do, that clowning and capering are out of place
in the midst of solemn ritual. Among the Hopi and Zuñi Indians of
the American Southwest, the clown is an important member of the
community, credited with special healing powers and a particularly
close relationship with the forces of nature. In return, he is allowed
the privilege of ignoring or deliberately violating ordinary social
conventions: he may use the coarsest language, play the lowest
pranks, mock the performance of the most sacred rites, without
fearing retaliation, or even loss of respect. He is permitted, even
encouraged, to be profane, boastful, gluttonous, and foolish, to defy
all the standards and customs of his community, since his clowning is
really a skillful dramatic commentary that illustrates and interprets the
laws and rituals he appears to ridicule. The clown's connection with
religion and natural mysteries will be encountered again in the drama
of ancient Greece and medieval Europe; the clown's role as commentator and social critic persists today as a universal element of world
theater.

The clown's first appearance on the historical stage can be safely
dated around the year 2270 B.C., at the beginning of the reign of Pepi
II, a pharaoh of the Egyptian Sixth Dynasty. Pepi came to the throne

when he was only six and is said to have ruled for ninety-eight years. When he was about nine years old, a trader named Harkhuf reported that he had acquired a "dancing dwarf"—possibly a pygmy from equatorial Africa—during an expedition to Nubia (present-day Sudan) far to the south. The young pharaoh was delighted with Harkhuf's discovery, and he dispatched Harkhuf a long, detailed letter, instructing him to bring "the dwarf that dances like a divine spirit" to his court with all possible speed "to rejoice and delight the heart of the King of Upper and Lower Egypt." Pepi promised Harkhuf all sorts of rewards and honors for himself, his sons, and all future generations of his family if he accomplished his mission, adding that it might be a good idea to keep a close watch on the journey down the Nile in case the pygmy should fall out of the boat. As a final precaution Pepi recommended that the trader "put vigilant men around him in his tent and change the guard ten times a night. For I desire to see this dwarf more than the products of Sinai and Punt" (two neighboring lands famous for their silver and gold mines). Unfortunately, after so much advance publicity the dancing dwarf disappears from history at this point (though probably not through any negligence on Harkhuf's part, since he ordered Pepi's letter to be carved on his tomb years later). We can only hope that the pygmy arrived safely and gave a performance memorable enough to delight the heart of the nine-year-old pharaoh.

§ SOCRATES AND THE PARASITE §

In ancient Greece the name "parasite" was given to a kind of wandering entertainer who sang for his supper in wealthy houses—or danced, told jokes, juggled, tumbled, or simply regaled his hosts with flattery, mimicry, and witty conversation. Some parasites were truly talented—it was a parasite who wrote the first treatise on gourmet cooking—others merely persistent, like the famous Zomos or "Soup," so called because he had never been known to miss the first course. At first the parasite's was an honorable calling (the word itself simply means "guest"); however, parasites seem to have worn out their welcome pretty quickly, and they appear in ancient Greek and Roman comedy as spongers and hangers-on, greedy, scheming, and obnoxious.

The Greek writer Xenophon described an amusing encounter

between his teacher, the great philosopher Socrates, and a parasite liberally endowed with both talent and persistence. Socrates and his companions had gathered for a convivial evening of good food, good wine, and good talk. The parasite wormed his way into the banquet, uninvited but intent on monopolizing both the dinner and the conversation. He began to interrupt the feast of reason by mimicking and insulting the invited guests; after a troupe of dancers appeared to entertain the company, he sprang up to supply his own preposterous parody. Accustomed to having the last word, Socrates called for a halt, but the parasite kept on with his clowning, while host and guests— with the exception of Socrates—roared with laughter.

Greek comedy is believed to have developed out of dances and choral recitations that accompanied certain religious festivals. (*Komos* means a "procession of revelers," and we can imagine that these early Greek festivals were a volatile mixture of the sacred and the profane.) In historical times comedies were performed in Athens during the spring festivals of Dionysus, the god of wine, intoxication, and fertility, in an amphitheater hollowed out from the hillside near his temple on the Acropolis. A panel of judges awarded prizes to the best comedy; the lists of prizes that survive indicate that the first comedies were presented in 486 B.C. The only one of these first comic playwrights who is much more than a name to us is Aristophanes. He lived from about 450 to about 387 B.C. and won four first and three second prizes. More important, the eleven of his forty-four plays that survive are the only extant examples of Athenian Old Comedy.

§ ARISTOPHANES §

Aristophanes was a man with a comic outlook on life, but he was interested in serious issues. He was essentially a conservative, suspicious of innovation, and he felt that the former greatness of Athens was gradually being replaced by fakery and mediocrity in all things. To a large extent he was right, the Golden Age of Athens *was* coming to an end; through most of his adult life, Athens was destroying itself in a seemingly endless and ultimately disastrous war with Sparta. Several of Aristophanes' plays express his earnest desire for peace and his impatience with the rabble-rousing politicians and incompetent generals who only succeeded in prolonging the war. Virtually all

Aristophanes' plays are satirical, critical of every aspect of life—from the deplorable condition of politics, philosophy, and the arts, the battle of the sexes, and the conflict of the generations, down to all the familiar problems of crowded city life: noise, traffic, dirty air, and ugly modern buildings. The topicality of Aristophanes' plays makes them seem very fresh and strangely modern—Athens was small enough that his many allusions to people and situations must have been instantly familiar to his fifth-century audience. But Aristophanes satirized many contemporaries whose lives we *are* familiar with. His portrait of Socrates in *The Clouds* is very funny (and quite unfair), making the father of modern philosophy out to be a sort of unscrupulous mad scientist. In *The Frogs* the tragedian Euripides appears to similar disadvantage, for Aristophanes preferred the earlier tragedies of Aeschylus and Sophocles. The unfortunate Euripides was an innovative and original dramatist who was not entirely appreciated in his lifetime; Aristophanes skillfully parodied him as a trivial versifier whose nonsensical declamations are echoed by a mocking chorus of frogs. *The Birds* was Aristophanes' most imaginative attack on the city and citizens of Athens. In the following adaptation of the opening scene, Euelpides and Pisthetairos, two gentlemen of Athens, stagger to the top of a high mountain. They have evidently been walking all day; Euelpides carries an enormous pack on his back, Pisthetairos a couple of pillows.

EUELPIDES Straight ahead?

PISTHETAIROS Straight ahead.

EUELPIDES We can't go straight ahead. If we do, we'll walk right off this mountain.

PISTHETAIROS Let's rest a minute.

EUELPIDES Are you certain we brought everything?

PISTHETAIROS Of course. I saw to it myself. Everything we need: pots, pans, skillets. We can cook the finest meal in the world, fit for the gods.

EUELPIDES But trees don't grow up this far. And we can't cook without logs. Did you think of that?

PISTHETAIROS I didn't forget anything. What do you think you've carried up here but logs?

EUELPIDES So, that's what's breaking my back!

PISTHETAIROS Besides our logs, you're carrying our clothes, our food, our tools, our . . .

EUELPIDES What, may I ask, are you carrying?

PISTHETAIROS *(pretending to stagger beneath the weight of his burden)* Why, these pillows! *(Euelpides takes the pillows.)*

EUELPIDES *(cooing)* I'll share your load, happily. *(More emphatically)* Now you share mine! *(He puts his pack on Pisthetairos' back; Pisthetairos falls face down to the ground. . . .)*

EUELPIDES That's one thing you didn't think of, eh?

PISTHETAIROS I can't move. You've buried me alive.

EUELPIDES Just lie there a minute and listen to me. I think we're in trouble.

PISTHETAIROS Impossible, Euelpides, I thought of everything when I planned this trip.

EUELPIDES Not quite!

PISTHETAIROS I brought the logs, the clothes, the food, the tools, and . . .

EUELPIDES You mean *I* brought the logs, the clothes, the food, the tools, and everything else except these pillows. Let me tell you something, Pisthetairos, you forgot one thing. . . .

PISTHETAIROS *(plaintively)* But I made a list.

EUELPIDES And still you forgot the most important part of any trip. . . .

PISTHETAIROS What's that?

EUELPIDES To find out where we're going.

PISTHETAIROS Oh, I never thought of that.

EUELPIDES And why not?

PISTHETAIROS It wasn't on my list.

(They exchange significant glances; Pisthetairos is on the verge of tears and Euelpides lifts him to his feet.)

EUELPIDES *(pensively)* Unless I'm very much mistaken, the road we're on ends right here. If we go down . . .

PISTHETAIROS *(whimpering)* We'll be right back where we came from.

EUELPIDES Back in our own backyard.

PISTHETAIROS In Athens. And one thing is clear: no matter where we are, it's better than there.

EUELPIDES Anywhere is better than Athens. It's true, as soon as you're out of that city, the air even smells better.

PISTHETAIROS We may be lost, but there's no noise here, no traffic, no screaming busybodies, no neighbor's dog barking. . . .

EUELPIDES *(visibly brightening)* No tax collectors . . . no poets spouting rhymes, no architects building marble columns . . .

EUELPIDES *and* PISTHETAIROS O Athens, hang your head in shame!

EUELPIDES That's right. Athens is a disgrace. We could never be happy there.

PISTHETAIROS We're agreed. *(He nods.)* We're not going back.

EUELPIDES Never.

PISTHETAIROS Never.

EUELPIDES Only one question.

PISTHETAIROS What's that?

EUELPIDES Where *can* we be happy?

> *(Again the men exchange significant glances; Pisthetairos finally breaks the silence.)*

PISTHETAIROS *(softly)* I planned everything else; you plan *that,* all right?

Having left Athens in disgust, Euelpides and Pisthetairos decide to build a perfect city called Cloudcuckooland, in the kingdom of the birds. A chorus of birds obligingly helps with the construction, but as soon as their utopian project is complete, the tax collectors, stone cutters, poets, politicians, and all the other pests of Athens, who are just as disgusted with one another, arrive on the mountaintop clamoring for admission as citizens of Cloudcuckooland.

Satire frequently urges the abandonment of outmoded ways, but in *The Birds* Aristophanes' satire is aimed as much at the folly of reformers as at the abuses they set out to correct. He believed that only a return to the simpler ways of the heroic past would restore Athens' greatness. In the end, of course, Aristophanes was no more successful than his hapless heroes Euelpides and Pisthetairos. In 404 B.C. Athens was finally decisively defeated by Sparta. The city had become a virtual dictatorship, intolerant of criticism. The fantastically inventive situations and critical choruses of *The Birds* and *The Frogs* gave way to a less daring preoccupation with everyday situations. After Aristophanes' death this became the focus of a new dramatic form called Middle Comedy—at least as far as we know, for of some five hundred plays produced in the next fifty years, only fragments survive today.

§ MENANDER §

New Comedy developed and refined the lost Middle Comedy, with a particular emphasis on stock character types in complicated domestic situations. The greatest of the New Comedy dramatists was Menander (c. 342–292 B.C.), the author of over a hundred plays (of which one complete play and large fragments of several others are still extant). Menander drew his characters from the ordinary people of Athens— creating models or stereotypes of almost every imaginable type or occupation—the loving father or the angry father, the honest son or the stupid son, the tricky slave, the braggart soldier, the parasite, the pimp, and the haughty courtesan; plus eunuchs and drunkards, charioteers and stableboys, mistresses and marriage brokers, widows and heiresses, farmers and fishermen, masochists and misogynists (self-tormentors and woman-haters). Menander's style was light and conversational, and he brought these stock characters realistically to life with delicate humanizing touches. His comedies are romantic, and their intricately constructed plots throw one obstacle after another in the path of his young lovers. But just as old comedies often ended with a feast, Menander's plays end with a marriage, if not two or three.

Menander was easily the most prolific and most popular of New Comedy playwrights. His realism was much admired in antiquity— "Menander or life, which of them imitated the other?" a classical critic exclaimed—and his plays were frequently produced and widely imitated on the Greek and Roman stage. A papyrus copy of a complete play, *The Grouch,* was discovered several years ago in Alexandria, Egypt. The title character, Cnemon, is a misanthrope—an embittered old man who despises all mankind, throws sticks and stones at passersby, and snarlingly chases visitors from his door.

A young man called Sostratus, who has fallen in love with Cnemon's daughter, is hanging around the grouch's doorway on the unlikely chance that Cnemon will take a liking to him and consent to their marriage. Sostratus, hardly encouraged by his first glimpse of his prospective father-in-law, remarks, "He certainly doesn't seem to be the friendly type, scowling and shouting like that even though he's all alone. And my gods, what a face!" Cnemon appears, complaining that no matter where he goes, there's always someone around to annoy him. He mutters that if he had the mythical powers of Medusa (who turned everyone who looked at her to stone), "I'd fill this place with statues." Gritting his teeth and clenching his fists, Cnemon continues his diatribe: "Life isn't worth living—if I could get some privacy, I'd hang myself!" Sostratus has heard enough. He hurries off to consult with his father's servant and figure out some way of ingratiating himself with this impossible old man. Cnemon goes back into his house, exclaiming, "What I have to put up with! I'm cursed, if you ask me!"

The grouch finally changes his ways when he is rescued after falling into a well. He comes to understand that he owes much more to his fellow creatures than he had ever imagined. "I guess the one big mistake I made was to think I was self-sufficient. I realize now how little I knew. It seems the only way we learn is by bitter experience." He resolves instantly to stop quarreling with his wife, and of course he gives his fond blessings to the marriage of Sostratus and his daughter.

Menander exercised a tremendous influence on later dramatists. Most of the comedies of Plautus and Terence are adaptations of his work, and through them, Cnemon's literary descendants came to include Shakespeare's Timon of Athens, Molière's misanthrope, and even Dickens's celebrated grouch Ebenezer Scrooge.

§ PARMENON'S PIG §

We have said nothing so far of the actors of antiquity, since almost nothing is known but a few of their names. The Greek biographer and moralist Plutarch tells us a little about one of them: Parmenon was a clown of the first century of our era who became famous for his extraordinarily lifelike imitation of a pig. Parmenon's virtuoso grunting inspired a flock, or rather a drove, of imitators, some of them very gifted, but none as popular as Parmenon. "Very good indeed" was the general verdict, "but nothing like Parmenon's pig!" One of Parmenon's competitors lost all patience with this state of affairs and concealed a real pig onstage, coached to grunt and squeal on command. Once more came the response: "Nothing like Parmenon's pig." The clown triumphantly seized the real pig and flung it into the audience, shouting that Parmenon's celebrity was "judged by opinion, not by truth." This became a proverbial expression, and Plutarch, as usual, was quick to point out the moral: audiences delight in an actor's realistic mimicry of what in reality might be upsetting or distasteful—a man convulsed with rage—or merely tedious or commonplace—a grunting pig. Long before Plutarch, though, the clowns of ancient comedy realized that exaggeration and incongruity played a large part in humor. They consequently made it their business to create larger-than-life characters rather than merely lifelike ones—for example, the ludicrous (frequently libelous) caricatures of Aristophanes, the vivid character types of Menander, and of course, the quintessential, proverbial pigginess of Parmenon's pig.

§ THEATER IN ROME §

Theater began when Rome was scarcely more than a village. When the Romans conquered Greece, as the Greeks were fond of saying, "the captors were made captive," culturally speaking at least: for several centuries Roman playwrights imitated and adapted the plays of Menander and the other dramatists of the Greek New Comedy. But performers of all sorts were welcome in the Roman theaters: actors, acrobats, athletes, dancers, wrestlers, jugglers, gladiators, and mimes. Pantomime was the only form of theater the Romans really originated, and it remained the most popular.

The original pantomimes were improvised performances of mythological stories, sung, danced, and acted on a simple stage, without dialogue, and with a great deal of vigor and vulgarity. (In this connection, clowns and fools were much in evidence.) Like the Greeks, the actors sometimes wore masks. With time the pantomime developed into quite a lavish spectacle; scenery, costumes, and special effects were introduced, and entire orchestras and choruses supplied the musical accompaniment. These Roman pantomimes came to resemble modern operas and ballets, and not the astonishingly simple one-man shows of Marcel Marceau, for example, which we tend to associate with the word "pantomime."

§ PLAUTUS §

The most original and imaginative of Menander's Roman imitators was Plautus (c. 254–c. 184 B.C.). (His name "Flatfoot" certainly suggests comedy, although it might simply have been his real name.)

Plautus came to Rome from Umbria, in Northern Italy, and became the world's first professional playwright, that is, the first to support himself solely by writing for the stage. He seems to have been quite successful—although, according to one story, a brief financial crisis forced him to take a job in a flour mill until he could turn out three new plays.

Even though Plautus borrowed plots and character types from Greek New Comedy, his plays, highly flavored with Latin puns and topical allusions to Roman life, were unmistakably his own. Shakespeare and Molière, in their turn, borrowed from Plautus, and the Broadway musical and film *A Funny Thing Happened on the Way to the Forum* is a mixture of scenes from no less than six of his comedies. Plautus would have approved. His plots are lively and hilariously complicated, his language bristles with wordplay, abuse, obscenity, and especially jokes—good and not so good—all set to the conversational rhythms of everyday speech. In addition his actors were constantly kept active by slapstick routines and chases, trickery, and bits of comic business, with frequent pauses for singing and dancing. Plautus's treatment of the typical stock characters of New Comedy was especially vivid and, once again, many of his finest creations were pressed into service by later writers: for example, the braggart soldier as Shakespeare's "very mountain of a man," Sir John Falstaff. The miser was borrowed by both Ben Jonson and Molière, and the identical twin brothers of *The Menaechmi* reappear in Shakespeare's *Comedy of Errors* and, several centuries later, in the Broadway musical *The Boys from Syracuse*.

Another favorite character who appears in several of the comedies was the tricky slave: quick-witted and unscrupulous, expert at lying, sowing confusion, and, especially, covering his tracks. His treachery and deception are in a good cause—generally helping his young master to get the girl—and with the general relief, and exhaustion, that follows the final unraveling of a Plautine plot, he always escapes punishment, however richly deserved.

In Plautus's *The Haunted House,* Tranio, the tricky slave, discovers that his master, Theopropides, has unexpectedly returned after three years' absence. Meanwhile, his son, Philolaches, has been leading a wild, carousing life and filling his father's house with his noisy drinking companions. Moments before Theopropides is expected to return, Tranio encounters the wayward son and a pack of his friends groping their way to the front door, bleary-eyed and worn out after a night on the town. One of them, in fact, has just collapsed in the doorway; Tranio steps over the unconscious figure and confronts his young master with the bad news.

TRANIO We've had it!

PHILOLACHES *(thickly)* What?

TRANIO Your father's here.

PHILOLACHES That's a good one. I thought you said, "Father's here." *(He slaps his thigh, laughs.)*

TRANIO I did. YOUR FATHER IS HOME!

PHILOLACHES Oh, for the gods' sake! Where is he?

TRANIO *(whispering)* On his way here, that's where.

PHILOLACHES *(shouting)* Who saw him?

TRANIO Me. I saw him. Damn it!

PHILOLACHES You're sure.

TRANIO Sure, I'm sure.

PHILOLACHES Sure, I'm finished. Unless you're kidding me. Say you're kidding, please.

TRANIO *(insulted)* Why should I lie to you?

PHILOLACHES *(pitifully)* What am I going to do? Tell me what to do.

TRANIO Get up and get these others out of here.

(Philolaches tries to lift his fallen comrade, struggles for a few moments, then falls down himself.)

PHILOLACHES My father is coming! Oh, no, my father is coming!

TRANIO *(helping Philolaches and his friend to their feet)* Leave it to me. You needn't worry about a thing.

PHILOLACHES My father is coming! Oh, no, my father is coming!

TRANIO *(guiding the young men to the door and helping them inside)* Quick, get inside and take your friends with you.

PHILOLACHES It's no use. I'm too terrified to move.

TRANIO Just do what I tell you. Can you do that?

PHILOLACHES Yes, I think so.

TRANIO Then make certain the house is locked completely from the inside. Make it look as if no one lives here. Close up everything, especially your mouths.

PHILOLACHES All right.

TRANIO And when the old guy knocks, nobody, but *nobody,* answers. Do you understand?

PHILOLACHES I've got it. Anything else?

TRANIO Just remember what I've said.

PHILOLACHES Very well. My life is in your hands, Tranio. *(He closes the door; the key clicks in the lock.)*

TRANIO *(looking at his hands)* Whether slave or master, it all depends on how well you use your hands—and head. Of course, anybody can get himself into a mess like this, but it takes talent, and a few brains maybe, to get out. And that's just what I'm going to do. *(He looks down the street.)*

(Enter Theopropides, carrying a traveling case.)

THEOPROPIDES Neptune be praised for delivering me safely home! *(Under his breath)* I'll never so much as put my foot in water again. After three years in Egypt, how happy my household will be to see me. *(He tries the door.)* Locked? And in the daytime? *(He scratches his head, and then knocks.)* Anybody home?

TRANIO *(appearing from one side of the house)* Who is at our door?

THEOPROPIDES *(warmly)* Tranio, my slave.

TRANIO My dear master. Is it really you? I am so glad to see you back. How have you been?

THEOPROPIDES But surely something is wrong here. Have you all lost your heads?

TRANIO *(puzzled)* Lost our heads?

THEOPROPIDES Yes, look at you, out in the street, with no one inside to answer the door. I pounded so hard I nearly knocked it down.

TRANIO *(aghast)* You what? Say you didn't? You touched . . . that door? *(He points.)* That door?

THEOPROPIDES It's my door. Why shouldn't I?

TRANIO You touched it?

THEOPROPIDES Yes, I touched it, you idiot. I pounded it! I knocked on it! I beat the daylights out of it. What's so wrong with that?

TRANIO *(lowering his eyes)* You shouldn't have done that.

THEOPROPIDES And why not?

TRANIO Sir, you really touched it?

THEOPROPIDES How the hell can you knock on a door and not touch it?

TRANIO You've done a terrible thing, sir. *(He blubbers.)* You've killed your family.

THEOPROPIDES *(with a start)* I've what? Don't say things like that. *(He pulls himself together.)* Now tell me what this is all about.

TRANIO *(with animation)* A great crime was committed in this house, many years ago, which we discovered only this last year. A guest was murdered inside, slaughtered by the man who sold you this house. And what is more, he buried the poor murdered, slaughtered guest in your basement.

THEOPROPIDES *(after a pause)* How do you know this to be true?

TRANIO Why, your son, late one night, when asleep in bed, suddenly screamed and was visited by the poor murdered, slaughtered guest moving toward him. . . .

THEOPROPIDES This was in a dream, you say?

TRANIO Yes, but the poor murdered, slaughtered guest spoke to him just the same, and said . . .

THEOPROPIDES But in a dream?

TRANIO Yes, in a dream. How could he talk to him when he was awake? After all, the guest was murdered and slaughtered sixty years ago. Pardon me, sir, but sometimes you can be pretty thick.

THEOPROPIDES I won't interrupt again, I promise.

TRANIO The poor murdered, slaughtered guest said, "Because my host murdered and buried me here without a funeral, they will not admit me to the spirit world. Now you move out, for no one may live here but me. This house is cursed!" That's what the poor murdered, slaughtered guest said. And it would take me hours to tell you the strange things that have been happening around here ever since that night.

(Theopropides stands dumbstruck; half-suppressed, drunken laughter comes from inside the house.)

THEOPROPIDES What's that?

TRANIO The door is rattling, sir. *(He faces the house.) He* did it. He touched the door. Not I!

THEOPROPIDES Who are you talking to?

TRANIO Oh, flee, master, before it is too late! *(Laughter is now distinctly audible inside.)*

THEOPROPIDES Why aren't you running, Tranio?

TRANIO Me? Why should I? I have done nothing to disturb the ghost. *(Laughter inside gets louder.)* Say your prayers, sir, and get out of here as fast as you can! *(He ushers the old man away from the door. The laughter rises to an uproar.)*

THEOPROPIDES *(clasping his hands in supplication)* Oh, holy Hercules, I call upon you to protect me from the ghost of the poor

murdered, slaughtered guest. . . . *(He disappears down the road.)*
TRANIO *(turning to the door)* That was a close one indeed. Hey, holy
Hercules, I hope you enjoyed my good work here.

Comedy of this kind, which derives its humor from a situation—
especially such a frenzied and precarious situation as this one—is
called a farce. The tricky slave, the prime instigator of many Plautine
farces, seems to be constantly tottering on the edge of disaster,
clothed only in the shabbiest fabrications and shivering with naked
terror. The comic tension created by Theopropides' unexpected arrival
mounts to near hysteria after Tranio's inspired powers of invention
begin to work on the gullible Theopropides; when the drunken
guffaws from behind the door threaten to expose the deception,
Tranio rises (or stoops) to even wilder flights of imagination. As
usual, this Plautine character type shows up again in later centuries—
Don Quixote's Sancho Panza and Don Giovanni's Leporello (in
Mozart's opera) show the same kind of desperate ingenuity in the
service of their monomaniacal masters; so does Passepartout in
Around the World in Eighty Days. (Even Mary Poppins is a less
excitable English example of the cunning servant.)

The other great Roman comedian was Terence (195 or 185–159
B.C.); six of his plays survive. He was born in Carthage and came to
Rome as the slave of a wealthy senator. His master recognized
Terence's gifts, provided him with a good education, and set him free.
He was introduced into a circle of cultivated Romans who encouraged
him to put his comedies on the stage, and the demanding Roman
public received them enthusiastically. After a number of stage successes, Terence traveled to Greece, perhaps in search of further cultural
polish, and was drowned on the return voyage.

Like Plautus, Terence relied heavily on Menander's comedies, but
he seems to have altered them rather freely (for which he was harshly
criticized by his pedantic rivals). He introduced several important
innovations in technique, notably, a romance involving two people of
the same social class (which, strangely enough, the Greeks had never
thought of) and a narrative built on two (or more) subplots (another
tremendous boon for later comic playwrights, Shakespeare in particular). Terence's style was more elegant and considerably subtler than
that of Plautus—whom Terence admired, by the way, in spite of his
"carelessness." Terence might be thought of as the inventor of the

sophisticated comedy of manners; his characters speak an urbane, cultured language, and Plautine punning and horseplay are conspicuously absent.

Rome produced several great comic writers after Terence, but no great playwrights. The most popular entertainment of the Empire was the circus (the only resemblance to the modern circus is that the audience was seated in a *circle*). In the Colosseum in Rome and the Circus Maximus and lesser arenas in every Roman city, audiences crowded onto high-tiered stone benches to witness chariot races or deadly combats between gladiators (who were usually slaves, convicts, or foreign captives) or against exotic wild animals; the Colosseum could even be flooded to stage mock naval battles, and under the later Empire, free Roman citizens, and at least one emperor, fought in the arena. In the late fifth century A.D. invaders from the north broke the power of Rome forever, and the circus, and for a time the theater, disappeared with the fall of the Empire.

· 2 ·

THE MIDDLE AGES
AND THE EARLY
RENAISSANCE

Mimes, Vices, Knaves,
Jesters, Fools, Simpletons,
and the Clowns of Hans Sachs and Others

FOOL

SIMPLETON

——————————————

After Rome fell, the theater and the circus disappeared; the great cities of the Empire were deserted by the players. The clown survived only as a traveling performer, singing and telling stories, juggling and tumbling in country marketplaces and trying to coax a few coppers from peasants and traders almost as poor as himself. The clown and his company, sometimes consisting of just his family, simply set up a small portable wooden platform and waited for a crowd to collect. They might find an appreciative audience, since strangers, especially entertainers, were a rare enough commodity—but traveling performers enjoyed none too good a reputation, deservedly so in many cases, and they were frequently treated like simple beggars, rogues, and vagabonds and "drummed out of town." Plautus and Terence might not have thought much of their performances, but these wandering players kept the tradition of the theater alive in Europe for hundreds of years.

§ MIMES §

Pantomime artists who were popular favorites in Roman comedy continued to flourish through the Middle Ages, unaffected by the disappearance of theaters, plays, and playwrights. Many of the medieval vagabond clowns were mimes. One of them, aptly named Vitalis (or "Lively"), left a brief biography in a dramatic verse epitaph. Evidently Vitalis was a great success, for he retired from the wandering life to settle down and enjoy his wealth. In his epitaph he remembers how even the tearful and grief-stricken smiled as he passed by, and boasts that "hearts leapt at my name." A gifted character actor, he brags: "When I spoke I so changed my face, my habit so altered, and tone, men thought that many were there where I stood all alone." He specialized in women's roles: "My gestures so womanly quaint, the shy blush done to the life!" He reflects mournfully that a thousand characters will follow him to the grave, and begs that all who read his epitaph might pray, " 'What joy, Vitalis, you gave! Where'er you may go from this earth, may happiness meet you there!' "

§ A CLOWN NAMED BESSY §

Popular theater during the Middle Ages returned to the most ancient traditions of pre-Christian, even pre-Roman Europe. The English Sword Dance play was performed during the Christmas season from earliest times until the beginning of the nineteenth century. Based on some now forgotten pagan ritual, this intricate folk dance celebrated the return of spring and the end of winter, the triumph of life against death.

The dance went like this: six youths would enter with wooden swords which they put together in various patterns to form stars, hearts, squares, and circles. The clown, called Bessy, wearing a foxfur cap with a long tail, introduced himself:

> My mother was burned for a witch,
> My father was hanged on a tree,
> And it's because I'm a fool,
> That nobody's meddled with me.

The Sword Dance continued in solemn, orderly fashion; but the ritual broke down quickly enough as Bessy wove in and out among the dancers, deliberately disrupting their stately dance. When he playfully interfered as they formed the final figure—all holding their swords touching tip to tip to make a hexagon—Bessy would be accidentally stabbed and die.

The dancers mournfully circled the body, each denying his part in the killing and accusing the others. A general brawl was prevented only by the timely arrival of the doctor. The doctor announced confidently that he could cure "all but a lovesick maid" by his art, and with many mysterious passes and impressive flourishes, he sprinkled a handful of snuff over the lifeless figure. Bessy sneezed lustily, hopped to his feet, shook hands with the doctor, and joined the company in wishing the audience a Merry Christmas, adding his own personal hope that everyone present would have "pocketsful of brass and cellars full of beer" in the coming season. This was Bessy's cue to pass the hat and collect enough brass from the crowd to stand the troupe a few rounds before their next performance. Bessy, or a similar clown character, rose from the dead every Christmas for over a thousand years, long after the original ceremonies of a vanished pagan religion had passed out of memory and the ancient Sword Dance had become no more than a high-spirited village entertainment.

§ THE VICE §

Like Bessy, the theater itself was reborn in the Middle Ages to celebrate Christian holidays and festivals. Even after Christmas and Easter plays were no longer performed inside the church and medieval theater had moved to the streets, it retained a strongly religious flavor. The characters in the famous morality play *Everyman* (a late-medieval masterpiece that is still acted today) have names like Good Deeds, Knowledge, Fellowship, and Strength; they are a well-meaning but solemn lot, given to long speeches full of lofty sentiment and good advice. In many medieval plays, including English and Scottish morality plays and interludes, action and comedy were largely the preserve of Vice. His name brands him as a personification of the Seven Deadly Sins, and since to the medieval mind vice and folly were much the same, he often dressed in a court jester's cloak, cap, and bells, and brandished a wooden dagger.

By the late Middle Ages the theater had drifted rather far away from its religious origins, and playwrights had abandoned the restrictive form of the morality play. Vice's energetic buffoonery was finally allowed to dominate whole comedies (while the likes of Good Deeds and Knowledge predictably vanished from the stage). Vice was no longer a manifestation of human folly and mortal sin; in fact, he had taken on several different names and become a very likable jester.

Later playwrights sometimes adopted him as their spokesman to make a particular point or observation. He appears as Merry Report in an interlude called *The Play of the Weather* written in 1533 by John Heywood, the unsung author of dozens of common proverbs such as "Love me, love my dog" and "Better late than never."

In Heywood's gentle fantasy Merry Report is a well-spoken buffoon who collects everyone's complaints about the weather—a miller wants only strong winds to turn his windmill, a beautiful girl only fair weather to preserve her complexion, and so on—and presents a petition to Jupiter, ruler of the skies, who agrees to review the case. Jupiter announces his decision: There will be enough different kinds of weather on different days to satisfy everyone. The medieval figure of Vice, ranting and flourishing his lath dagger, is hardly recognizable as Merry Report, though in later guises, such as Jack Juggler, he gets some of his own mischief back.

§ JACK JUGGLER §

Another English Vice made his appearance around 1555 in a play called *A New Interlude for Children to Play, Named Jack Juggler, Both Witty, and Very Pleasant.* Its anonymous author conceived the idea of mixing the familiar rogue and a dash of instructive morality with one of Plautus's funnier plots: the comedy of mistaken identity *The Menaechmi.* In the original play identical twin brothers are accidentally separated at birth and remain ignorant of each other's existence until they both arrive quite by chance in the same street in the same city. The author of *Jack Juggler* decided it would be both witty and pleasant to improve on Plautus's classic situation.

The rascally Vice Jack Juggler resolves to have a bit of malicious fun with the hapless Jenkin Careaway, a slow-witted, inefficient pageboy who can spend all day delivering a single garbled message. Jack dresses in Jenkin's master's livery and stands in front of Jenkin's master's house, proclaiming that *he* is the page Jenkin and that Jenkin must then be someone else altogether. With relentless wit and baffling logic, driven home by a few kicks and a little arm twisting, Jack gets poor Jenkin so confused that he begins to think that Jack must be right. When Jack finally asks, "Who art thou?" Jenkin, completely intimidated and by now quite convinced, answers, "Nobody but whom it pleaseth you certain!"

The sluggish Jenkin finally works out his identity crisis and goes home to tell his master and mistress of his strange encounter. They give him another beating for being so gullible. The moral—to avoid tricksters and sharp types clever enough to steal your very personality—is very much upstaged by the practical jokes of Jack Juggler.

§ FOOLS AND JESTERS §

The fools and jesters of the Middle Ages and the early Renaissance feasted in palaces and castles at the pleasure and under the protection of kings and great magnates. One German fool had a town named after him by an admiring duke. A jester performed before the Pope in the Vatican; another rode into battle beside the King of France. A Florentine fool was thought learned enough to teach Latin to the children of the Duke of Tuscany. Henry VIII's buffoon became the king's friend and constant companion and was gratefully remembered in his will. By the later Middle Ages the fool was a necessary ornament to a royal court; kings and queens coveted and collected accomplished knaves and jesters, sometimes trading them or presenting them as gifts to their fellow sovereigns as they would a prized painting or a favorite horse.

This is not to say that all medieval fools were necessarily gifted entertainers. The term "fool" included dwarfs and grotesques, the physically deformed and the mentally defective (often unwilling or helpless captives—idiots and madmen—who were detained for the cruel amusement of royalty). Royal records list salaries for "keepers" of fools of this kind, yet this term is misleading, for it also refers to the many pampered court fools who had their own valets and attendants and lived in comfort like little princes and princesses.

The fools we are concerned with here were fools by choice and not by accident; though often dwarfs themselves, they only mimicked feeble-mindedness in the practice of an honored and exacting profession. As Viola says of the clown Feste in Shakespeare's *Twelfth Night,* "This fellow's wise enough to play the fool. And to do that well craves a kind of wit." Apparently many medieval fools were well educated as well as witty. Apart from the fool we have already met who doubled as an instructor of Latin, we learn of another who secretly took a degree at the University of Pisa, although his master had forbidden it.

Other fools specialized in prophecies and won great reputations as fortunetellers. At the French court, jesters preached mock sermons ridiculing the clergy; they sounded so impressive and learned that for a while the friars and chaplains faced serious competition.

The fool's more usual occupation was not prophesying and sermonizing but storytelling. Performing before the entire court and taking all the parts himself, he selected from his inexhaustible store a fable or folk tale that suited a particular occasion or could be slyly embellished to comment on some topical event at court. Like Scheherazade in the *Arabian Nights,* whose life depended on 1001 nights' worth of storytelling for an insomniac tyrant, the court fool's livelihood depended on his ability to collect or compose a virtual lifetime's supply of stories, tales, and quips.

Other fools sought the royal favor through music and poetry, by singing songs and playing instruments or reciting verses of their own composition. One German fool was appointed Professor of Poetry at the University of Wittenberg, Hamlet's alma mater. Perhaps this was simply the self-indulgent joke of his princely master, although his Latin verses were said to be quite competent.

Of course, most of us would rather watch an accomplished clown trip over his feet and spill a pot of gravy over himself than listen to a recitation of polished Latin verse. Medieval monarchs were certainly no different. The court buffoon's principal duty was to garnish the king's supper with pranks and practical jokes—the noisier and messier the better—interrupting the courtiers' conversation with funny faces and ridiculous capers or leaping up on the table to do furious battle as if the roast pig were a wild boar.

As these examples imply, the fool was permitted to do or say pretty much what he pleased—a freedom that other subjects must have envied. The fool spoke his mind with embarrassing frankness; empty flattery and tedious ritual were favorite targets for his pointed wit. Acting as an informal master of ceremonies, he was free to cut short a courtier's windy speech or a councilor's boring discourse, and this made him a powerful figure at court. The fool was permitted these remarkable liberties because, in turn, he allowed the king himself a kind of liberation from the stifling etiquette of his own court. Many fools enjoyed particular favor. One French fool, a dwarf called Thony, was the pet of three kings, Henry II, Francis II, and Charles IX. Henry insisted that Thony dine with him and announced that anyone who mistreated this tiny dignitary would be punished most severely.

According to one story, William the Conqueror's fool once saved his master from a plot against his life. The conspirators were thoughtless enough to discuss their plans to kill the king and seize his castle in the fool's presence, thinking that such a simpleton would be none the wiser. When they arrived on the appointed night, William and his fool and a formidable guard were ready to receive them.

The costume of the medieval fool was derived from the one worn by the King of Fools, the central figure of the traditional Feast of All Fools. (This was a kind of carnival celebrated by students and young people on the first of the year; they chose the ugliest or the silliest of their members to serve as their king and paraded him through the town.) We hear of an Italian fool who fell sick with grief and humiliation because, as he told his doctor, his mistress had failed to outfit him in a proper "fool's dress with ears." This was a hooded cap down to his shoulders, with asses' ears attached—sometimes bells or a cockscomb—and an oval cut for his face. His jacket of motley—a patchwork of brightly colored cloth—reached to his waist; below that, snugly fitting tights, sometimes complete with a tail. His soft shoes or slippers allowed complete freedom of motion; sometimes he even went barefoot. Another set of bells at the ankles completed the jester's costume. Even female fools dressed in this traditional costume at the glittering and eccentric Renaissance court of Mantua. Isabella and Beatrice d'Este maintained a special section in the ducal palace reserved for their bustling household of dwarfs and fools, where, it is said, they married and raised families of their own.

The jester carried a *marotte*, a stick with a miniature "fool's head" carved at the top. Some fools used this wooden-headed prop like a ventriloquist's dummy, carrying on animated conversations with the marotte; others tied a beanbag to the staff to make a rattle or a handy but harmless weapon against pomp and circumstance.

We have already mentioned Henry VIII's fool. This was William Somers, whose gift for phrasemaking and face-making brought him into Henry's service in 1525. Like many famous jesters, Somers was a dwarf, or almost one—very short, lean and stooped, rather like a hunchback. As the king's jester he became a national figure, the subject of songs and plays, but he never sought the limelight. Somers preferred to wait silently in the shadows until the king called for him. Henry in turn preferred no man's company more than that of Will

Somers. They improvised verses while out riding together: Henry, a talented amateur poet, set the subject and supplied the first lines; Somers, the professional, took care of the bawdy conclusion. In his last years Henry suffered from gout and swollen legs, and often only Somers was allowed to come near him. One historian believes that Somers was foremost in Henry's thoughts during the last ten years of his life, yet, unlike most royal favorites, he did nothing to take advantage of the situation; his only ambition was to please the king.

We don't know exactly how he went about this; no one thought to leave an account of his clowning, except to mention his funny faces and gestures, riddles and witty remarks, and the pet monkey that often rode on his shoulders. One of Henry's portraits shows Somers standing behind him—slight and serious, in strange contrast to the robust figure of "bluff King Hal."

Princes of the church also kept fools. Henry's great councilor Cardinal Wolsey had a famous fool called Patch, who was said to be a cousin of Somers. And in fact, after Henry had the cardinal beheaded, he invited Patch to join his cousin at court. Noblemen and wealthy citizens hired fools to entertain at weddings, baptisms, and other happy occasions, and fools performed in towns on feast days and holidays for folk of all degrees. The fool was a star performer in mystery plays, on pageant wagons (enclosed stages on wheels), at fairs, in marketplaces, taverns, and courtyards. Anywhere in the medieval world where a crowd could collect, where there might be a few coins to spare or an untapped keg of beer, there was a stage for fools, knaves, and jesters.

Unlike a stage actor who assumes a character's identity for a few hours, the fool spent his lifetime "playing the fool," always in character, always alert to a comic cue or a moment's inspiration for some fresh masterstroke of folly. Different fools took on different personalities. There were sad fools and silly fools, simple fools and subtle fools, grotesque fools, obnoxious fools, even serious fools, like Will Somers. The aristocrat of the profession, the fool who intrigues us most today, was the wise and witty fool, like Feste, the jester who wins Viola's praise in *Twelfth Night* or, another of Shakespeare's creations, the clever and heartbreaking Fool of *King Lear*.

In Germany the fool was called the *Naar*. In his most popular form he seems to have been a sixteenth-century import from England, since he went under the name of "the English John." (People have always tended to believe that real stupidity of a professional caliber must come from some other country.) Even after the original English companies went home, the English John stayed on as a naturalized German fool. He wore ridiculously oversized shoes, like a medieval Charlie Chaplin, a splendid coat, and a huge floppy hat that required constant attention to keep it on his head. Sixteenth-century Englishmen had a reputation for heavy drinking, and English John stumbled around the stage in a beery haze, misdirecting messages and chatting confidentally with the audience, asking their advice or how they liked the other actors—whom he interrupted freely and frequently in the middle of their scenes.

French fools, called *sots,* appeared perhaps as early as 1276 in short playlets, *soties,* which often contained political or religious satire, sugar-coated with cap-and-bells buffoonery. Sometimes the fool was shown as the Prince of Sots, a popular monarch who governed the country with an even hand and, in effect, acted as a mouthpiece for dissent and social criticism. This sort of thing required as much courage as showmanship to put on, for the sot did not have the court fool's license to speak freely on such serious subjects and often found himself in trouble with civil and religious authorities.

§ THE SIMPLETONS OF HANS SACHS §

Clowns in medieval farces often appear as foolish country folk who are only too eager to be duped and cheated by plausible rogues from the big city. Smug citizens of the German trading city of Nuremberg must have been especially gratified on carnival days to see their country cousins in this ridiculous light in the popular folk comedies of the poet Hans Sachs (1494–1576).

In *The Wandering Scholar from Paradise* a tramping student asks a farmwife for a handout, mentioning that he comes from Paris. The foolish woman understands him to say "Paradise" (she had never heard of Paris) and presses on the astonished student an armful of money and new clothes to take to her late husband, who himself has dwelt in Paradise since his death the year before. She explains that her new husband is a wealthy farmer who would never begrudge the poor man a few necessities. The student hurries off, more than satisfied with this explanation. The farmer hears of all this when he arrives home and gallops off to overtake the student before he can get too far. But when he does catch up with him, it never occurs to the farmer that this respectable scholar is the man he's looking for. He asks the student to watch his horse while he searches the neighborhood for the thief. He returns to find that horse and scholar have vanished, along with the clothes and the money. He decides to make the best of this regrettable state of affairs by telling his wife that he has given the student his horse to hasten him on his way to Paradise; his wife is delighted with this generous stroke and hurries off to fix him his favorite dinner.

The townspeople in the carnival crowd could have a hearty laugh at such typical peasant foolishness, while countryfolk, in town for a rare holiday, were no doubt struck by the likenesses to their neighbors back home of Sachs's gullible bumpkins.

§ THE FARCE OF THE WORTHY MASTER §
PIERRE PATELIN

This best-known and still most often performed of medieval secular farces was probably written about 1470, although it is set in a small French village around the year 1400. As the play begins, Master Pierre and his wife find themselves penniless and in rags—he is a lawyer whose well-founded reputation as a scoundrel and a swindler has driven off all his clients.

Master Pierre sees a way out of his difficulties and devises a scheme for living on credit. First he visits the draper and picks out an expensive bolt of cloth to make his wife a new gown. Unable and unwilling to pay, he invites the draper to share a fine roast goose supper the next day, when he will gladly pay for the cloth as well. After Master Pierre leaves, the draper, a bit of a rogue in his own right, reveals that he has charged him double the fair price, even with the roast goose and wine thrown in gratis.

Master Pierre returns home, presents his delighted wife with his prize, and coaches her in her part in his scheme to dupe the draper. The next day Pierre takes to his bed, draws the curtains, and sends his wife out to deal with the draper.

WIFE *(whispering)* Speak in a whisper!
DRAPER What for? What's the trouble?

WIFE My poor husband's at death's door these last eleven weeks! *(She sobs loudly but unconvincingly.)* Boo hoo! Boo hoo!

DRAPER Your husband bought six yards of my very best cloth—he owes me nine francs and a goose dinner!

WIFE But he hasn't left his bed these twelve weeks—and kindly keep your voice down. He's dying.

DRAPER But he was just in my shop yesterday!

WIFE Not so loud!

DRAPER Pay me my money and I'll go quietly.

WIFE Out of the question. He's been sick these thirteen weeks!

DRAPER *(a little agitated)* And I sold him my very best cloth.

WIFE No, no, no! He's been on his deathbed these fourteen weeks!

DRAPER Such a lovely bit of blue cloth. *(Sobs himself now, more realistically.)*

WIFE I tell you, the poor man hasn't left the house these fifteen weeks!

(Master Pierre groans behind the curtain, as if in delirium.)

PIERRE Everything's turned black and yellow—stop the braying of that jackass. *(He tumbles out of bed, pretends not to recognize the draper, and goes scurrying around the room, shrieking.)*

PIERRE Demons! They've come for me!

WIFE *(indignant)* Now see what you've done!

DRAPER *(ruefully)* You're right. I've learned my lesson. Always get the cash, never give credit.

WIFE *(sobbing again)* Now get out of here and leave us in peace.

DRAPER Maybe I *am* a little crazy.

WIFE *(seizing the upper hand)* Go back and take a look in your shop. Perhaps the cloth is still there.

The draper stumbles outside to clear his head. As soon as he comes to his senses, he bursts back inside Pierre's house and discovers the Patelins dancing arm in arm, celebrating their triumph, perhaps prematurely. The draper roars louder than ever for his money and takes out after Master Pierre. They circle the room a few times, until Pierre collapses, suddenly and dramatically, on his bed.

PIERRE Farewell—I die!

The draper has started to doubt his sanity all over again—and the thought that he has worried an innocent invalid to death is too much for him. He makes a hurried exit.

On his way home the draper meets the shepherd who looks after his flocks. The shepherd greets him with the news that all his sheep have died. Suspecting another trick, the draper accuses the shepherd of stealing his sheep and darkly announces that he will see him in court. The shepherd goes off to see if Master Pierre will take his case.

The shepherd is as big a rogue as Master Pierre or the draper. He cheerfully confesses to Pierre that he roasted the sheep and sold the wool. He promises Pierre a share of the booty if he wins his case in court. Master Pierre has come up with another stratagem; he tells the shepherd that no matter what anyone asks him, he must answer with a simple "Baa."

The case goes to trial. The draper is unable to contain himself; he keeps interrupting the proceedings to denounce Master Pierre and demand payment for the cloth. Accusations and denials fly so freely that the judge gets confused, forgets about the shepherd, and adjourns the court. Master Pierre gloats. Not only has he fleeced the draper, but he gets a gold crown for defending the crooked shepherd. Master Pierre confronts his client:

PIERRE A very successful defense, don't you think?
SHEPHERD Baa . . .
PIERRE First rate, I thought.
SHEPHERD Baa . . .
PIERRE It's all right, the trial's over. You can talk now.
SHEPHERD Baaa . . .
PIERRE And as for the fee you mentioned for my services . . .
SHEPHERD Baaa . . .
PIERRE Hand over that gold crown, my man!
SHEPHERD Baaaaa . . .
PIERRE (indignant) What kind of trick is this?
SHEPHERD Baaaaa . . .
PIERRE (sputtering incoherently) You rogue, you cheat, scoundrel
. . . wretch . . . knave . . .

The shepherd bleats faster and faster, then frisks away like a spring lamb, while Pierre seethes with fury. Master Pierre consoles himself by recalling how cleverly he cheated the draper and how the simple shepherd could never have cheated *him* without his masterpiece of trickery.

These fools, jesters, knaves, rogues, and Vices, for all their slyness, are trustworthy witnesses to medieval man's love of laughter and buffoonery. We can still learn much of his society and psychology from the swaggering Vice and the rascally Patelin, and perhaps more important, we can understand how the jesting of fools like Will Somers and the follies of Hans Sachs's country clowns taught kings and common folk to see themselves more clearly. But a new age of comedy was still to come. The art that began with the ragged players of the Dark Ages became in the sixteenth century the great Italian popular theater, the *commedia dell'arte*.

· 3 ·

THE ITALIAN COMEDIANS

Harlequin, Pantalone, the Doctor,
Pulcinella, the Captain,
and Their Friends

Harlequin

Between 1560 and 1760 a small invasion of touring Italian actors brought a distinctly new kind of comedy across the Alps to Western Europe. This was the *commedia dell'arte.* The name implied simply that the performers were professionals, unusual in Renaissance Italy, where most of the theatrical performances were provided by enthusiastic if inexperienced gentleman amateurs in the princely courts and universities. These amateur companies relied heavily on the Greek and Latin classics, current imitations of ancient drama, or topheavy mythological pageants—forgotten today and in their own time never as popular as the exuberant commedia dell'arte. The commedia players dispensed with playwrights altogether, ancient or modern, created their own characters, and made up their plots as they went along. Instead of a script a comedian worked from a simple outline or plot summary, called a *scenario,* with notations of tested routines and bits of surefire dialogue to tie the improvised scenes together. Beyond that, he was on his own.

To make the comedian's life a little easier, he always played the same role—once a Harlequin always a Harlequin—every performance of his life. Actors spent years developing and perfecting a polished, larger-than-life comic character or "mask," named for the traditional false face that made Harlequin or Pulcinella or Pantalone instantly recognizable to an audience.

Actors brought their masks to life with original and extremely elaborate comic routines called *lazzi.* These might be jokes or pantomime sequences, involving one or more characters, sometimes sung or danced to musical accompaniment. The mask known as Harlequin, for example, might make a mad dash after an imaginary fly, crashing into scenery, tripping over his own feet, and possibly blundering through the audience in hot pursuit of his invisible quarry—which he finally tracks down and devours with pantomime gusto, after first daintily removing the wings.

Here are a few typical lazzi that might help the hard-pressed commedia dell'arte characters out of dramatically sticky situations: Pulcinella is being marched off to prison. He stands on his dignity, protesting that he can't go without tying his shoelaces first; bending over, he makes for his shoes, instead grabs the legs of his captors, knocks their heads together and prudently exits, leaving the field to the anguished officers. In another lazzo a starving Pulcinella and companion come upon a sumptuous feast laid out before them. Just as they grab their forks, the banquet table picks itself up and gallops offstage, leaving the disappointed scoundrels staring after it in astonishment. Once more, Pulcinella is confronted by his archenemy, the Captain, who demands to know the name of his sweetheart. Pulcinella replies guardedly that it begins with "O," if the Captain would care to guess it. The Captain tries and fails with "Orsola, Olimpia, Orcana." In fact, "Rosanna" turns out to be her name. To the infuriated Captain's objection, the clown replies, "And if I spell it with an 'O,' what's that to you?" and slips away while the Captain executes the grimace the modern stage knows as the "slow burn."

In the commedia the actor was everything. The brief sketches that survive show how the comedian's "arte," which permitted great improvisational freedom, also demanded skillful coordination from the troupe. Their brand of fast-paced physical comedy could come off only with precise timing and perfect teamwork. Comedians started learning their routines in early childhood, since many of the great commedia troupes—the Gelosi, the Andreini, the Naselli, and the company of the Most Serene Duke of Mantua—were family companies in which parents passed their masks on to their children. Each family polished and perfected a repertory of lazzi that were handed down along with the masks. Family disputes could often be imperceptibly woven into the cheerful violence of the commedia, and families vied with one another in perfecting the dizzying acrobatics that accompanied their gibes and combats. Audiences outside Italy, who couldn't make head or tail of the jokes and patter, still appreciated what they could see. Handstands, headstands, walking on stilts and the tightrope, all with imaginative variations and personal embellishments (one comedian could box another actor's ear with his foot, another could turn a somersault while holding a full glass of water without spilling a drop), made the commedia the liveliest of the arts.

The vitality and perennial popularity of the commedia had very much to do with the rich and varied cast of characters which sprang from the apparently inexhaustible imaginations of the actors. A mask would be called onstage to suit the dramatic needs of a chosen scenario, or frequently because it was a favorite with the crowds in a particular region (many of the masks were said to be natives of a city or province in Italy). Local jokes and topical references—an effortless way of flattering an audience, then as today—were eagerly collected by the comedians, and provincial theatergoers devoured with particular relish the buffooneries of a mask that made their neighbors and compatriots look truly as ridiculous as they had always suspected them to be. However, the genuine appeal of the commedia characters scarcely depended on their origins in local folklore—audiences all over Western Europe, who might not know a Neapolitan from a Venetian, could howl with laughter at Pulcinella and Pantalone just the same.

§ HARLEQUIN (ARLECCHINO) §

The liveliest and most popular of the commedia clowns was also one of the oldest. Said to be a native of Bergamo, he makes his first appearance in a portrait dated 1570. He usually sported the familiar patchwork costume that was his trademark, with a black half-mask and a sword or stick to complement his mischievous and excitable stage personality. The patchwork design was standardized by the seventeenth century as a pattern of blue, red, and green triangles linked by a yellow braid. Although Harlequin began his career as a sort of grinning simpleton, later interpreters of the mask shaped him into a complex and cunning character, recalling the trickster of antiquity, who played the fool in order to put something over on his duller adversaries or out of a simple fondness for making trouble. Harlequin quickly became an international celebrity—Alberto Noselli, who originated the role, took his company to Spain, played there for ten years, and later appeared before the French court in Paris in 1571 and 1572.

§ PANTALONE §

The senior member of the commedia troupe, Pantalone typified the stubborn, interfering father, the inevitable target of ridicule in an age of arranged marriages and stern parental discipline. Pantalone was a Venetian, and as befitted a citizen of that prosperous city, a merchant, though not always a successful one, sometimes even bankrupt. Rich or poor, Pantalone was always portrayed as a vigorous old codger with a formidable temper and a healthy respect for the value of a ducat. Like a character in a modern "generation gap" comedy, Pantalone was baffled and infuriated by his children's ingratitude. They perversely resisted his clumsy attempts to make a "respectable" match for them and clung persistently to their poor-but-honest sweethearts. By the final curtain, though, love would triumph over Pantalone, and the gruff old miser resigned himself to the happy ending, showing at last an unsuspected streak of generosity and good humor. Pantalone was traditionally dressed in red, with a long black robe and yellow slippers, a fat purse dangling from his belt and a half-mask dominated by an enormous beaked nose, broadly suggesting Pantalone's two over-whelming preoccupations—his own business and other people's.

§ THE DOCTOR §

Pantalone's hometown, Venice, was known throughout Europe as the citadel of sharp-trading middle-class respectability. Pantalone's best friend, the Doctor, was a product of the Northern Italian city of Bologna, famous for its great university—and its sausage. His enor-mous bulk wrapped in the billowing black robes of a university graduate, the Doctor spoke an extravagant brand of learned double-talk, as well as misusing and mispronouncing words, spouting pom-pous, silly clichés and sprinkling his harangues with unintelligible phrases from imaginary foreign languages. He was identified various-ly as a doctor of medicine or philosophy, eager to share his ignorance of any subject with everyone he came across. Many of Pantalone's most preposterous intrigues sprang from the Doctor's overheated imagination, and the two of them were often shown plotting together, arm in arm, Pantalone bristling with indignation, the Doctor's sweeping mustaches and sausage nose beating time to the rhythms of his senseless conversation.

§ PULCINELLA §

This Neapolitan clown was Harlequin's only serious rival in fame and popularity. He was traditionally dressed all in white, except for his small dark and wrinkled mask, and a long tunic that ballooned above his waist and was cinched with a tight cord. He wore the kind of long pointed hat we call a dunce cap. His spindly legs, long beaky nose, and slightly humped back gave him the look, at least to one observer, of a "topheavy chicken"; his jerky, hopping "hen step" and clucking voice completed the resemblance.

A versatile character, he was equally incompetent as a lawyer, an artist, a doctor, a servant, a pirate, or a dentist; as with Harlequin, his moods were fleeting and changeable. He chose to be clever or stupid, brave or cowardly, irritating or ingratiating, as his fancy dictated. Always greedy, Pulcinella never passed up an intrigue that would win him a free dinner at someone else's expense. He was often cruel—his wit could be cutting as well as charming—and he delighted in the lowest of low comedy (one of his coarser tricks was urinating onstage in full view of the audience).

The lusty, pleasure-loving Pulcinella left a flock of theatrical descendants. In seventeenth- and eighteenth-century Germany he took the name of Hanswurst or Jack Sausage, a hot-tempered rogue who inherited Pulcinella's boundless appetite for the good things in life, sausages in particular. Even the English puppet character Punch, the wife-beating tyrant of the Punch-and-Judy shows, owes his name and his hot temper to his Italian ancestor.

§ THE CAPTAIN §

Very much like the "braggart soldier" in ancient Roman comedies, this boastful veteran fooled no one with his unlikely reminiscences of imaginary campaigns; beneath his glittering uniform beat the heart of a genuine coward. His romantic conquests were equally imaginary; women drew him out for the sake of his preposterous stories and ridiculed him the minute his beribboned back was turned. The Captain rarely wore a mask—probably out of vanity—and his costume was usually a military uniform of the period with as many plumes, ruffles, buttons, and braids as could possibly be piled on, a wide ruff collar, and a short cape which accentuated his swaggering warlike poses. When Italy was dominated by Spanish invaders and adventurers, the Captain suddenly became very Spanish in costume and accent, an impudent and undoubtedly stinging attack by the comedians on the dignity of their foreign oppressors.

§ THE WOMEN §

At first women were forbidden by law to perform in public, but during the sixteenth century several Italian states relaxed their ban and several accomplished actresses won international reputations in the commedia.

The most celebrated of the commedia dell'arte actresses was Isabella Andreini (1562–1604). She played the mask of a young woman in love, the *Inamorata,* a role well suited to her grace and beauty. Together with her husband, she headed the Gelosi troupe, performing before many of the great princes of Europe during her triumphant twenty-six-year career—not only as an actress, but as a poet and playwright. After a successful engagement in Paris, where she and her colleagues charmed commoners and courtiers alike, she died in childbirth in Lyons on the return journey. The entire population of Lyons walked in her funeral procession in a touching and unprecedented tribute to a foreign actress. She had been so much the star of the Gelosi company that her husband had no choice but to disband the troupe after her death.

The Inamorata, the role that won Isabella Andreini her glittering reputation, was the most popular and one of the most demanding of the female masks. Actually, the Inamorata went *un*masked, the better to display her beautiful and expressive face to appreciative audiences, and instead of a traditional costume she wore the fashionable gown and jewels of an elegant young lady in society, or at least as close an approximation as the troupe's budget permitted. The Inamorata's appearance on the stage was more than merely decorative—she was expected to sing and dance expertly and perform on musical instruments.

Women also played courtesans, gossips, old women, wives and

mothers, and Harlequin's female counterpart, Arlecchina. The saucy maidservant or *soubrette* was extremely popular; Columbine, a soubrette who was often in love with Harlequin, is the best known of the female masks today. She was the particular favorite of the French, and countless representations on the stage and in the decorative arts have made her the enduring symbol of flirtation and the most celebrated coquette of all times.

§ THE *ZANNI* AND OTHER CLOWNS §

Harlequin was only one of a great number of commedia clowns collectively called the *zanni*—the origin of the English word "zany." The zanni were sometimes portrayed as fumbling, inefficient servants but gifted mischief-makers. Inexplicably, their masters frequently relied on them to carry out the complicated plots and delicate intrigues that were the mainstays of the typical commedia scenario; predictably, their indiscretions and incompetence only deepened the confusion, bringing no end of trouble down on their masters' and their own empty heads. Other zanni simply ignored the play altogether—obliviously interrupting the action, chatting casually with the audience, and bringing everything to a complete standstill until their fellow players indignantly hustled them offstage.

Piero, better known by his French name of Pierrot, was the most serious of the commedia clowns. His sadness, honesty, and simplicity provided the commedia with many touching moments of "tragic relief." Pierrot is often unhappily involved in an unrequited romantic triangle with Harlequin and Columbine, and like them, Pierrot survived the demise of the commedia and remains a familiar figure today in paintings, plays, and ballets.

Another commedia clown with a flair for tragedy is Pagliaccio. He is best remembered as the character played by the lovestruck actor Canio in Leoncavallo's opera *I Pagliacci.* Pagliaccio's baggy white costume—with tall conical hat, billowing white sleeves and breeches, and red pompom buttons—helps the unhappy Canio conceal his suffering from his fellow players, including his rival and his beloved, though he lets the audience in on the secret in several memorable full-throated arias.

Mournful operatic clowns are all very well, but Harlequin, Pantalone, and the other stars of the commedia certainly deserve the last laugh. A crowd has gathered around the open-air stage in the city square. The painted backdrop shows us that the scene is Venice, with a fine house on the right and a canal on the left, and centerstage, a large cannon. Harlequin enters and stops short when he sees an audience crowded around the tiny stage, many shading their eyes against the afternoon sun. He jumps up, spins around in the air, bows very low, and turns to address the crowd.

HARLEQUIN You know, I love trouble. All kinds. The more trouble I cause, the better I feel. *(He runs around the stage beating the scenery with his stick, hoping someone will try to stop him or chase him off.)* But right now, I'm miserable. Do you know why? That's right. NO TROUBLE. If I don't find some soon, I'll die.
   Enter Franceschina, maidservant to Pantalone. Harlequin runs to greet her.)
FRANCESCHINA I will tell you nothing. *(Harlequin trails at her heels.)* No, I won't tell you what terrible sorrow plagues my master's house. *(She points to the house on the painted backcloth.)*
HARLEQUIN What else won't you tell me?
FRANCESCHINA I won't tell you how miserable my mistress is.
HARLEQUIN Don't tell me MORE!
FRANCESCHINA I won't tell you how my master suffers.
HARLEQUIN Don't tell me another word.
FRANCESCHINA I won't tell you why I am beside myself.
HARLEQUIN Why are you beside yourself?
FRANCESCHINA I won't tell.
HARLEQUIN *(with a long sigh)* Franceschina, I am very sorry to hear the bad news.
FRANCESCHINA Who told you?
HARLEQUIN You just did. *(Laughing, he jumps in the air, twirls, and bows low before her.)*
FRANCESCHINA *(threatening Harlequin with her fist)* You rogue, you tricked me! If I weren't in a hurry to fetch a doctor, I'd tell you a thing or two! *(She exits, leaving Harlequin baffled.)*
HARLEQUIN I wonder what could be wrong at Pantalone's house? Ah, here comes the Captain. Maybe he knows.
   (Enter the Captain, marching smartly. At Harlequin's "Good morning" he salutes.)

HARLEQUIN *(returning the salute)* Perhaps *you* can tell me what has happened to Pantalone?

CAPTAIN I can tell you about the time I captured the wild King of Sardinia, about the battle of . . .

HARLEQUIN Is he ill?

CAPTAIN Ill? He's dead.

HARLEQUIN Oh, no. Poor old Pantalone. *(He hangs his head.)*

CAPTAIN Not Pantalone. The wild King of Sardinia. I removed his head myself. The biggest I've ever seen . . . took four men to carry it away . . .

HARLEQUIN *(realizing he won't get any information from the Captain)* Captain, the enemy approaches. We await your command, sir.

CAPTAIN Where are my troops?

HARLEQUIN In San Marco Square, Captain. *(He points.)* Only you can save us, sir.

CAPTAIN *(marching offstage)* Every man, woman, and child to arms. Your captain comes!

HARLEQUIN *(to audience)* It's no more than he deserves for not telling me about Pantalone.

(Enter Franceschina with the Doctor. Harlequin runs to meet them, but Franceschina pushes him aside and escorts the Doctor into the house, slamming the door in Harlequin's face.)

HARLEQUIN Well, *he* won't be any use, no matter what the trouble is. The Doctor's the world's greatest authority on ignorance.

(Enter Pantalone from the house, yawning and rubbing his eyes.)

HARLEQUIN Old friend, how are you?

PANTALONE Go away. I'm sleepy.

HARLEQUIN *(to himself)* Is that all? And I thought he was sick. *(To Pantalone)* Is your wife ill?

PANTALONE She has everlasting hiccoughs!

HARLEQUIN HICCOUGHS! You mean she goes *hic-cup, hic-cup, hic-cup?*

PANTALONE All day and all night. The only sleep we get is between hiccoughs. I'm exhausted.

HARLEQUIN Just from the sound of hiccoughs? *(He lets go with a chorus of hiccoughs.)*

PANTALONE Please! Don't do that. It's driving me crazy!

HARLEQUIN But everybody knows how to cure hiccoughs.

PANTALONE Yes, I know cures. The Doctor knows cures. Even my wife knows cures. But not one works!

HARLEQUIN Has she had water?

PANTALONE Almost an oceanful, and still she hiccoughs.

HARLEQUIN Has she held her breath?

PANTALONE Till she turns blue. But when she stops, those awful watchamacallits start again.

HARLEQUIN Have you fired a pistol at her?

PANTALONE I want to cure her, not kill her.

HARLEQUIN Let me do it for you.

PANTALONE What? Shoot her?

HARLEQUIN It would be an honor *(he jumps, spinning in the air)* to do you a favor. I promise to cure her affliction, if not one way, then another. And all I ask is one gold piece.

PANTALONE You will have it the moment she stops hiccoughing.

HARLEQUIN Good. Now, ask your wife to step out here and meet Dr. Harlequin.
> *(Pantalone exits. Harlequin fetches a bucket of water, scampers up a ladder, and leans over the doorway.)*

HARLEQUIN *(with an evil laugh)* A good soaking should make the musical lady forget her hiccoughs!

PANTALONE *(offstage)* Come, good wife, a walk will do you good. *(Pantalone enters, stands in the doorway.)* See how bright the day is—the air is warm and dry. *(Harlequin empties the bucket and its contents drench Pantalone, who shakes and shivers and screams that he is drowning.)*

ISABELLA, *Pantalone's wife (laughing uproariously)* Yes, very dry, I see.

PANTALONE Harlequin! Where are you?

HARLEQUIN *(leaping off the ladder, bowing deeply)* Right here.

ISABELLA Don't scold him, husband. A little water never hurt anyone.

HARLEQUIN *(whispering to Pantalone)* If she feels that way, she won't mind a little swim. *(He sticks out his foot to trip Isabella, but Pantalone stumbles over it instead and falls into the canal. He thrashes about wildly, screaming for help.)*

ISABELLA *(now laughing hysterically)* A little water never hurt anyone. *(She and Harlequin drag Pantalone from the canal, wet and furious.)*

PANTALONE *(sputtering)* Harlequin, I will have you arrested for this.

HARLEQUIN Oh, no, you will pay me for this. Haven't you noticed? Your wife is cured of the hiccoughs.

ISABELLA *(delighted)* Why yes. I laughed them away.

HARLEQUIN Completely gone!

PANTALONE Not completely. Haven't *you* noticed? *I've* been hiccoughing ever since you pulled me from the canal. I can't stop. *(Hiccoughing uncontrollably, he swings at Harlequin, who ducks and darts out of reach.)*

HARLEQUIN For another gold piece, I'll cure *you.*

ISABELLA Pay him, Pantalone, pay him.

PANTALONE I'd rather have the hiccoughs than pay that rascal. *(He hiccoughs violently.)* Well, maybe I wouldn't. All right. Two gold pieces. *(He hands Harlequin the money.)* Now cure me.

HARLEQUIN Immediately. *(Looking about, Harlequin notices the cannon and swings it around toward Pantalone.)*

PANTALONE *(alarmed)* Harlequin, I beg you, don't fire! *(Unconcerned, Harlequin strikes a match.)*

PANTALONE *(falling to his knees)* Don't do it, Harlequin. I beseech you. *(Suddenly he looks up, amazed.)* Wait! Cease fire! I've stopped hiccoughing.

HARLEQUIN Of course you have. A good scare works as well as a good laugh.

ISABELLA Oh, thank you, Harlequin. We're both cured.

HARLEQUIN It's been a good morning's work, except *(his face darkens)* now that the trouble's gone, I'm miserable again.

ISABELLA Trouble always finds you, Harlequin. Don't worry.

HARLEQUIN *(even sadder)* What could happen to me? I never stand still long enough for anything to catch me. *(He hiccoughs loudly.)*

PANTALONE *and* ISABELLA TROUBLE!

PANTALONE *(smirking)* The hiccoughs may not have caught you but you seem to have caught the hiccoughs.

HARLEQUIN *(dazed, pounding his stick and crying)* It's a trick!

PANTALONE On you for once.

HARLEQUIN *(hiccoughing)* But I don't know any more hiccough remedies.

PANTALONE Then you really *are* in trouble. There will be another gold piece for you, *Doctor* Harlequin, if you cure yourself. *(He *escorts Isabella to the door.)* Let's go inside, my dear, where it's a bit quieter.

HARLEQUIN *(convulsed with hiccoughs)* This can't happen to me! First she gets them, then he gets them, now I have them. There's nobody left to get them. *(He sags, defeated. Then, looking at the audience, he brightens.)* Oh, yes, there is. I'll give my hiccoughs to YOU! *(He leaps into the air and spins around, looking like himself again.)*

(The sound of a small hiccough comes from the audience.)

HARLEQUIN I heard you. Now *you've* got them! *(He points to a boy in the crowd. The boy looks up, smiles, and hiccoughs. A second and third hiccough come from the back of the audience.)* Listen, you all have them! And I'm cured! *(The entire audience, familiar with the routine and more than willing to join in, hiccoughs in unison.)* What wonderful trouble I've caused! *(Harlequin leaps in the air, spins around, beats the scenery with his stick, waves goodbye, dashes offstage.)*

By the middle of the eighteenth century, the commedia dell'arte had enjoyed three hundred years of uninterrupted popularity in half a dozen countries—a long and successful run by any standards. Perhaps too long and too successful, at least in the opinion of a young Italian lawyer turned performer and playwright named Carlo Goldoni (1707–1793). He felt that this noisy improvised street theater—its "stage" a hasty scaffolding thrown up in an inn courtyard or public square—was ready for retirement, ready to give way to formal, "legitimate" theater, presenting real plays written by real playwrights, like himself in fact. There had been such plays, of course, but in Italy they had never provided much serious competition for the fascinating simplicity and infinite complexity of the commedia. Goldoni was determined to beat the comedians at their own game, and gradually he did. He lured their audiences out of the streets and into his theater with his own fresh satirical comedies, which were just as lively as the commedia and a great deal more original. But even Goldoni's popular comedies and stinging essays could not entirely kill the commedia; Goldoni himself was not above bringing the much-abused masks out of retirement for an extra engagement in one of his own plays.

Echoes of the commedia survive in the comedies of Shakespeare and Molière, and Harlequin and company can still be seen today in

Milan, in the Tivoli Gardens in Copenhagen, and in several regional theaters in the United States.

The imported commedia tradition also provided strong competition for native playwrights in France until the early eighteenth century, but it reached England as living, popular theater only a few decades before it was about to die out on the Continent. Long before, around the middle of the sixteenth century, the English had created a theater of their own, which developed out of the medieval mystery plays and was heavily influenced by classical Latin drama and the literature of Renaissance France and Italy. Historians call this period the Elizabethan Age, but lovers of the theater are more likely to think of this extraordinary first flowering of creativity and vitality as the Age of Shakespeare.

· *4* ·
THE ELIZABETHANS

Jig Makers, Richard Tarleton,
William Kempe, Robert Armin,
and the Clowns of Shakespeare

Richard Tarleton

Robt Armin   Will Kempe   A Playwright

———————

Elizabethan England was a theatrical nation: Elizabeth and her court lived a kind of perpetual costume drama where wit and elegance were the stuff of everyday life. Londoners crowded the theaters in which plays and masques—elaborate pageants combining music, mime, and poetry—were given. In the streets crowds gathered to applaud jugglers, tumblers, and jig makers—dancers and clowns who performed skits with music and dialogue. The cruel sports of cockfighting and bearbaiting provided a less artistic brand of excitement. Music of every kind—from serious chamber concerts to bawdy ballads—found enthusiastic audiences. At court and in the great houses, whose spacious banquet halls could easily accommodate companies of actors presenting full-dress plays, minstrels sang and told stories while fools and jesters tossed out witty and witless remarks indifferently.

Her Majesty's lesser subjects packed the inn courtyards where wandering players set up their platform stages, while in the market square, buffoons and acrobats vied for the attention of the jostling crowds. Comedies were given at fairs in summer; the traditional mystery plays were still an important part of the Christmas and Easter celebrations. Playacting was fostered in the schools and universities. The choirboys in the royal chapels and churches performed plays in verse that attracted huge crowds and even threatened the livelihood of the professional actors in the playhouses. One of them, William Shakespeare, apparently a little anxious about the box-office receipts in his own Globe Theatre, included in *Hamlet* a satirical gibe at the "little eyases," likening the high-pitched voices of the boy actors to the earsplitting shrieks of a nest of baby hawks. Less sensitive Londoners flocked to see them nevertheless, and the choirboy-actors continued to thrive.

Elizabethans of every station passionately craved shows and spectacles. Her Majesty and most of her subjects would have agreed with Touchstone, Shakespeare's jester in *As You Like It*, when he remarked, "It is meat and drink to me to see a clown." The careers of three celebrated clowns spanned the Elizabethan Age, from the queen's accession in 1558 to her death in 1603; performing in palaces, playhouses, or open pastures, these gifted comedians were lionized by their countrymen and ranked among the great men of the age.

§ RICHARD TARLETON §

Queen Elizabeth's famous jester was "discovered" quite accidentally while he was feeding the pigs on his father's farm. A servant of the Earl of Leicester stopped to ask the boy a question and was so taken with his replies, which were double-edged, sad and funny at the same time, that he insisted that Richard be sent to perform at court. The delighted queen discovered that bandying words with the quick-witted jester could "undumpish" her completely, banish her black moods and lift her low spirits, certainly far more effectively than the solemn attentions of her physicians and councilors. Richard's unique access to the throne made him an esteemed and privileged member of the royal household, with ambassadors and courtiers competing for his favor.

A contemporary visitor to Elizabeth's court left us a brief glimpse of Tarleton at work. The jester approached the throne with poker face and pompous tread, and with a juicy piece of meat concealed beneath his jacket. The queen's lapdog, Perrico de Faldas, scenting the hidden prize, gave furious chase, while Tarleton dodged behind furniture and skidded over the polished marble floor. Cornered at last, Tarleton defended himself manfully with sword and staff, but the ravening Perrico proved the stronger. Tarleton threw himself on his face at the queen's feet, begging to be spared from the monster. This proved too much for the royal composure—and Elizabeth could barely summon words to dismiss Tarleton from the presence. Our eyewitness does not record whether Perrico got the meat or the joke, but we can still appreciate Tarleton's frantic burlesque of the courtier's bravado and the stately ceremonies of court.

Tarleton's specialty was extemporaneous verbal dueling with his audiences, a kind of rapid-fire ad lib comedy that became known as "Tarletonizing." The Elizabethans delighted in paradoxes, puns, and wordplay of all kinds, and Tarleton's popularity was enormous. His grinning likeness peered out from shop and tavern signs everywhere—a stocky little man with a squinting, quizzical expression, dressed in a russet-colored clown's suit. His short bandy legs were uncommonly nimble, and he joined in the lusty jigs and comic dances that followed performances in the playhouses, accompanying himself on the pipe and tabor (a small drum which a skillful musician could play with one hand). He also composed his own comic songs and wrote several plays, and not surprisingly, compiled an enormous collection of jokes, published in a volume entitled *Tarleton's Jests* ten years after his death.

Tarleton lived happily until 1588, the year of the great English victory over the Spanish Armada. Hours before his death he scribbled a hasty note to a nobleman who had known him at court, begging him to look after his six-year-old son as a last tribute of friendship to the dying jester. Tarleton's most enduring honor was to come from Shakespeare's Prince Hamlet. Picking through the bones unearthed by the gravediggers in the churchyard, he comes across the skull of Yorick, his father's jester "dead these twenty years" and addresses "the chopfallen skull" with affectionate irony: "Alas, poor Yorick! I knew him, Horatio; a fellow of infinite jest, of most excellent fancy; he hath borne me on his back a thousand times; and now how abhorred in my imagination it is! My gorge rises at it. Here hung those lips that I have kissed I know not how oft. Where be your gibes now? your gambols? your songs? your flashes of merriment, that were wont to set the table on a roar?" The impermanence of even the most spirited and fanciful of men was a favorite theme of Elizabethan writers, and critics today think that in choosing a symbol of that vital human spark, Shakespeare recalled "the wonder of his age," the jester Richard Tarleton.

§ WILLIAM KEMPE §

This Elizabethan clown first appeared on London stages in the 1580s.

He became a truly international celebrity, performing in Holland in 1585 and at the Danish court of Elsinore, the setting of *Hamlet,* in 1586. He may have ventured as far as Italy, since he returned to England with a trunkful of crowd-pleasing lazzi and commedia dell'arte flourishes. The improvisational liberties that he took with a script annoyed Hamlet's creator, William Shakespeare, who objected to Kempe's grimaces and gestures and to the quick laughter he extracted from his adoring public. Hamlet had nothing but scorn for ad-libbing comics like Kempe: "And let those that play your clowns speak no more than is set down for them." Impromptu comic interruptions in a serious scene were particularly galling, and Shakespeare had Hamlet warn the traveling players at Elsinore that "that's villainous and shows a most pitiful ambition in the fool that uses it."

Well before Kempe's behavior had become "villainous," Shakespeare had created a number of characters especially to display the clown's talent for portraying fumbling rustics who are naïve, and even stupid. Costard in *Love's Labor's Lost* is "a most simple clown" and an "unlettered small-knowing soul," who hopelessly tangles an already overburdened plot by delivering two love letters to the wrong ladies. ("Clown" in this connection means a rustic or an ignorant countryman and not just a jester or a simpleton.) Dogberry, the officious, word-fumbling constable in *Much Ado About Nothing,* announces that the night watch "have indeed comprehended two aspicious persons" and portentously informs an unimpressed prisoner: "O villain: thou wilt be condemned into everlasting redemption for this." Kempe would probably be pleased to learn that Dogberry's most famous line—"comparisons are odorous"—is almost always misquoted. When Launce of *Two Gentlemen of Verona* remarks that his sour-tempered dog Crab "has no more pity in him than a dog," we are reminded of the true simpleton's instinct for confusion. In *A Midsummer Night's Dream* Shakespeare created Kempe's greatest role, Nick Bottom, the weaver and would-be actor. His conceited determination and fussy incompetence are oversized and incongruous, but entirely human—even when, by enchantment, he appears with the shaggy head of a donkey and plays a torrid love scene with the Queen of the Fairies. Possibly a donkey's head and a juicier part were Shakespeare's way of dealing with Kempe's mugging and scene-stealing; at any rate, we know Kempe was destined for the role, since in the earliest surviving text of the play the dramatist sometimes identified the character as "Kempe" instead of "Bottom."

After he left the Globe, Kempe took his act on the road, in a way that would have delighted the literal-minded Constable Dogberry. In February 1600 he danced all the way from London to Norwich, nearly a hundred miles away. Kempe bowed and saluted the crowds of well-wishers lining the road, never missing a step, and proudly displayed his boots in the Norwich town hall to commemorate his incredible feat. Afterward Kempe admitted that he had danced himself "out of this world," went back to acting and clowning, and made another tour of Italy and Germany before his death, sometime after 1603.

§ ROBERT ARMIN §

Shakespeare must have been delighted to find in Robert Armin such a brilliant replacement for the unruly Kempe. Born about 1569, Armin was apprenticed to a goldsmith and spent seven years learning that exclusive trade. The goldsmith was a prince among craftsmen, a skilled artisan who dealt with nobility, and so was expected to speak, act, and write with the ease and grace of an Elizabethan gentleman. Armin began writing while still an apprentice—first, short topical sketches, later a play (in which he took four of the parts when it was performed) and a humorous psychological treatise with the promising title *Fool Upon Fool or a Nest of Ninnies*. As a young actor, Armin is said to have been the pupil and protégé of the great Tarleton; in 1599 he joined Shakespeare's company at the Globe Theatre. With an actor of Armin's comic gifts in the company, Shakespeare was free to develop comic roles of greater depth and complexity. Fumblers and bullies like Costard and Dogberry gave way to the subtle, witty philosophical jesters of *Twelfth Night* and *King Lear*—the character that modern scholars call simply Shakespeare's Fool.

The Fool's language is fantastic, yet inspired by a logic hovering between elegant paradox and outright nonsense. Bottom and Dogberry make us laugh by straining to become what they obviously are not. (Bottom imagines that "to eat no garlic" is enough to make him an actor. Dogberry thinks his rhetorical flourishes will cloak him in the law's majesty instead of merely burying him in confusion.) In contrast, Armin's fools are happy to be as they are, and they see the world quite clearly as it is. The Fool takes advantage of the jester's prerogative to laugh at us, and we are forced to see his point and join in the laughter.

Touchstone in *As You Like It* starts out as a slightly Kempish character, but he soon shows himself a rueful, philosophical, very worthy fool. Touchstone sees around him a world turned upside down, where virtue and wisdom are driven into exile in the wilderness, and he is moved to regret "that fools may not speak wisely when wise men do foolishly." In fact, he is much admired for his wit and eloquence, and envied by some who would be fools themselves. In *Twelfth Night* Viola, the heroine, admiringly tells the witty jester Feste that his profession is "as full of labour as any wise man's." Armin himself made a great point of this in his own writings: in a world so full of fools by nature, an artful fool must give himself up to careful study and long preparation to become truly remarkable for his foolishness.

The Fool in Shakespeare's tragedy *King Lear* serves as chorus and commentator, observing with the wise man's insight and speaking with the jester's frankness. The Fool instructs Lear in the practice of folly, a lesson which might have come from Armin's own book. He explains to Lear the difference between himself, the "sweet fool" in motley, and Lear, the bitter fool, a father ruled by his children, a king who gives up his kingdom. "Callst thou me fool, boy?" Lear asks. "All thy other titles thou hast given away, that thou wast born with," replies the Fool. The Fool mocks Lear to teach him wisdom, laboring "to outjest his heartstruck injuries" as he follows the half-mad king into the fury of a storm on the desolate heath. But Lear, "the natural fool of fortune," has fled from folly into madness where the wise Fool's bitter jests and witty lessons can no longer reach him.

Historical records of the Elizabethan theater are disappointingly scarce; we know little more of Armin's life than a few dates and a handful of anecdotes. Armin's writings show us a man of learning and curious psychological insight, but only from Shakespeare's plays can we imagine the extraordinary clowning of Robert Armin, the wise fool and comic philosopher of Touchstone's pleasant greenwood and Lear's blasted heath.

The weaver Nick Bottom and his fellow amateur players try their hand at a different kind of tragicomedy in *A Midsummer Night's Dream.* Here Bottom, Snug the joiner, Flute the bellows-mender,

Snout the tinker, and Starveling the tailor meet for a casting confer-
ence at the house of Peter Quince the carpenter.

§ SHAKESPEARE'S CLOWNS IN §

A MIDSUMMER NIGHT'S DREAM

QUINCE Is all our company here?

BOTTOM You were best to call them generally, man by man,
according to the scrip.

QUINCE Here is the scroll of every man's name which is thought fit,
through all Athens, to play in our interlude before the Duke and
Duchess on his wedding day at night.

BOTTOM First, good Peter Quince, say what the play treats on: then
read the names of the actors; and so grow to a point.

QUINCE Marry, our play is "The most lamentable comedy and most
cruel death of Pyramus and Thisbe."

BOTTOM A very good piece of work, I assure you, and a merry. Now,
good Peter Quince, call forth your actors by the scroll. Masters,
spread yourselves.

QUINCE Answer as I call you. Nick Bottom, the weaver?

BOTTOM Ready! Name what part I am for, and proceed.

QUINCE You, Nick Bottom, are set down for Pyramus.

BOTTOM What is Pyramus? a lover or a tyrant?

QUINCE A lover that kills himself, most gallant, for love.

BOTTOM That will ask some tears in the true performing of it. If I do
it, let the audience look to their eyes! I will move storms. . . .

QUINCE Francis Flute, the bellows-mender?

FLUTE Here, Peter Quince.

QUINCE Flute, you must take Thisbe on you.

FLUTE What is Thisbe? a wandering knight?

QUINCE It is the lady that Pyramus must love.

FLUTE Nay, faith, let not me play a woman—I have a beard coming.

QUINCE That's all one: you shall play it in a mask, and you may
speak as small as you will.

BOTTOM An I may hide my face, let me play Thisbe too. I'll speak in
a monstrous little voice: "Thisne, Thisne!" "Ah, Pyramus, my
lover dear, thy Thisbe dear, and lady dear."

QUINCE No, no; you must play Pyramus; and Flute, you Thisbe.
BOTTOM Well, proceed.

. . . .

QUINCE Snug, the joiner, you the lion's part. . . .
SNUG Have you the lion's part written? Pray you, if it be, give it me;
   for I am slow of study.
QUINCE You may do it extempore; for it is nothing but roaring.
BOTTOM Let me play the lion too. I will roar that I will do any man's
   heart good to hear me. I will roar that I will make the Duke say
   "Let him roar again; let him roar again!"
QUINCE An you should do it too terribly you would fright the
   Duchess and the ladies that they would shriek; and that were
   enough to hang us all.

. . . .

BOTTOM . . . But I will aggravate my voice so that I will roar you as
   gently as any sucking dove. I will roar you an 'twere any
   nightingale.
QUINCE You can play no part but Pyramus; for Pyramus is a
   sweet-faced man; a proper man as one shall see in a summer's
   day; a most lovely, gentlemanlike man. Therefore you must
   needs play Pyramus.
BOTTOM Well, I will undertake it. . . .

Quince distributes the parts, asking the company to learn them by
the following night, when they will meet in the woods outside town to
rehearse the play by moonlight. As agreed, they meet on a green plot
in a clearing, which will serve them as a stage.

QUINCE . . . We will do it in action as we will do it before the Duke.
BOTTOM Peter Quince!
QUINCE What sayest thou, Bully Bottom?
BOTTOM There are things in this comedy of Pyramus and Thisbe
   that will never please. First, Pyramus must draw a sword to kill
   himself, which the ladies cannot abide. . . .

. . . .

STARVELING I believe we must leave the killing out. . . .
BOTTOM Not a whit. I have a device to make all well. Write me a
   prologue, and let the prologue seem to say we will do no harm

with our swords, and that Pyramus is not killed indeed; and for the more better assurance, tell them that I, Pyramus, am not Pyramus, but Bottom the weaver. This will put them out of fear.

. . . .

SNOUT *(unconvinced)* Will not the ladies be afeard of the lion?

STARVELING I fear it, I promise you.

BOTTOM Masters, you ought to consider with yourself, to bring in (God shield us) a lion among ladies is a most dreadful thing; for there is not a more fearful wildfowl than your lion living; and we ought to look to't.

SNOUT Therefore another prologue must tell he is not a lion. . . .

QUINCE Well, it shall be so. But . . . there is another thing. We must have a wall in the Great Chamber; for Pyramus and Thisbe, says the story, did talk through the chink of a wall.

. . . .

BOTTOM Some man or other must present Wall; and let him have some plaster . . . about him to signify Wall; and let him hold his fingers thus, and through that cranny shall Pyramus and Thisbe whisper. *(He spreads his thumb and forefinger as far as they will stretch.)*

QUINCE If that may be, then all is well. Come, sit down every mother's son, and rehearse your parts. . . . Speak, Pyramus! Thisbe, stand forth!

BOTTOM *as Pyramus*
Thisbe, the flowers of odious savours sweet—

QUINCE Odours—odours!

BOTTOM *as Pyramus*
   . . . odours savours sweet.
   So hath thy breath, my dearest Thisbe dear.
   But hark, a voice! Stay thou but here awhile,
   And by and by I will to thee appear. *(Exit.)*

FLUTE Must I speak now?

QUINCE Ay, marry must you; for you must understand he goes but to see a noise that he heard, and is to come again.

FLUTE *as Thisbe (in a high-pitched, squeaky voice)*
   Most radiant Pyramus, most lily-white of hue

. . . .

   I'll meet thee, Pyramus, at Ninny's tomb.

QUINCE "Ninus' tomb," man! Why, you must not speak that yet.
That you answer to Pyramus. . . .

At this point the rehearsal is interrupted by the mischievous
hobgoblin Puck, who casts a magic spell on Bottom, giving him the
head of a donkey. But on the appointed night the ill-prepared players
assemble in the palace of Theseus to present their interlude to the
wedding company.

THESEUS (*reading the evening's program*)
　"A tedious brief scene of young Pyramus
　And his love Thisbe; very tragical mirth."
　Merry and tragical? Tedious and brief? . . .
PHILOSTRATE (*the Master of Revels*)
　A play there is, my lord, some ten words long,
　Which is as "brief" as I have known a play.
　But by ten words, my lord, it is too long.
　Which makes it tedious. For in all the play
　There is not one word apt, one player fitted. . . .
THESEUS
　What are they that do play it?
PHILOSOSTRATE
　Hard-handed men that work in Athens here,
　Which never laboured in their minds till now,
　And now have toiled their unbreathed memories
　With this same play against your nuptial.
THESEUS
　And we will hear it. . . .

Theseus calls for the play to begin, and Quince opens with the
Prologue, distorting its meaning ludicrously by pausing for punctua-
tion in all the wrong places.

QUINCE
　If we offend it is with our good will.
　That you should think we come not to offend
　But with good will. To show our simple skill,
　That is the true beginning of our end.

Consider then we come but in despite.
We do not come as minding to content you,
Our true intent is. All for your delight
We are not here. That you should here repent you
The actors are at hand, and by their show
You shall know all that you are like to know.

The members of the audience comment on Quince's mistakes among themselves but remain outwardly polite as he introduces the players and their parts. In his opening speech as Pyramus, Bottom addresses the wall:

BOTTOM *as Pyramus*

. . . .

O night, O night, alack, alack, alack,
I fear my Thisbe's promise is forgot.
And thou, O wall, O sweet, O lovely Wall,
That standest between her father's ground and mine,
Thou wall, O wall, O sweet and lovely Wall,
Show me thy chink to blink through with mine eyne.
    (Wall holds up his fingers.)
Thanks, courteous wall; Jove shield thee well for this.
But what see I? No Thisbe do I see. . . .

FLUTE *as Thisbe*

O wall, full often hast thou heard my moans
For parting my fair Pyramus and me. . . .

BOTTOM *as Pyramus*

I see a voice. Now will I to the chink
To spy an I can hear my Thisbe's face.
Thisbe!

FLUTE *as Thisbe*

My love! Thou art my love, I think?

BOTTOM *as Pyramus*

Think what thou wilt, I am thy lover's grace,
And like Limander am I trusty still.

FLUTE *as Thisbe*

And I like Helen till the Fates me kill;

. . . .

BOTTOM *as Pyramus*

O, kiss me through the hole of this vile wall!

FLUTE *as Thisbe*

I kiss the wall's hole, not your lips at all.

BOTTOM *as Pyramus*

Wilt thou at Ninny's tomb meet me straight way?

FLUTE *as Thisbe*

Tide life, tide death, I come without delay.

   (Exeunt Bottom and Flute.)

SNOUT *as Wall*

Thus have I, Wall, my part discharged so;
And being done, thus Wall away doth go.

   (Exit.)

   . . . .

HIPPOLYTA This is the silliest stuff that ever I heard.

THESEUS The best in this kind are but shadows; and the worst are no
   worse, if imagination amend them.

HIPPOLYTA It must be your imagination, then, and not theirs.

THESEUS If we imagine no worse of them than they of themselves,
   they may pass for excellent men. Here come two noble beasts in:
   a moon and a lion.

   (Enter Snug as Lion and Starveling as Moonshine.)

SNUG *as Lion*

You, ladies—you whose gentle hearts do fear
The smallest monstrous mouse that creeps on floor—
May now, perchance, both quake and tremble here,
When Lion rough in wildest rage doth roar.
Then know that I as Snug the joiner am
A lion fell, nor else no lion's dam,
For if I should as lion come in strife
Into this place, 'twere pity on my life.

   . . . .

FLUTE *as Thisbe*

This is old Ninny's tomb. Where is my love?

SNUG *as Lion*

O!

   (Lion roars. Flute as Thisbe runs off.)

DEMETRIUS Well roared, Lion!

THESEUS Well run, Thisbe!

HIPPOLYTA Well shone, Moon! Truly, the moon shines with a good grace.

(Lion tears Thisbe's mantle. Exit.)

THESEUS Well moused, Lion!

(Enter Bottom as Pyramus. He discovers Thisbe's bloodied mantle.)

BOTTOM *as Pyramus*

. . . .

What dreadful dole is here?
Eyes, do you see?—
How can it be?
O dainty duck, O dear!
Thy mantle good—
What, stained with blood!

. . . .

Come tears, confound;
Out sword, and wound
The pap of Pyramus.
Ay, that left pap,
Where heart doth hop.
Thus die I—thus, thus, thus.
   (He stabs himself.)
Now am I dead,
Now am I fled;
My soul is in the sky.
Tongue, lose thy light;
   (Exit Starveling as Moonshine.)
Moon, take thy flight;
Now die, die, die, die, die.
   (He dies.)

. . . .

   (Enter Flute as Thisbe.)

FLUTE *as Thisbe*

Asleep, my love?
What, dead, my dove?
O Pyramus, arise!
Speak, speak. Quite dumb?
Dead, dead? . . .

Come, trusty sword,
Come blade, my breast imbrue!
  (She stabs herself.)
And farewell friends.
Thus Thisbe ends.
Adieu, adieu, adieu!
  (She dies.)
. . . .

BOTTOM *(starting up)* . . . Will it please you to see the epilogue, or to
  hear a Bergomask dance between two of our company?

THESEUS No epilogue, I pray you; for your play needs no excuse.
  Never excuse; for when the players are all dead, there need none
  to be blamed. Marry, if he that writ it had played Pyramus and
  hanged himself in Thisbe's garter, it would have been a fine
  tragedy. And so it is, truly, and very notably discharged. But
  come, your Bergomask; let your epilogue alone.

The performance ends with the clowns' dance, and the gathering
disperses, leaving the night to Puck and the King and Queen of the
Fairies. And Shakespeare's clowns to the ages.

· 5 ·

THE CLOWN'S
SUPREMACY
IN FRANCE

*Tabarin, Turlupin,
Gautier Garguille, Gros Guillaume,
Jodelet, and the Clowns of Molière*

TABARIN and his hat

The Imaginary Invalid.

Tartuffe: The Hypocrite

Monsieur Jourdain: The Would-be Gentleman

Molière
in stage costume
as Sganarelle

Harpagon:
The Miser

MOLIÈRE and his characters

The seventeenth century was the golden age of French drama. The stately neoclassical tragedies of Racine and Corneille, as well as the satirical comedies of Molière, were subsidized by Louis XIV with a characteristically lavish hand. Troupes of actors, comedians and tragedians alike, followed the Sun King and his court to his magnificent new palace at Versailles. At the same time, a lively, less dignified popular theater, direct descendant of the medieval farces and soties, continued to flourish in the streets of Paris without benefit of royal patronage. Or more accurately, without official royal patronage, for we know of at least one instance in which Louis's grandfather, Henry IV, intervened to rescue a company of farce players from their harshest critics, the Paris magistrates.

Henry was a forthright military man, too preoccupied with his armies and his mistresses to leave much time for the arts. Still, he was a popular monarch—affectionately remembered by the French people even today—who shared his subjects' simple tastes, including a fondness for farcical comedy. One evening in 1607 the king and his party attended a performance at the Hôtel de Bourgogne. The farce pictured three royal tax collectors ransacking a poor man's house; when they incautiously lifted the lid of an enormous chest, three devils leaped out, shoved the men inside, and slammed down the lid. The audience, including Henry and his retinue, roared their approval, but the actors were hauled off to prison for this deliberate insult to the royal dignity. Henry overlooked the offense and laughingly signed the warrant for the actors' release; the comedians paraded back to the theater in triumph and finished their run under royal protection.

Parisian comedians had other worries besides overzealous tax collectors and unappreciative magistrates. They complained bitterly that they were losing their audiences to a rascally pack of peddlers— clowns, musicians, and acrobats hawking homemade herbal medicines in the streets. Parisians willingly bought these worthless elixirs, balms, and powders in gratitude for the performances, and doctors too began to feel the pinch of competition. The street-hawking clowns were roundly denounced as charlatans, which of course they were, but their seventeenth-century medicine shows impudently continued to prosper, and the medicines apparently did no one but the doctors any harm.

§ TABARIN AND HIS HAT §

The most famous of these entertaining fakers was Tabarin. This clown advertised his dubious remedies with genuinely inspired manipulations of a simple comic prop—an oversized, wide-brimmed floppy felt hat. The hat could take on almost any shape, and Tabarin assumed a different comic character to fit each one. Audiences watched enthralled, eager to see how many characters could emerge from Tabarin's celebrated hat. A book appeared around 1622, devoted to *The Pleasant and Delightful Fantasies of Tabarin's Hat,* and a portrait medallion was even struck of Tabarin, his hat pushed up in a pair of long pointed ears, giving him a slightly satanic look.

Tabarin worked with his brother, Mendor, who played the foppish, foolish aristocrat to Tabarin's cunning valet. Master and servant argued such questions as whose backside was the more honorable— the pampered gentleman's or the humble peasant's, which knew only the open air; when Mendor boasted of his noble birth, announcing grandly that blood made the man, Tabarin claimed precedence for himself, since his father had been a butcher.

Evidently Tabarin was something of an upstart offstage as well. One of his critics, a doctor, demanded he be banished from Paris for enriching himself by swindling the people; instead, Tabarin retired with his fortune after seven years of "practice" and installed himself in a handsome villa on the outskirts of the city. The local squires were none too happy to have a vulgar street performer in their midst, and in

1626 Tabarin was fatally shot, in a hunting accident, his neighbors explained. At least the unfortunate Tabarin was assured a sort of immortality—in French, someone who plays the fool is still said to *"faire le tabarin."*

§ THREE PARISIAN CLOWNS §

The Hôtel de Bourgogne—whose company was so graciously and unexpectedly rescued from prison by Henry IV—was the first professional theater in Paris and the home of three other famous clowns with the intriguing names of Turlupin, Gautier Garguille, and Gros Guillaume. Turlupin means "a sorry fellow," though he cut a pretty natty figure in his tailored tunic with a short cape, large upturned hat, long hair, and neatly trimmed beard. Turlupin seems to have based his costume and character on Brighella, one of the brazen, deceitful zanni of the commedia dell'arte, and, true to form, Turlupin specialized in picking pockets while staring his victims straight in the eye.

Turlupin frequently shared the stage with Gautier Garguille, a gangling creature whose oversized head and staring eyes gave him his nickname of "Gargoyle." Parisians relished his dry wit and his ability to twist his spidery limbs with the double-jointed agility of a contortionist. The third member of the trio was Gros Guillaume—"Fat Willy"—a clown who draped himself in a tentlike tunic down to his knees, and cinched a belt around his chest, with another around his waist, so that his already enormous belly preceded him like a bad reputation. Guillaume had been a baker in his youth and is credited with the discovery of the comic and cosmetic properties of flour. Guillaume whitened his face with flour (the modern Whiteface clown uses greasepaint) with plenty to spare for sneezing around the stage and blowing in his partners' faces.

The three sang comic trios together, often songs they composed themselves. This was their specialty number—and it must have been an extraordinary sight—which never failed to pack the house. According to legend, after Gros Guillaume's death, his partners too died, broken-hearted, within the week. A touching story but probably not a true one, though such stories were inspired by the kind of precision teamwork and timing that the clowns of the commedia might have admired. Gautier Garguille left a comic "testament," a popular form with contemporary satirists. It is dated December 45, 24666; he wills his costume and his jokes and routines to various colleagues before leaving for an engagement in the next world. There was more to this than Gautier's playfulness; Molière and lesser comedians of the next generation owed much to the comic legacy of Gautier Garguille, Turlupin, and Gros Guillaume.

Jodelet, another performer who furthered the clown tradition, specialized in playing the valet, a role often appearing in French comedy no doubt due in part to the popularity of Jodelet himself. He was famous for speaking with a whining nasal twang, apparently the result of smallpox, which he turned to comic advantage. He wore a fuzzy short growth of curls covering his chin and lower face. After escaping from a fire that destroyed the Marais Theater, he was depicted as a frightened clown, his head wrapped in a cloth (except for his face) and his hat in his hand, stepping through flames that leaped at his heels and engulfed his cloak. An inscription says he lost every possession in the fire and begs for help to restore him to his customary good humor.

§ MOLIÈRE §

Louis XIV did everything in his power—which was considerable—to make his monarchy "grand, noble, and delicious" (as he put it) and his court the most brilliant in Europe. Accordingly, handsome pensions and commissions were readily made available to artists, authors, and architects who appealed to Louis's exquisite taste, or his insatiable appetite for flattery. Surely one of the best bargains of his long and extravagant reign was the thousand pounds a year paid to the honorary royal bedmaker, an actor and playwright named Jean-Baptiste Poquelin de Molière.

At first, young Jean-Baptiste seemed destined to follow the family trade of furniture making and inherit his father's resounding title, Upholsterer in Ordinary to the Royal Court. His father sent him to a Jesuit academy, where the students put on Latin plays as part of the rigorous classical education; his grandfather had already introduced him to the livelier performances at the Hôtel de Bourgogne. According to one story, his father became suspicious of these excursions and demanded angrily, "What do you want to make of the boy? An actor?" The boy's grandfather replied simply, "I wish to Heaven he might become as good a comedian as Bellerose" (one of the stars of the Hôtel de Bourgogne). In fact, after a flirtation with philosophy and the law, Jean-Baptiste abandoned his studies and his career in his father's furniture factory to pursue his true loves—the theater and, coincidentally, a charming actress named Madeleine Béjart. Jean-Baptiste joined Madeleine and her four brothers and sisters in a company that they optimistically called the Illustrious Theater (it was at this time that Jean-Baptiste took the stage name of Molière, to shield the family name of Poquelin from theatrical notoriety).

The Illustrious Theater's Paris debut in 1643 was a complete disaster. The company went bankrupt in two years, and Molière's exasperated father had to bail him out of debtor's prison. The company prudently decided on an extended provincial tour to sharpen their skills on duller, less demanding audiences. It was thirteen years before they risked a return to Paris, and this barnstorming apprentice-ship turned the Illustrious Theater into a seasoned professional company. Their director and manager, Molière developed into a versatile character actor and a playwright of startling originality. In the last years of their tour they had enjoyed the patronage of a royal governor in the south of France. After their triumphant Parisian comeback in 1658, they quickly attracted the attention and the patronage of the king's brother, and through him, the young king himself. Louis—then barely twenty—was an avid playgoer and enthu-siastic amateur actor (apparently quite a good one, for a king); he became both patron and champion of Molière's company. A theater in one of the royal palaces was turned over to Molière; as an especial mark of royal favor, Louis stood godfather to Molière's son.

The king's favor shielded Molière from the fury of his critics (particularly after the production of *Tartuffe,* a satire of a pious hypocrite which got Molière much disliked by the clergy, and *Don Juan,* which was variously interpreted as an attack on Louis's pleasure-seeking court and an incitement to clear immorality). Both plays were banned, but Louis placidly defied the Tartuffes at court by increasing Molière's pension to a substantial six thousand pounds and placing the troupe—now renamed the King's Players—under his official protection. The court may have preferred less biting entertain-ments, but fortunately for us and for Molière, Louis's taste set the fashion and Molière's comedies were very much to Louis's taste. Molière gave his last performance in 1673; although he was dan-gerously ill, he insisted on going on against the advice of his doctors.

The play was *The Imaginary Invalid,* with Molière in the title role; he collapsed onstage and died a few hours later. It was only through Louis's personal intervention that an actor—even a great one—was permitted a Christian burial, although only secretly, at night, and without ceremony. Eight years after Molière's death, the Hôtel de Bourgogne company and the King's Players were combined by royal decree; the new company came to be called the Comédie-Française, the French state theater, which still flourishes today as the magnificent "House of Molière."

Molière's close association with the Béjarts lasted until his death (Molière's wife was Madeleine's younger sister, or perhaps her daughter—no one seems quite certain). All the comedies were written with the particular players in mind, and of course Molière reserved many of the best roles for himself. Molière's was a comedy of characters rather than situations. He made a particular social type the target of his gentle satire, usually as the embodiment of some prevalent vice of contemporary Parisians. And Molière was an unerring if affectionate critic—his characters are masters of self-deception, single-mindedly intent on making themselves ridiculous, and quite incapable of realizing it. They may be humbled, they are almost always outwitted, but they are never stripped of their illusions. We have already mentioned *Tartuffe* and *Don Juan*—Molière's version of the legendary Spanish libertine; in *The Miser* we meet Harpagon—so stingy that he will not give you good morning but only lend it. In *The Doctor in Spite of Himself* and *The Imaginary Invalid,* Molière satirizes quack doctors and their hypochondriacal patients; in *The Learned Ladies,* the overeducated literary ladies of the *salons;* and in *The Misanthrope,* a satire of the emptiness of court life, Molière seems to be satirizing Molière.

As we have noted, Molière owed much to the commedia dell'arte and the farce tradition—broad comedy of intrigue and trickery; he also admired the intricacy, urbanity, and realistic social portraiture of Roman comedy. (He had learned enough Latin from the Jesuit fathers to produce a French verse adaptation of Plautus's *Amphitryon.*) Molière made the farce elegant and respectable, ancient comedy topical and contemporary; he was a keen observer of all classes of French society, and he cocked an especially ironical eye at the pretensions of the prosperous middle class, the bourgeoisie.

In Molière's time many French men and women of bourgeois origin were infiltrating the aristocracy. Louis awarded titles of nobility to officials who served him well, and wealthy, ambitious bourgeois who simply paid well. Social climbers on the lower rungs of Parisian society contented themselves with ostentatious displays of wealth and the slavish imitation of aristocratic manners. Molière's Monsieur Jourdain in *The Would-Be Gentleman* was the good-hearted but simple-minded model of such a "bourgeois gentleman." Molière's audiences—the genuine aristocrats at court and comfortable Paris bourgeois who had already "arrived"—must have enjoyed the earnest attempts of the newly rich M. Jourdain to purchase polish and refinement. He hired a flock of tailors, tutors, and instructors to make him into a man of fashion, with all the tastes and accomplishments of the "people of quality," and a couple of footmen to impress his callers just by looking expensive in their powdered wigs and livery.

In this scene from *The Would-Be Gentleman* the Music Master and the Dancing Master greedily anticipate M. Jourdain's arrival by gloating over the princely fees they expect to charge for his lessons in gentility.

MUSIC MASTER In this man Jourdain we both have the person we need . . .

DANCING MASTER But it would be nice if he possessed a little understanding of what we teach him and what we represent.

MUSIC MASTER Still the money is good, and that is what we both need just now.

DANCING MASTER True, but more than money I crave applause—it is the thing I live for. And nothing distresses me so much as the artist who must perform for fools. But to share one's artistic gifts with people who truly appreciate our beauty is pure joy, like no other.

MUSIC MASTER I agree exactly, but even an artist cannot live on applause . . . and this Jourdain, however poor his judgment, makes up for it in cash. . . .

DANCING MASTER . . . Cultivated persons should be above vulgar considerations of money.

MUSIC MASTER Still, I notice you don't refuse our friend's pay.

DANCING MASTER Definitely not. . . . But nevertheless I still wish that along with his fortune he had some taste.

MUSIC MASTER So do I. But, after all, that is what we are here for, to help him—so far as we can . . .

DANCING MASTER Be still! He is here.

(Enter M. Jourdain in an elaborate dressing gown, followed by two footmen who remain in attendance just inside the door.)

JOURDAIN Here we are, gentlemen. What will it be today? Some more of your fooleries?

DANCING MASTER Fooleries?

JOURDAIN You know—whatever it is you call your la-de-das. Your singing and dancing, that's it.

DANCING MASTER Oh, *that's* what you mean.

JOURDAIN *(showing off his printed dressing gown)* I had this Indian robe done up expressly for me.

DANCING MASTER Very handsome indeed.

JOURDAIN People of quality, the tailor tells me, go about this way in the morning.

MUSIC MASTER It's very you. *(He winks knowingly at his fellow artist.)*

JOURDAIN And my footmen? How do you like them? . . .

DANCING MASTER Both are splendid.

(Calling for the footmen to take his robe, M. Jourdain steps forth in red velvet pants and a green velvet jacket.)

JOURDAIN How do you like my exercise suit?

DANCING MASTER *(astonished by the clashing colors)* Just the thing.

JOURDAIN Well, then, let's begin . . .

MUSIC MASTER *(self-importantly)* I would like you to hear a serenade. . . .

JOURDAIN *(to his footmen)* Bring me my gown again so that I can hear better. No, I think I can hear better without it. On the other hand, give it back. I am at my best with it on. *(The footmen pass the gown back and forth while M. Jourdain makes up his mind.)*

(When the song has been sung, the Music Master waits for M. Jourdain's verdict.)

JOURDAIN It puts me to sleep. Couldn't you speed it up here and there?

MUSIC MASTER The music must fit the words.

JOURDAIN I knew a song once. How did it go?

DANCING MASTER I have no idea!

JOURDAIN It had to do with a sheep.

DANCING MASTER A sheep?

JOURDAIN Yes. Ah! *(He sings a dreadful song in doggerel.)* Isn't that pretty?

MUSIC MASTER *(sarcastically)* Oh, very!

DANCING MASTER And you sing it so well.

JOURDAIN Yet I have never learned music.

MUSIC MASTER But you must, just as you are learning to dance. The two arts are closely related.

DANCING MASTER And add to one's sense of beauty.

JOURDAIN Do people of quality learn music, too?

MUSIC MASTER Of course!

JOURDAIN Then I'll learn it. But I don't know where I'm going to find the time what with fencing lessons and philosophy lessons . . .

MUSIC MASTER Philosophy is important. But music, sir, music is . . .

DANCING MASTER Music and dance. If you learn music and dance you need nothing else.

MUSIC MASTER But music, sir, is the most useful art of all.

DANCING MASTER And dance the most necessary to mankind!

MUSIC MASTER All the disorders, all the wars in the world today, are the result of not learning music.

DANCING MASTER All of man's troubles, all of history's miseries, the blunders of politicians, the failures of great leaders, all result from not knowing how to dance.

JOURDAIN How is that?

MUSIC MASTER What is war but a lack of unity among men?

JOURDAIN True!

MUSIC MASTER But if all men studied music, wouldn't they learn to live in harmony? . . .

JOURDAIN You are right.

DANCING MASTER And when a man makes a mistake, in his private life, in running the government, in commanding the army, don't we say that he is out of step?

JOURDAIN We do.

DANCING MASTER And being out of step comes from not knowing how to dance.

JOURDAIN True enough. Both of you are correct.

DANCING MASTER We want you to see the importance and usefulness of music and dance.

JOURDAIN I do. I do.

M. Jourdain cheerfully muddles through his lessons in dancing, fencing, spelling, and elementary elocution (he learns "the correct pronunciation of the vowels and consonants"). Finally, he asks the philosophy instructor for advice on a matter of some delicacy.

JOURDAIN I want you to assist me in a little note that I can drop at the feet of a certain countess.

PHILOSOPHER Of course. . . . Do you want it to be in verse?

JOURDAIN No, no, I'll have none of your verse.

PHILOSOPHER Then it's to be in prose?

JOURDAIN No. I don't want it in verse *or* prose.

PHILOSOPHER But it must be in one or the other.

JOURDAIN Why?

PHILOSOPHER Because, my dear sir, that's all there is to express yourself with: verse or prose.

JOURDAIN You mean there's nothing but prose or verse?

PHILOSOPHER That's right. Everything that's not prose is verse and everything that's not verse is prose.

JOURDAIN And when talking as I am now, what is that?

PHILOSOPHER Prose.

JOURDAIN *(astonished)* Really! And when I say, "Nicole, bring my slippers" or "Give me my nightcap," that is prose?

PHILOSOPHER Yes, sir.

JOURDAIN Upon my word! I've been speaking prose for more than forty years without knowing it.

As dramatist, performer, director, and social critic, Molière was a clown of genius, perhaps the greatest France has ever known. Each year the Comédie-Française reminds us that we are still the happy benefactors of roles he created for himself to play more than three hundred years ago.

·6·

THE
RESTORATION AND
THE EIGHTEENTH
CENTURY

Fops, British Harlequins and Pantomimes,
Sheridan's Clowns, America's Jonathan
and France's Figaro

Figaro

Sir Novelty
Fashion

―――――――――――――

In the generation after Shakespeare's death in 1616, the English stage was dominated by escapist "tragicomedies," full of swordplay, seduction, and in the eyes of those harshest of critics, the Puritans, "hideous obscenities." The Puritans seized control of London in 1642 and the playhouses were closed for eighteen years. A few reopened after the monarchy was restored, but for several decades the theater was no longer a popular entertainment. Its audiences were exclusive and aristocratic—and Restoration comedies reflected the brilliantly superficial world of a society preoccupied with fashion and appearance: gallants and gossips, flirtatious ladies of fashion and their fatuous husbands, who came to the theater to admire and be admired, and incidentally to see themselves satirized on the stage. The Restoration ideal of perfection of manners and elegance of dress was personified by the figure of the fop; the greatest of these was the actor, dramatist, and "nationally celebrated coxcomb" Colley Cibber (1671–1757).

Cibber might have been created by Molière, perhaps as The Would-Be Tragedian or Comedian in Spite of Himself. Painfully aware of "the insufficiency of [his] voice," his small size, and "dismal, pale complexion," as he puts it in his autobiography, Cibber nonetheless clung to his fantasy of playing the tragic hero to the queen-sized tragic heroines of Mrs. Bracegirdle, an imposing leading lady of the Restoration stage. Cibber's first few appearances in minor parts were scarcely encouraging. He philosophically shrugged his narrow shoulders and set out to write a comedy showcase for his unappreciated gifts. *Love's Last Shift; or the Fool in Fashion,* featuring Colley Cibber as the gossipy, overdressed dandy Sir Novelty Fashion, was a great success. Realizing that "tis not *what* we act, but *how* we act what is allotted us, that speaks our value," Cibber went on to exploit his talent for making himself ridiculous in the roles of Lord Foppington and Sir Fopling Flutter.

Although he managed the Drury Lane Theatre for thirty years (1710–1740) and finally became the poet laureate of England, Cibber never quite succeeded in getting people to take him seriously. He is largely remembered today because several eminent men of letters, the poet Pope and the novelist Fielding, among them, persisted in making fun of him. Cibber probably looked on this as simply good publicity. Like Sir Novelty, he wanted nothing more than to be noticed.

Here comes Sir Novelty, showing off his extravagant fop's wardrobe to two young ladies, Narcissa and Hillaria, in a fashionable London garden:

SIR NOVELTY Pray, madam, how do I look today? The town does talk of me, indeed; but, the devil take me, in my mind I am a very ugly fellow.

NARCISSA Now you are too severe, Sir Novelty.

SIR NOVELTY Not I, burn me. For heaven's sake, deal freely with me, madam, and if you can, tell me one tolerable thing about me.

NARCISSA Oh, Sir Novelty, it is hard to know the brightest part of a diamond.

SIR NOVELTY You'll make me blush, stop my vitals, madam. *(In an aside to the audience)* Egad, I always said she was a woman of sense. Strike me dumb, I am in love with her.

NARCISSA I'll warrant there's not a tailor in town but has got rich by you.

SIR NOVELTY I must confess, madam, I am for doing good to my country.

Sir Novelty stops fishing for compliments momentarily to gossip. He starts by criticizing the wardrobe of young Mr. Worthy, with whom Narcissa is secretly in love.

SIR NOVELTY . . . the devil take me if I did not meet him in a coat with buttons no bigger than nutmegs.

HILLARIA There I must confess you outdo him.

SIR NOVELTY Oh, dear madam, why mine are not above three inches in diameter.

HILLARIA But methinks, Sir Novelty, your sleeve is a little extravagant.

SIR NOVELTY Nay, madam, there you wrong me; mine does but just reach my knuckles. But my Lord Overdo's covers his diamond ring. *(He hides his hand in his sleeve.)* I don't question but this very suit . . . the garter, the sword knot, the large button, and the long sleeve, were all created or revived by me. In a word, madam, there has never been anything agreeable for these ten years past, but your humble servant was the author of it.

Sir Novelty explains his custom of visiting all the playhouses in a single night—so that all of London will have a chance to see him leaving.

SIR NOVELTY But if I do stay a play out, I always sit with my back to the stage.

NARCISSA Why so, sir?

SIR NOVELTY Then everybody will imagine I have seen it before, or that I am jealous of who talks in the King's box. And thus, madam, do I take more pains to preserve a public reputation than ever any lady took after the smallpox to recover her complexion.

For all his outsized personal ambitions and preposterous affectations, Colley Cibber made a genuine contribution to English theater. The pleasant, sentimental comedies that Cibber wrote and produced played a large part in softening and transforming the flashy cynicism of the Restoration stage and making way for the comedies of manners perfected in the late eighteenth century by Goldsmith and Sheridan.

§ JOHN RICH §

Pantomime was introduced into England by an eccentric comic genius named John Rich (1692–1761). There had been English Harlequins before Rich, but Rich's *Harlequin Sorcerer* in 1717 was the first really successful Harlequin play. Rich had inherited the Lincoln's Inn Fields Theatre from his father and continued to manage it himself; as Harlequin, Rich the actor rescued Rich the manager from serious financial difficulties. He repeated his triumph every season until his death in 1761, and the Harlequin "panto" still remains a popular English Christmas entertainment today.

Rich was a strange and complicated man, an actor who despised all other actors and a manager who hated audiences. (At least he seems to have been very fond of cats—at one time as many as thirty shared his household and accompanied him everywhere except onstage.) Rich's contempt for serious drama doubtless prompted him to produce John Gay's enormously popular *Beggar's Opera* in 1728. Gay's satirical ballad opera, the ancestral English musical comedy, was a bold attack on political corruption, Italian opera, and much else besides. After an unprecedentedly long run of sixty-two nights, London wits remarked that success had made Gay rich and Rich gay. That would have been quite out of character for Rich, but we know in any case that it did make him richer. The profits enabled him to build the Covent Garden Theatre in 1732, which became the only serious rival to Colley Cibber's Drury Lane.

Since Rich sincerely believed that he was England's greatest actor—at least the equal of the great tragedian of the Drury Lane Theatre, David Garrick—he had no other ambition than to keep surpassing himself. The first half of a typical Rich pantomime was a mythological tableau with rapid scene changes and elaborate special effects (backstage at his new Covent Garden Theatre was a thicket of ropes and machinery). The second half, the real show—designed to show off Rich's own masterful comedy of motion—was devoted to Harlequin's pursuit of Columbine.

Rich's Harlequin owed little to the familiar commedia figure; from his new English name, Lun, to his fresh repertory of comic and acrobatic routines, he was very much Rich's creation. Masked and completely silent, Lun was still spectacularly expressive—he conveyed momentary bafflement, for example, by scratching an ear with his foot. Pathos was a Rich specialty, and he made Lun's farewell to Columbine especially touching. Rich's best-remembered routine came from *Harlequin Sorcerer*. When Lun Junior asked his father how the human race came to be, Rich pantomimed a giant egg being hatched by the rays of the sun. Kneeling, he slowly chipped his way out of the imaginary shell; he cautiously felt his way along the stage, gaining courage, then standing upright he confidently strode away. One admiring spectator commented, "Every limb had its tongue, and every motion a voice which spoke with most miraculous organ to the understanding and sensations of the observers."

Characteristically, Rich was unmoved by such tributes, and the amused contempt he felt for his public only increased with success. Before going on to give such a performance, it was his custom to peep through the curtain and count the house, then say, sneering, "What, are you there? Well, much good may it do you!"

§ HENRY WOODWARD §

Audiences kept coming to Covent Garden, doubtless to Rich's exasperation, and Garrick, the manager of the Drury Lane Theatre, was driven to adopt desperate remedies to remain in competition. Garrick was commonly reckoned (except by Rich) to be the greatest actor in England. He had made his reputation in Shakespearean drama, and he championed the revival of Shakespeare's great tragedies, sometimes staging them more or less as they were written—often restoring the cuts and throwing out the bizarre revisions and adaptations made by earlier actors and playwrights. Nevertheless, Harlequin was added to the Drury Lane repertory, since as Garrick explained in a rueful prologue to the 1750 season:

> Sacred to Shakespeare was this plot designed,
> To pierce the heart, and humanize the mind,
> But if an empty house, the actor's curse,
> Shows us our Lears and Hamlets lose their force,
> Unwilling we must change the nobler scene,
> And, in our turn, present you Harlequin,
> Quit poets, and set carpenters to work,
> Show gawdy scenes, or mount the faulting Turk,
> For though we actors one and all agree
> Boldly to struggle for our vanity,
> If want comes on, importance must retreat;
> Our first great ruling passion—is to eat.

Garrick cast a handsome young actor named Henry Woodward as Drury Lane's Harlequin. Woodward was a "highly ingenious" mime (he had been trained by Rich himself); moreover, Garrick felt that the novelty of a talking Harlequin would be a powerful lure for London audiences after thirty years of Rich's silent comedy. Woodward's pantomime technique, not as original and innovative as Rich's, recalls the traditional lazzi of the Italian comedians. He was famous for his emotional "attitudes"—poses struck to music suggesting anger, jealousy, fear, and so on—and a mimetic gift for sucking imaginary oranges and gobbling invisible currants and gooseberries off a stem with such realism that spectators swore they could see the pits he pretended to spit out on the stage.

Woodward also came close to equaling Rich in displays of temperament—he was especially rude on the nights he played Harlequin. Only Garrick could put up with him, perhaps because he had to—at least until Woodward took off for Dublin to co-manage his own theater, leaving Garrick to hunt in vain for a new Harlequin. Woodward never seriously challenged John Rich's popularity, but at least his success as Harlequin permitted Garrick and his fellow players to have their Shakespeare and eat too.

§ SHERIDAN'S CLOWNS §

Garrick's successor was Richard Brinsley Sheridan (1751–1816), who became director of the Drury Lane company in 1776, a year after his first great success, *The Rivals,* which was written when he was only twenty-three. Together with Garrick's close friend Oliver Goldsmith, Sheridan popularized a witty new "comedy of manners," brilliant and satirical, but without the smirking undertones of Restoration comedy. Sheridan's best-known creation is Mrs. Malaprop, a talkative and opinionated matron whose unequal struggle with the language leaves the stage strewn with limping, mangled phrases—"a nice derangement of epitaphs," as she put it, or "malapropisms," as we say today. Mrs. Malaprop's name comes from the French *mal à propos*—"unsuitable" or "inappropriate" (a "malapropism" is a word similar in sound to the right one but ludicrously different in meaning)—and she practiced a kind of cheerful linguistic butchery that might have left even Constable Dogberry appalled. (Jimmy Durante, Gertrude Berg—creator of the kitchen-window philosopher Molly Goldberg—

and Archie Bunker are three inspired twentieth-century descendants of Mrs. Malaprop.)

In this scene from *The Rivals,* Mrs. Malaprop tells Sir Anthony Absolute of the difficulties she has had rearing her niece, Lydia Languish:

MRS. MALAPROP There, Sir Anthony *(she points to Lydia),* there sits the deliberate simpleton who wants to disgrace her family, and lavish herself on a fellow not worth a shilling!

LYDIA Madam, I thought . . .

MRS. MALAPROP You thought, Miss! I don't know any business you have to think at all. Thought does not become a young woman. But the point we would request of you is, that you will promise to forget this fellow—to illiterate him, I say, quite from your memory.

SIR ANTHONY Aye, this comes of her reading!

LYDIA What crime, madam, have I committed to be treated thus?

MRS. MALAPROP Now don't attempt to extirpate yourself from the matter; you know I have proof convertible of it. But tell me, will you promise to do as you're bid? Will you take a husband of your friend's choosing?

LYDIA Madam, I must tell you plainly, that had I no preference for anyone else, the choice you have made would be my aversion.

MRS. MALAPROP What business have you, Miss, with *preference* and *aversion?* They don't become a young woman; and you ought to know, that as both always wear off, 'tis safest in matrimony to begin with a little *aversion. (Sends Lydia to her room.)* You are fit company for nothing but your own ill-humours.

Sir Anthony suggests that Lydia's impertinence and independence are "the natural consequences of teaching girls to read." At most, he argues, young women should be allowed to learn the alphabet and the numbers from 1 to 20. Mrs. Malaprop responds with her own views on the education of women:

MRS. MALAPROP Observe me, Sir Anthony. I would by no means wish a daughter of mine to be a progeny of learning; I don't think so much learning becomes a young woman; for instance—I would never let her meddle with Greek, or Hebrew, or Algebra, or Simony, or Fluxions, or Paradoxes, or such inflammatory branches of learning. Neither would it be necessary for her to handle any of your mathematical, astronomical, diabolical instruments. But, Sir Anthony, I would send her, at nine years old, to a boarding school, in order to learn a little ingenuity and artifice. Then, sir, she should have a supercilious knowledge in accounts. And as she grew up, I would have her instructed in geometry, that she might know something of the contagious countries. But above all, Sir Anthony, she should be mistress of orthodoxy, that she might not mis-spell, and mispronounce words so shamefully as girls usually do. And likewise that she might reprehend the true meaning of what she is saying. This, Sir Anthony, is what I would have a woman know, and I don't think there is a superstitious article in it.

Lydia's most ardent suitor is one Bob Acres, a simple country squire who comes to the resort of Bath, the setting of *The Rivals,* in the hope of making a good impression on the susceptible Lydia. Acres tries to adapt to the world of fashion by making himself over as an elegant, affected fop. He succeeds admirably, and here he explains to his friend Captain Absolute the reason for his transformation.

BOB Lydia . . . could never abide me in the country, because I used to dress so badly—but odds frogs and tambours! I shan't take matters so here. My hair has been in training some time. *(He removes his hat, revealing a luxuriant hairdo, full of paper twists, pins, and combs.)* . . . The side curls are a little restive but the hindpart takes to the new arrangement very kindly. Odds triggers and flints!

CAPT. ABSOLUTE Bob, I observe you have got an odd kind of a new method of swearing—

BOB Ha! Ha! You've taken notice of it? 'Tis genteel, isn't it?

CAPT. ABSOLUTE Very genteel, and very new, indeed . . .

BOB Damns have had their day.

Bob Acres swaggers offstage, proud of his fashionable new clothes and his remarkable innovations in the field of "sentimental swearing."

§ AMERICA'S JONATHAN AND §
FRANCE'S FIGARO

Another country boy's arrival in the big city is the subject of Royall Tyler's *The Contrast* (1787), the first American comedy. Colonel Manly introduces his manservant Jonathan, a New England farmboy, to the strange sights of New York. Jonathan finds the city a little bewildering at first—when he goes to the theater, he imagines that he has mistakenly blundered into the mansion of the elegant notables he sees on the stage. Unlike Bob Acres, Jonathan sticks to his country manners and steady Yankee habits and forces the city slickers to accept him on his own terms. Jonathan's humor is a typical frontier mixture of sly understatement and wild exaggeration—he apologetically admits that he knows only 190 verses of "Yankee Doodle," but he adds that his girl friend back home can sing it all the way through to the end. For Tyler and his countrymen, Jonathan, with his simple patriotism, Yankee integrity, and homespun humor, embodied all that was best in the American character. Jonathan was also the first stage expression of the folklore of the frontier—and Tyler's forthright Yankee with a fondness for tall tales is still recognizable in the later humor of Davy Crockett and Mark Twain and the twentieth-century comedy of Will Rogers and Andy Griffith.

Another spokesman of the common man in an age of revolution was Figaro in Beaumarchais's *The Marriage of Figaro*. More familiar today in the comic-opera adaptations of Mozart and Rossini, Figaro is the resourceful valet of a rather dissolute nobleman, the theatrical descendant of the tricky slave of antiquity and the cunning servant of the commedia. Beaumarchais (as was Sheridan) was an active friend of the American Revolution. When *Figaro* was produced in 1784, five years before the French Revolution, the Paris censors condemned certain scenes as subversive; Figaro's attack on aristocratic privilege, as the censors clearly recognized, was nothing less than a clown's serious affirmation of the rights of man.

In the last act of the play, Figaro confronts the count with a defiant declaration of equality: "Because you are a great lord you think you are a great genius. Nobility, wealth, honors . . . it all makes a man so proud! What have you done to earn so many advantages? You took the trouble to be born, nothing more. Apart from that, you're a common type. Whereas I, lost in the herd, had to exert more skill merely to survive than has been spent for a hundred years in governing this country. And you want to tangle with *me!*"

Figaro proved that laughter is the most humanizing, as well as the most critical, force mankind possesses. In using it, he pleaded the cause of freedom and made his point. In one French dictionary the entry under "Figaro" reads: "Another of the causes of the French Revolution." For when the comic servant became the symbol of the common man, the oppressed found the strength to declare in unison: "And you want to tangle with *me!*"

· 7 ·

NINETEENTH-CENTURY CLOWNING

*Early American Clowns, Joseph Grimaldi,
Two Clowns Named Rice, Harrigan and Hart,
Gilbert and Sullivan, and Others*

"Joey"
(Joseph
Grimaldi)

Punchinello   Pantaloon   Harlequin

On September 21, 1786, a New York City advertisement announced a forthcoming performance by a certain Mr. Pool, who claimed to be the first American ever to exhibit such remarkable "Feats of Horsemanship" as mounting three galloping horses at once, standing up in the saddle, and jumping over a bar. Actually, John Sharp had produced a similar entertainment fifteen years earlier in Salem, Massachusetts. But Pool's real claim to originality is more important to our story, for his advertisement also boasted, in bold type, that "A CLOWN will entertain the Ladies and Gentlemen."

Exhibitions of horsemanship and clowning were already popular in England. In 1770 the equestrian showman Philip Astley presented a variety show combining his own displays of "activity on horseback" with the rough-and-tumble antics of Billie Button, the first true circus clown. In an enclosed area not far from Westminster Bridge, Astley astonished Londoners by riding at a gallop while standing on his head, dressed in the colorful scarlet uniform of the light dragoons. Billie's activity on horseback apparently emphasized falling as much as riding, and a number of other clowns whose names appear in Astley's advertisements were soon following Billie's hilarious example around the single ring of Astley's wooden amphitheater. Encouraged by the success of these entertainments, Astley built a new grandstand to seat three thousand spectators and added trained animal acts, acrobats, tightrope walkers, and tumblers—bringing together for the first time on one stage all the ingredients of the modern circus.

Astley's success in London and later Paris inspired a flock of imitators, and clowns appeared on every bill. Charles Hughes, a fashionable riding master, styled his company as The Royal Circus, a mark of particular favor. In 1792 Hughes's pupil John Bill Ricketts brought the circus, complete with clowns and tightrope artistes, to his riding academy in Philadelphia. President George Washington, himself a noted rider, attended in April 1793. He was so impressed with Ricketts's hornpipe danced on the saddle of a galloping horse, and the antics of Mr. Merryman, the clown, that he came back the very next night, bringing the First Lady with him. The local press gave Ricketts a rave notice, recommending the circus as the very thing "to dispel the gloom of the thoughtful, exercise the lively activity of the young and gay, or to relax the mind of the sedentary. . . ." When Ricketts took his show on tour, a company of actors in New York presenting a sophisticated comedy preferred to cancel its performance rather than compete with the circus, prompting the satirical comment that "Sheridan and *The School for Scandal* gave way for Ricketts and Clown."

His triumphant tour concluded, Ricketts began to produce his own plays in an elaborate new playhouse he built himself in Philadelphia. His colorful pantomimes and gaudy spectacles dominated the theatrical life of the new nation's capital. Unfortunately, Ricketts's special effects were so painstakingly realistic that the flames of hell enveloping the rascally hero in the final scene of *Don Juan* set fire to the theater and burned it to the ground. Ricketts's career in America was at an end. He resolved to return to England but was drowned at sea—a melodramatic exit for a showman who had done so much to establish the circus and the clown as permanent fixtures of American popular entertainment.

During this period traveling road companies not only brought the circus to the seaboard towns and larger cities but also reached out into the thinly settled frontier wilderness. Travel was slow, an actor's life difficult and dangerous, but amusements were few and laughter was always welcome.

§ JOHN DURANG, PIONEER CLOWN §

John Durang was one of the first American entertainers whom we can truly call a clown. He was born in Pennsylvania in 1768 and died there in 1822 after a long and astonishingly varied career as an actor, dancer, musician, equestrian, acrobat, tightrope walker, artist, designer, and puppeteer. He began his lifelong involvement with the circus and the theater as a boy of eight, playing the character of Mercury in a mythological pageant in Philadelphia, part of our nation's first Fourth of July celebration. (He remembered proudly that Benjamin Franklin himself was present when he was fitted for his costume.) He never passed up a chance to perform in public ("Music and dancing was my attraction"), and, still stage-struck at fifteen, he ran off to Boston to join a magic-lantern troupe.

Shortly afterward he attracted the attention of Lewis Hallam the Younger, a noted actor-manager, and became a member of his Old American Company. In his *Memoir* Durang recalls the excitement on nights that George Washington visited Hallam's playhouse. Attended by a troop of soldiers posted around the theater, the general made his entrance. Dressed in black velvet and accompanied by his "trusty dog," Washington was ceremoniously escorted to his seat in the half-darkened theater by the company's star comedian, bearing a lighted candle.

Durang's own watercolor illustrations for his book have left us a vivid portrait of this amusing man in action. He specialized in quick-change "before and after" transformations. He first appeared onstage as a tiny man, three feet tall, decked out in an elegant red suit and high-plumed headpiece; his unsophisticated audiences roared with laughter as the tiny man suddenly vanished, leaving a six-foot woman wearing a long dress and apron standing in his place. Another illustration from the *Memoir* shows Durang costumed as Harlequin, black-masked and posed impudently on his pedestal, club tucked under his arm. He stands poised in the ballet fifth position, ready for a sudden mischievous leap from his pedestal, a furious attack on the painted cloth backdrop with his club—capped by one of the expert acrobatic routines that were Durang's particular pride.

This versatile pioneer clown was equally at home playing Shakespeare's Richard III before a Pennsylvania Dutch audience in their own German vernacular, staging puppet shows for children, riding horses, tumbling on the slack rope, supporting a human pyramid on his shoulders, acting, directing, building and painting sets, and coaching his child actors in the exacting technique of pantomime. For much of his life he toured widely up and down the eastern seaboard, with one extensive stay in Canada. His audiences were farmers at county fairs, settlers in remote frontier villages, and hunters and fellow wayfarers at roadside taverns. Although Durang was by no means a great artist, his company brought a brief taste of fantasy and excitement to people whose lives were still basically harsh and primitive, just as had the strolling players of medieval Europe centuries before.

§ JOSEPH GRIMALDI §

The comic character that most of us associate with the word "clown"—now universally known by the nickname Joey—was originated by Joseph Grimaldi around the turn of the nineteenth century.

Grimaldi was born in London in 1778, the illegitimate son of an aging Italian dancing master then appearing in pantomimes and a young dancer in the chorus of the Drury Lane Theatre. At an extremely early age (his *Memoirs* claim he was only a year and eleven months old) Joe made his professional debut in the Harlequinade. This lively art form had undergone some changes since Rich's day and in fact came to resemble the frantic spectacle of the Italian original more than Rich's sensitive pantomime tableaux. To these exotic ingredients, English actors added homelier flavorings from their own fairy tales and popular novels. For instance, *Harlequin Whittington* introduced Harlequin into the familiar story of Dick Whittington and his cat; *Harlequin Gulliver, Harlequin and Cinderella,* and *Harlequin and Mother Goose* were also whipped up into elaborate holiday confections. The original story line served primarily as a showcase for singers, dancers, and specialty performers of all sorts. The rapidly moving plot involved very little dialogue and consisted mainly of one continuous chase, frequently interrupted by the entrance of acrobats, animal acts, ballet sequences, and satirical comments on fashion, manners, and topical events. The bewildering pace of the spectacle was helped along by stage illusions, transformation scenes (one location was dissolved into another before the spectators' eyes without bringing down the curtain), and striking special effects— apparitions, royal processions, land and sea battles, explosions, burning castles, natural wonders, and supernatural miracles. This was the popular theater to which Joseph Grimaldi was born.

Tyrannized by a cruel and eccentric father, Joey meekly played whatever role he was ordered to perform. Joey's father preferred to keep him out of school for eight months of the year and earning a salary on the stage (sometimes two salaries, for at one time Joey was appearing in two different theaters on the same night). Joey had nothing but warm memories of the life he led at his boarding school in Putney, but all too soon his father whisked him back to London to rehearse for a new pantomime season. The elder Grimaldi, then in his seventies, apparently could not bear to see the boy happy. His fellow actors described him as a true monster—strong, wicked, and unpredictably violent. As an old man, Joe could still recall the thrashings he received, how his father lifted him "by the hair of his head" and set him down in a corner of the green room (the actors' backstage waiting room), warning him that he dared "to move at his peril."

"Clever little Joe," as the other actors in the company called him, could not sit still for very long. As soon as his father left, he tumbled out of the corner, showing off some stunt he was practicing to add to his stage monkeyshines. (In fact, his impersonation of a mischievous monkey was one of his first notable successes. Dressed in a long-tailed monkey suit, a chain wrapped around his waist, he was led about the stage by his father, who would lift and twirl him around at great speed at the end of the chain. In the middle of one performance the chain snapped, hurling Joe out past the footlights, over the heads of the orchestra, and far into the audience. He landed, dazed but unhurt, in the arms of an old man who had been avidly taking in the show and was surprised to find its star performer sitting in his lap.)

With his father safely out of the theater, the boy could rehearse for hours on end, or at least until someone called out, "Joe! Joe! Here's your father!" Then he would hurry back to his corner and pick up where he had left off, whimpering and wailing as though he hadn't stopped since his father had left. Before too long the actors began to sound the warning simply because they loved to watch Joey's incredible transformation on the cue of his father's real or imagined footsteps at the stage door.

Joe was only nine when his father died, but he was already a veteran actor and was readily engaged by such well-known London theaters as Sadler's Wells, Covent Garden, and Drury Lane. He remained active and successful in pantomime, although not until the unprecedented success of his *Harlequin and Mother Goose* in 1806, when he was twenty-eight, did he win a truly national reputation.

Joe's essential comic gift was the uncanny mobility and expressiveness of his face and body. Whether he was playing the Clown of the Harlequinade, Bob Acres, or one of Shakespeare's comic characters, Joe's glances, winces, and scowls instantly projected his volatile emotions to the farthest reaches of the gallery. His nose seemed almost to roam at will around his face. His busy tongue darted out irrepressibly, slyly punctuating a joke or signaling heartfelt but inexpressible feeling. His jaw, a contemporary recalled, had the power to lower his chin an alarming distance down his waistcoat, taking his ears along with it. His famous grin was said to travel across his plump face from ear to ear, then, just as suddenly, to retreat into a frown or grimace.

His rubbery features were made up to exaggerate his bushy eyebrows and stretch his forehead up to the blue topknot on his otherwise bald head. His eyes sparkled through painted circles, as though they were staring through two large knotholes. The patterns painted on his cheeks varied from one character to the next; for example, two tilted red triangles emphasized the expressive eyes, nose, and mouth of the Clown. This makeup, applied over a base of pure white, supplied the basic funny face on which clowns still compose their own greasepaint variations today.

Stocky and muscular, Grimaldi possessed total command of his agile body; he could move as nimbly as any dancer. "Every limb of him had a language," boasted an admirer, who added that his Clown need not speak because his movements said everything. All the same, Grimaldi developed a good speaking and singing voice, which he put to excellent use in routines and songs written especially for him. These songs became identified with the character of the Clown over the years, and Joe's audiences clamored for them wherever he appeared.

Grimaldi was an expert swordsman, and his roles frequently called for dueling scenes in which he could scamper about, narrowly escaping extinction through skillful acrobatics. When not fighting with swords, he swallowed them, or at least pretended to, some with blades of enormous size. In a single performance he might have to take dangerous falls and leap and tumble vigorously around the stage until he was exhausted. He was often on the verge of collapse by the time he made his last exit. Yet he boasted in his *Memoirs* that he never wore padding of any kind to minimize the inevitable bruises and other hazards of his profession.

All these impressive abilities would not have earned him the title "King of Clowns" if he had not also been a tireless inventor of new acts and tricks. Joe and his fellow players were expected to come up with a fresh assortment of special effects for each new pantomime. Many required props, costumes, and sets made according to his exact specifications. Since Joe was also a skillful carpenter, he could easily provide a model for each new design.

If sets or props were unavailable, Grimaldi could improvise brilliantly with whatever he could scrape together. Once he arrived at a theater in Birmingham only to discover it had none of the equipment necessary for pantomime. He asked the manager what sort of properties he could locate on short notice for that evening.

"What? Properties!" shouted the manager. "You London stars require a hundred things where we country people are content with one. However, whatever you want you shall have." And with that he sent his errand boy out to the market for a pig, a goose, and two ducks, explaining that "Mr. Grimaldi wants some properties and must have them."

Naturally enough, Joe thought the manager had completely misunderstood his request or was playing some sort of bizarre joke. But, sure enough, in a few minutes the company exploded with laughter as the boy dutifully returned bearing the "properties," loudly protesting their sudden and involuntary involvement with the stage. Whatever the manager might have understood by "properties"—and we might well wonder ourselves—Joe decided the joke would do perfectly for his first performance in Birmingham.

The curtain rose and the Clown came on, wearing an old livery coat with two enormous pockets, a duck's head poking out from each, the pig under one arm, the goose under the other, and a basket on his back overflowing with carrots and turnips. The audience howled at the sight of the countrified clown, who looked like nothing more than a walking marketplace. This was the sort of theater the good folk of Birmingham could lustily appreciate. Joe was called back for three encores of the comic song "Tippitywitchit," and the house was packed for all four nights of Joe's engagement.

Grimaldi introduced his "Joey" on the Drury Lane stage in 1800. The new clown quickly supplanted Harlequin as the star of the pantomime. Joey was a clown with an insatiable appetite—gobbling down countless strings of sausages and ropes of macaroni, trays of tarts, bowls of pudding, innumerable oysters—and a bit of a drunkard as well. Grimaldi himself was a man of well-developed appetites, and as Joey he stretched his considerable offstage capacities to truly superhuman limits. Joey was also an accomplished and indiscriminate thief. Pies and legs of mutton, lighted candles and kettles of boiling water vanished into his bottomless pockets with sleight of hand unmatched until the advent of Harpo Marx. Joey took his inevitable thrashing just as shamelessly, with howls of outraged innocence and humiliation. His revenge was just as swift; he could deal out kicks and smacks from the most unexpected quarters and leave his tormentors sore and smarting, but none the wiser. Yet for all his earthiness and vulgarity, Grimaldi's Joey remained warm-hearted and essentially human, and even the most genteel London society roared with laughter at his unrestrained antics.

Joey was just as abandoned in his courtship of Columbine, sighing, swooning, and flirting, regaling her with useless presents and discordant serenades; but the chase (usually in hot-blooded pursuit of his rival Harlequin) was the real test of his ingenuity. He might be tossed into a fiery furnace, for example, but it took him only a few moments to get himself out and set off again after Harlequin. Joey took on a variety of curious disguises in the course of these adventures, and the quick-change became Grimaldi's specialty: he might become a ballerina, a talking bird, a tomcat, a dwarf, or a doll. His most famous stage creation was a "wondrous verdant man" pieced together in seconds from cabbages and turnips, with carrots for fingers. Of course, as soon as this intriguing creature came into existence, it got into a furious quarrel with its creator, "old Joe Frankenstein" (in the words of a writer affectionately recalling the scene many years later).

Grimaldi's greatest success was *Harlequin and Mother Goose or the Golden Egg,* which ran for more than ninety performances in 1806–1807. Dispensing with the gaudy sets and spectacular effects customary since Rich's time, *Mother Goose* was a (comparatively) simple story; Grimaldi played Squire Bugle, who, with his lady love, Colinette, and the rest of the cast, is transformed by Mother Goose into a traditional character in the Harlequinade. The squire, of course, becomes the Clown—banqueting at a table suspended in midair and bombarding the stage with crockery, fleeing from a swarm of bees, running through a whole wardrobeful of disguises that burlesqued the latest fashions, and winding up somehow in an undersea tableau.

Grimaldi, working for the most part on a bare stage with a few simple props, was the entire show, and critic and public finally recognized Joey as the extraordinary comic personality that he was, far more than just another raffish and amusing pantomime character. Years later, Dickens and Shaw both paid tribute to the originality of Grimaldi's creation in almost identical phrases. Shaw put it simply: "Grimaldi's clown was his own."

Grimaldi retired early from the stage, his health broken. He lived until 1837, and his last years were particularly lonely and unhappy. It is said that he never recovered from the loss of his first wife, who died while still quite young, and he seems to have always led a rather somber and solitary life, only happy when pursuing his two offstage passions of raising pigeons and collecting butterflies. (As a painful joke of the period had it, he was "grim all day," though he delighted audiences at night.) According to a charming but doubtful story, Grimaldi once sought the advice of a doctor during one of his frequent bouts of depression. The doctor's recommendation: "There's only one cure for you, my man. You must go at once to see the clown Grimaldi."

§ TWO AMERICAN CLOWNS NAMED RICE §

Thomas "Daddy" Rice (1808–1860), the father of the American minstrel show, began his career playing bit parts and working as a stage carpenter, lamplighter, and prop man, like many an aspiring actor who will do anything as long as it is somehow connected with the theater. From the first he specialized in "blackface" parts. (It was the curious custom of white actors in the nineteenth century to darken their faces with burnt cork in order to play black characters.) Rice played a variety of comic servant roles, at least until he hit upon a single character who made his fortune.

Although the conventions of blackface comedy scarcely encouraged realistic or sympathetic portrayals of black people, Rice was in fact a keen observer of Southern black speech and mannerisms. One day in 1828 he noticed from his dressing-room window an old man sweeping up a livery stable next door to the theater. The man had a pronounced limp, and as he swept he sang a song with dozens of verses, all ending with the refrain, "Wheel about, turn about, do jis so. An' ebery time I wheel about I jump Jim Crow!"—the words "jump Jim Crow" accompanied by a peculiar hopping step on his lame leg. Rice bought the Jim Crow song from the old man, borrowed the step, and the old man's nickname, Daddy. Rice's ragged "Daddy" character, with his odd croaking voice and hopping Jim Crow dance, became an immediate success, and before long a national craze. In the early 1830s Washington, New York, and London went successively "Jim Crow mad"; thus Daddy Rice was one of the first American entertainers to establish a European reputation. Before the Jim Crow mania subsided, Rice introduced full length "Ethiopian Operas," forerunners of the blackface minstrel shows of the 1840s and 1850s. The minstrel shows added garish costumes and energetic song-and-dance routines, and unfortunately retained the crudely condescending racial stereotypes that were both implicit and explicit in Rice's routines and all-blackface comedy. The phrase "Jim Crow" acquired ominous connotations after the Civil War, but blackface and other forms of broad ethnic humor that seem tasteless and even vicious today were universally accepted, and persistently popular, on the nineteenth-century stage. The minstrel show, the first truly American theatrical form, endured into the early twentieth century, and Rice himself went on from Jim Crow and the well-known Christy Minstrels to even greater public adulation, touring in the antislavery melodrama *Uncle Tom's Cabin*.

Dan Rice, Daddy's contemporary, occupies a less controversial place in the American imagination. With his distinguished goatee and top hat, blue leotard and red and white tights, "the original American white face clown" is also thought by many historians to have been the model for "Uncle Sam." He supplanted the Yankee type called Jonathan (who reappeared often in comedies that followed *The Contrast*) about the time that Rice was at the height of his career. Rice began as a strongman, catching cannonballs on the back of his neck, and as straightman to a gifted sequence of performing animals, starting with an educated pig called Lord Byron. Other Rice protégés included talking horses, ornery comic mules, and pigs trained to spell the word P-I-G by arranging printed placards, to answer questions with a prearranged system of grunts, or to select the American flag from a box of flags of many nations and, as a finale, wave the flag in their mouths while rising patriotically to attention on their hind legs.

Rice became famous as "the modern Shakespeare jester," first by answering questions from the audience with appropriate Shakespearean quotations, and later, by retelling the stories of *Hamlet* and *Romeo and Juliet* in backwoods colloquial language. Rice played showboats and one-ring circuses across the country, and before long he was billing himself, with complete accuracy, as "America's favorite clown." Rice's manner was easy and conversational, and his appearance was particularly striking (an ex-strongman on horseback wearing an Uncle Sam suit was, after all, bound to command the respect of even the most unruly frontier audience).

Rice counted President Zachary Taylor, hero of the Mexican War, and Abraham Lincoln, another accomplished backwoods humorist, among his friends, and at the peak of his popularity he seriously considered a try at the presidency himself. His candidacy never materialized, but he did turn from Shakespeare to political satire, voicing sensible opinions from the saddle in vivid frontier language— much like the nationally celebrated cowboy-philosopher of the 1920s and 1930s, Will Rogers. A benefit performance in 1850, by and for Dan Rice, attracted so many Washington notables (President Taylor and his Cabinet, Stephen A. Douglas, Daniel Webster, John C. Calhoun, and Henry Clay) it was said that the government came to a complete standstill for a day. Some time later, President Taylor made Rice an honorary colonel for his "great service rendered in entertaining mankind."

After the Civil War Rice returned to the showboats for a successful comeback (with a new attraction, Excelsior, the blind wonder horse). At the peak of his career, Rice made as much as a thousand dollars a week (equivalent to perhaps five times as much today), but heavy drinking and financial mismanagement reduced him to poverty. He died in 1900, a forgotten man.

§ HARRIGAN AND HART, §
CLOWNS OF NEW YORK CITY

By the 1870s New York City had become a city of immigrants; the term "melting pot" was not coined until almost forty years later, but the process was already well under way. A rich variety of ethnic types seemed to step straight off the docks in New York harbor onto the music-hall stages of a half-dozen big cities; contemporary humorists were amused and fascinated by the immigrants' stubborn reluctance to abandon the dress, speech, and manners of the Old Country, their struggles and inevitable conflicts with new customs and new realities, as well, of course, as with each other. Just as Dickens found a rich vein of humor in the shabby settings of his London boyhood, the playwright and actor Edward Harrigan wandered the crowded, noisy streets of Manhattan's Lower East Side, notebook in hand, chronicling the everyday alarms and small catastrophes of immigrant life. Harrigan's musical farces were dominated by the Mulligan Guards, a self-appointed peace-keeping force of liquor-loving Irishmen, but in their riotous maneuvers, the Guards encountered the full complement of genial ethnic stereotypes—Italian, German, Jewish, Chinese, black, and Yankee, all of whom populated the New York streets in the late nineteenth century.

Harrigan was born in New York City of Irish-American parents, who had little sympathy for his theatrical ambitions. He ran away from home while still in his teens and supported himself for five years on the road as a singer, banjo player, and dialect comic. His partner, Tony Hart, only sixteen when he began his long collaboration with Harrigan, had grown up performing in circuses, saloons, and minstrel shows between occasional stints in reform school. Hart also had a flair for dialect comedy (and for female impersonations realistic enough to fool a city detective). The team performed comic dialogues written by Harrigan and eventually recruited their wives and other relatives into the act and finally acquired their own theater.

The Mulligan Guards were an instant success, and Harrigan obligingly provided them with enough songs and sketches to prolong their adventures through many seasons in the 1870s and 1880s. Dogs and cats joined the two families onstage in a chaotic and convivial round of picnics and parades, dances, marches, chowders, and Christmas banquets, enlivened but rarely interrupted by fistfights, frantic chases, explosions, and collapsing ceilings. The comic formula discovered by Harrigan and Hart, the slapstick situation comedy, is still very much with us, and its success went a long way toward making the Irish immigrant a familiar and accepted figure in an America that was still suspicious of such uninhibited new citizens as the Mulligan tribe and the other exotic arrivals that crowded Harrigan's stage.

§ GILBERT AND SULLIVAN §

The long collaboration between a lawyer turned lyricist named

W. S. Gilbert (1836–1911) and composer Arthur Sullivan (1842–1900) produced fourteen satirical operettas and several dozen memorable comic characters. Sir Joseph Porter of *HMS Pinafore,* Ko-Ko of *The Mikado,* the Duke of Plaza-Toro in *The Gondoliers,* and Mad Margaret in *Ruddigore,* among many others, have given Gilbert and Sullivan's original Savoy Theatre company and thousands of later Savoyards, amateur and professional, their finest comic hours. A great many indeed in the case of Sir Henry Lytton, for example; he played nothing but Gilbert and Sullivan in his fifty years on the English stage from 1884 to 1934. Several years ago even Groucho Marx made his "G and S" debut with a highly original interpretation of the villainous Ko-Ko in a television production of *The Mikado.*

Gilbert and Sullivan themselves considered their best work to be *The Yeoman of the Guard, or the Merryman and His Maid.* The "merryman" of the title is Jack Point, a philosophical jester who speaks for all clowns, and for his creators, as he announces just after his entrance: "We are merry folk who would make all merry as ourselves. For, look you, there is humor in all things, and the truest philosophy is that which teaches us to find it and to make the most of it."

Here the Lieutenant interviews Jack Point as a prospective jester:

LIEUTENANT What are your qualifications for such a post?

JACK Marry, sir, I have a pretty wit. I can rhyme you extempore; I can convulse you with quip and conundrum; I have the lighter philosophies at my tongue's tip; I can be merry, wise, quaint, grim, and sardonic, one by one, or all at once; I have a pretty turn for anecdote; I know all the jests—ancient and modern—past, present, and to come; I can riddle you from dawn of day to set of sun, and, if that content you not, well on to midnight and the small hours. Oh, sir, a pretty wit, I warrant you—a pretty, pretty wit! *(He sings:)*

> I've jibe and joke
>> And quip and crank
> For lowly folk
>> And men of rank.
> I ply my craft
>> And know no fear,

> But aim my shaft
>> At prince or peer.
> At peer or prince—at prince or peer,
> I aim my shaft and know no fear!

Still not satisfied, the Lieutenant sets Jack a test of his talent for improvisation.

LIEUTENANT Say that I had sat me down hurriedly on something sharp?

JACK Sir, I should say that you had sat down on the spur of the moment.

LIEUTENANT Humph! I don't think much of that. Is that the best you can do?

JACK It's always been much admired, sir, but we will try again.

LIEUTENANT We will suppose that I caught you kissing the kitchen wench under my very nose.

JACK Under *her* very nose, good sir, not under yours! *That* is where *I* would kiss her. *(Bobs his head, pleased with himself.)* Do you take me? Oh, sir, a pretty wit—a pretty, pretty wit.

Gilbert and Sullivan were disappointed with the reception of their tragicomic masterpiece. Their devoted public was enchanted by Jack's pretty wit, but ill-prepared to see the merryman lose his maid to a rival and suffer the pangs of unrequited love—all the trials of the grand-opera hero played out in the grim shadow of London Tower. (In some productions Jack Point actually dies as the curtain falls.) This portrayal of the jester as the tragic victim of his art may have puzzled Victorian Londoners, but their Elizabethan ancestors would have smiled with recognition at this witty descendant of Shakespeare's Fool.

Here are a few more popular clowns of the nineteenth century, captured at much happier moments by contemporary posters, prints, photographs, and accounts by amused eyewitnesses:

John Ducrow performed with his English equestrian family; a Joey clown in the best Grimaldi tradition, he wore whiteface makeup with a single tuft of hair topping his bald head, a sunburst collar, and a striped leotard with baggy balloon pants painted with large circles. In his famous "Tea and Supper Party" routine, Ducrow set a table, complete with tea service, for his bewigged and fashionably costumed guests: two well-behaved circus ponies, who daintily sat down to tea at Ducrow's invitation. Ducrow placed large napkins around their necks, poured tea, and passed the cake tray—sometimes with his feet—in solemn parody of the national teatime ritual.

The Irish-American actor and playwright John Brougham satirized mid-nineteenth-century cultural and political life in a series of topical comedies with titles like *Much Ado about a Merchant of Venice* (a travesty of Shakespeare) and *Columbus el Filibustero* ("filibusteros" were American adventurers who led private armies in a number of notorious attacks on friendly Caribbean countries). *Po-ca-hon-tas, or the Gentle Savage* ridiculed the current Hiawatha craze for books, plays, and poetry romanticizing the American Indian.

One evening the Wallack Theatre, where Brougham was presenting *Po-ca-hon-tas,* was filled to capacity, in spite of a heavy snowstorm. The actress playing Pocahontas failed to show up, however; she had in fact eloped and no understudy was prepared to take her place. Never a man to disappoint an audience, Brougham suggested to his fellow actor Charley Walcott, "Suppose we do *Po-ca-hon-tas* without Pocahontas." The audience quickly fell in with the joke as Walcott stepped forward to explain, "This is what Miss Pocahontas would remark if she were present." After delivering her lines himself, Walcott remarked absently, "Where is Pokey?" "Lost among the icebergs on Broadway," Brougham replied pointedly. "Ah, but if she were here I know she would answer you in this way. . . ." The play continued smoothly enough, with Brougham and Walcott supplying all the missing Pocahontas speeches, until the final scene, when the script required Brougham to join the hands of Walcott and Pocahontas in marriage. This at last could hardly be done with a purely imaginary bride, and Brougham's wandering eye fell on a broom standing in a corner of the stage. Struck by a happy inspiration, Brougham seized the broom and presented it to Walcott, beaming. "Take her, my boy, and be happy." Soon the story of how a broom came to play a starring role on Broadway was all over town, and Brougham's outrageous improvisation, "*Po-ca-hon-tas* without Pocahontas," was actually held over for a number of repeat performances.

Dicky Usher was a special favorite with London schoolboys, since he told jokes sent in to him by his audience as a regular part of his act, and his performances at Astley's Circus in the early nineteenth century were always well attended by his expectant young contributors. On one occasion in 1809 his audience gathered on the banks of the Thames awaiting his widely advertised voyage from Westminster to Waterloo Bridge in a washtub drawn by a pair of geese. The tiny craft hove into view with all present and correct—the geese bobbing along on the current and Dicky, in the tub, waving jauntily to his well-wishers on the bank. Even as Dicky came in closer to shore, the spectators did not notice the underwater towrope that ran from the tub to a large boat sailing unobtrusively downstream. Dicky had more than made up in showmanship for what he might have lacked in seamanship, and the crowd roared its approval.

A Berlin ringmaster named Tom Belling made a notable contribution to clowning, as with so many great discoveries, quite by accident. Belling was a versatile performer, an expert equestrian, aerialist, and acrobat. But novelty as well as skill is of the essence in the circus, and one night in 1864 the last few minutes before the performance found him rummaging hopefully through an old costume trunk in search of a new comic identity. A shabby dress coat and a frayed wig, worn back-to-front, made Belling look as if he had his head screwed on backward. A touch of greasepaint added a brilliant red nose, and the effect of drunken disorientation was complete. By this time, though, the clowns had already started their act. The manager mistook Belling for one of the regular clowns, chided him for missing his cue, and shoved him into the ring. Belling, hampered by his unwieldy costume, stumbled into the spotlight and took a splendid fall, face down. The crowd shouted "Auguste!"—a slang nickname for anyone who was especially hapless or clumsy—and Belling, still slightly dazed but with his performer's instincts unimpaired, picked himself up and promptly fell down again, to another burst of laughter and applause. The clumsy Auguste clown of the modern circus still trips and stumbles, slaps and gets slapped, very much in the tradition of mishap and confusion that surrounded his accidental birth.

Joseph Grimaldi had created the first great modern clown near the beginning of the century, and by the end hundreds more were performing on stages, in circus rings, and out of doors, all over the world.

·8·

THE
CLOWNS
OF ASIA

The Vidushaka *of India, the* Ch'ou *of China,*
the Kyogen *of* Japan, *and the* Punakawan
of Java

<hr/>

The clown took on many roles in the traditional societies of Asia. His talents were as varied as his Western counterpart's; he might be an actor in a court theater or a traveling performer in a back-country village, an acrobat, a poet, a singer, a jester, a juggler, or a storyteller. From earliest times the Asian clown has been a satirical commentator on religion and society, an interpreter of an ancient heritage of folklore and mythological drama. In many cultures the clown has served as a mediator between the state and its subjects: often in the past, as the common man's spokesman and friend at court, or in present-day China and Indonesia, as an unofficial comic propagandist and popularizer of new governmental programs. The Asian clown's techniques, whether in the service of tradition or social change, have been much the same as those of the great clowns of the West: puns and wordplay, parody and satire, repetition and exaggeration, vivid characterization, even malapropism (though without the benefit of Mrs. Malaprop's excellent example). The clown has taken strikingly original and varied forms in the folk theater of India, the classical drama of China and Japan, the shadow plays of Indonesia, and in the theater and folklore of every country of Asia.

§ INDIA §

The classical drama of India is one of the world's oldest, based on the even more ancient Sanskrit epics, the *Mahabharata* and the *Ramaya-*

na, first compiled between the eighth and second centuries B.C. The intricate rivalries of the gods, heroes, and kings of Hindu mythology furnished dozens of ready-made plots, to which were added elements from popular legend and folklore; for example, these early Sanskrit dramatists quite reasonably provided their kings with complete royal households, often including a court jester or *vidushaka.* The word means "one who mocks or heaps abuse on others," and the vidushaka is a rather petulant jester and a master of invective often given to rhapsodies of complaint and self-pity when he is not hurling insults.

Madhavya in the Sanskrit play *Shakuntala,* written around the beginning of the fifth century A.D., is such a vidushaka character (although he brightens up noticeably as his fortunes take a dramatic turn for the better). Madhavya serves a young king who has come across Shakuntala, the beautiful daughter of a hermit, while hunting deer in the forest, and has fallen passionately in love with her. Madhavya takes it upon himself to distract his lovesick young master, who now spends his days pining for Shakuntala.

Madhavya arrives exhausted from the rigors of the hunt, complaining that the king has kept him too busy even to eat or drink. "I can no longer control my bones. My poor bruised legs! My aching crippled feet!" he moans, and begs for a day off to restore himself.

The king, who has apparently not been listening, replies "Madhavya, you have never beheld anything worth seeing, for you have not yet gazed upon the most perfect creation in the world."

Madhavya, playfully pretending to misunderstand, replies with a bit of outrageous flattery, "How can you say that when I see Your Majesty standing before me at this very minute?"

Once again, the king ignores Madhavya's clowning and answers mildly, "It is only natural that we consider our friends perfect, but I was referring to Shakuntala."

Madhavya tries to reason with the king, pointing out how absurd it would be for him to marry the daughter of a hermit.

"One so beautiful," the king explains, "surely must be divine, a celestial being left on earth and found by a holy man."

Madhavya realizes the futility of trying to distract his master or dissuade him from returning to seek out Shakuntula, and offers to help him in his quest.

"Friend Madhavya," the king replies, "you were my playmate in childhood and my mother has considered you a second son. Go home and take my place until I return: act the part of a son to the queen."

Instantly rising to his new station in life, the jester insists, "You must let me travel in a manner becoming the king's younger brother."

The king obligingly offers his entire retinue to accompany Madhavya on his journey, and the jester announces proudly, "Already I feel quite like a young prince."

"This is indeed a very giddy fellow," the king remarks to himself as he hurries off to find Shakuntala, while Madhavya busies himself with preparations for his royal progress to the queen's palace.

The vidushaka disappeared from Sanskrit theater in the eighth century, banished by a playwright called Bhavabhuti, who had no use for such frivolous characters in his solemn religious dramas. The jester surfaced again at the court of India's later Muslim rulers; one Mogul emperor prized his jester as "a jewel" (and another jester took his duties so seriously that it was said that he would have rather lost his wife than a good joke). As in medieval Europe, jesters formed a hereditary caste, and professional skills and privileged status passed from father to son through many generations.

In the popular theater the irascible clowning of the vidushaka was replaced by the *Bhana,* who performed satirical monologues on life at court and other subjects of current interest. These were interspersed with comic songs and poems, and heavily spiced with "double entendre"—a kind of wordplay in which an apparently innocent word or phrase is used in a context which hints at a second meaning, usually off-color. Topical farces were also presented, with actors portraying comic drunkards, canting priests, and lascivious courtiers.

The modern Indian folk theater has carried on this irreverent tradition. In Kashmir, for example, a play may begin with a long Muslim prayer, followed by a mock-religious travesty performed by two clowns called *maskharas.* Today, plays are performed in India's several dozen spoken languages rather than in classical Sanskrit, but clowns still open a performance with an improvised prologue in a question-and-answer form that derives from the epic *Mahabharata;* the prologue may offer comments on topical matters or an exposition of the subject of the play itself. Even after the play has begun, the clowns may interrupt the action to demand an explanation of what is going on, so that even the simplest spectator will be sure to keep up with the plot. In many parts of India the clowns' bantering dialogue may be the only source of information on current events for an isolated and illiterate but avidly curious rural population.

§ CHINA §

The clown first appeared in China as a jester and court entertainer during the Chou dynasty (c. 1027–256 B.C.), the classical age of Chinese art and philosophy. Shih Hwang-ti, a grim conqueror with a hatred for the ancient classics and a passion for monumental architecture (the Great Wall of China was constructed during his reign) was the founder of the succeeding Ch'in dynasty. The emperor pursued his obsessions with ruthless efficiency: scholars were persecuted and virtually every copy of the great works of the Chou dynasty was burned; whole populations were conscripted into forced labor gangs and wealthy provinces were reduced to famine by ruinous taxes. According to legend, only one man at court dared to oppose the tyrant's will, the jester Yu Sze.

As the story has it, when the Great Wall was completed, the emperor announced to his astonished councilors that even this formidable achievement—one of the greatest engineering feats of the ancient world, an immense stone barrier strongly fortified and extending more than fifteen hundred miles along the mountainous northern frontier—was unsatisfactory. In addition, he wanted the gigantic blocks of rough-hewn stone finished, painted, and decorated. The councilors, of course, remained prudently silent, aware of the horrible cost in money and lives of the emperor's new caprice, yet even more impressed by the certainty that their own lives would be forfeited by any sign of opposition. Instead, they sought out Yu Sze, the emperor's favorite, and begged him to dissuade his master from carrying out this insane project.

Yu Sze himself was keenly aware of the price he stood to pay for even hinting at disloyalty or disobedience, but when the emperor next mentioned his incredible scheme, Yu Sze simply began to laugh, rolling on the floor and howling so that tears streamed down his cheeks, until even the emperor began to smile in recognition of his folly, and finally rescinded the order. Whether or not the Ch'in emperor actually considered decorating the Great Wall, writers of Chinese history have always been reluctant to pass up a good story with a neat moral tag: the foolishness of even the most absolute tyrant is powerless against the laughter of a courageous, sensible clown like Yu Sze.

The Pear Garden, founded in A.D. 714, was one of the world's first acting schools. In about the year 1000 the actors and dancers of the Pear Garden began to re-enact scenes from Chinese history and mythology. Influenced by theatrical styles from different regions of China, these performances developed into the Chinese classical theater of the fourteenth and fifteenth centuries, a sophisticated dramatic form of great subtlety and complexity. Plays of as many as thirty acts lasting many hours were performed on a simple platform surrounded by low railings set up in a palace or temple courtyard; two doors at the rear of the stage allowed for entrances and exits. Scenery was minimal, no more than a table and chairs, which were variously arranged to indicate different interior settings. Costumes and makeup, considerably more intricate and very beautiful, served as similar cues for the imagination of the spectators. The conventions of pantomime permitted an actor standing on a bare stage to convey by precisely stylized gestures that he was crossing an unseen mountain range or drowning in an imaginary ocean.

Roles in Chinese classical drama are classified into four basic types: male roles; female roles; "painted faces," representing gods, statesmen, bandits, or courtiers; and clowns. A clown's face is made up in an elaborate pattern of black markings on a symbolic area of white, identifying him immediately as a comic servant, foolish mandarin, soldier, priest, vagabond, matchmaker, witty jester, or interfering mother-in-law. The clown often sports extravagant whiskers and drooping mustaches; exaggerated shadows around his eyes intensify his comic gestures and grimaces. The other actors are required by convention to declaim in an elevated, artificial style, while the clown, as a distinctly lower-class type, speaks a colloquial dialect and freely embellishes his set speeches with rambling ad lib commentaries full of topical and sexual allusions. But for all his coarse-grained realism and improvisational freedom, the clown too is subject to conventions dictating everything from the exact pitch of his voice to the way he points his little finger. As in all the arts of traditional China, from temple architecture to classical cooking, Chinese dramatists and actors seek a perfect balance of opposing forces, in which comedy is as necessary and therefore as precisely regulated as tragedy.

There are two styles of clowning: *wen* involves verbal play and *wu* physical comedy and acrobatics. Apprentice actors all undergo the same basic course of study for six years; then, at the age of twelve, they begin to specialize in one of the four categories and spend the rest of their careers perfecting their chosen roles.

The Peking Opera, also called the Peking Theater, is a nineteenth-century outgrowth of the classical drama. Characters and action are developed through similar conventions of makeup, costume, and pantomime. The audience knows immediately not only who a character is—ghost, courageous general, or treacherous councilor—but quite likely what he is going to do next, since the plays are based on familiar historical or legendary tales. Troupes compete to present the most striking and original production of a traditional plot through music, dance, mime, and dialogue; the effect depends on the grandeur and pageantry of the ensemble scenes, and most of all, on the sensitivity and technical virtuosity of the individual actors. The written texts of the operas, like the commedia dell'arte scenarios, are basically plot summaries, with extremely precise stage directions: instructions on the correct pantomime technique of riding a galloping horse, catching birds, or cutting one's throat with an ax. The Peking Opera makes its demands on the audience as well—performances of several plays in one evening, easily lasting six or seven hours altogether, are quite common.

The opera follows the classical drama in its division of roles into four categories; the clown, called the *ch'ou,* plays an impressive variety of comic characters. In *Ssu Lang T'an Mu (Ssu Lang Visits His Mother)* the ch'ou form a chorus of mandarins—wearing the court dress of black robes and red caps, each adorned with a long peacock feather—who guard the palace of the Dowager Empress. They speak in unison, or in alternate lines, offering single-minded and singularly ineffective advice to the Princess, who has been tragically separated from her mother, the Empress. After several false starts, the clown councilors finally hit on the correct plan; mother and daughter are reunited, and the play ends happily.

In *Hu Tieh Meng (The Butterfly Dream)* the ch'ou character is the resourceful servant boy, Tung Erh, who is sent out to buy a coffin, and coolly hoodwinks the coffin merchant, haggling quite shamelessly until he gets the price he wants. When he cannot control situations, he scampers away from them.

The Peking Opera still flourishes in Taiwan and Hong Kong, and in the overseas Chinese colonies of Southeast Asia. But in today's China many of the plays in the older repertory, condemned as undesirable relics of the feudal past, have been replaced by "revolutionary" operas commemorating Red Army victories or illustrating the teachings of Chairman Mao. Romantic stories of ancient princesses and the exploits of legendary heroes have given way to "The Red Detachment of Women" and the determined struggles of politically conscious peasants against reactionary landowners. Nevertheless, the acrobatic swordplay between the Red Army hero and the tyrannical warlord with his ferociously painted face would be delightfully familiar to a Chinese audience of the nineteenth, or even the sixteenth, century.

§ JAPAN §

Japanese classical drama can also be traced to court entertainments of the eighth century, based on even earlier religious rituals and performed by a hereditary caste of dancers and mimes under the protection of the emperor. This troupe was eventually joined by storytellers, jugglers, and acrobats who, in the twelfth century, began to present short sketches. By the fourteenth century these had evolved into the famous Noh dramas and their comic counterparts, the *Kyogen* plays. Noh plays are lyrical and romantic, and usually depict the tragic conflict of passion with social and familial obligations; in the farcical Kyogen, characters deal with the momentary crises of everyday life. Canons of dramatic harmony, similar to the Chinese, prescribe that the Kyogen be presented as an interlude between two Noh performances. Today about 250 of these comedies remain in the repertory of the Nomura School of Tokyo and the Shigeyama School of Kyoto, which together make up the National Comic Theater of Japan. Membership in these companies is still a matter of birth as well as talent: Manzo Nomura is a sixth-generation direct descendant of the founder of the Tokyo school, which he directs today; Sengaro Shigeyama, an actor in the Kyoto company headed by his father, is the twelfth in his line. These companies have made a number of successful foreign tours in the last twenty years (most recently to the United States in 1975), and several Kyogen actors have been designated by the Japanese government as "National Living Treasures" and "Intangible Cultural Treasures of Japan."

Kyogen plays are short, simple sketches of high and low life; gods, demons, priests, lords, and ladies share the Kyogen stage with peasants, woodcutters, quack doctors, swindlers, monkeys, and, of course, the ever-present comic servants. In *Boshibari (Tied to a Pole)* Taro and Jiro have raided their master's wine cellar once too often. The master takes Jiro aside and enlists his aid in catching Taro and tying his outstretched arms to a bamboo pole. Jiro, imagining he has got off scot free, chuckles at his comrade's discomfiture, while his master slips a rope over *his* shoulders and binds his arms securely behind him.

After their master leaves, Taro and Jiro decide to make the best of a bad business, since at least they can still sniff the wine if not taste it, and head straight for the cellar—or rather, they walk in circles to indicate a pantomime staircase. The servants throw themselves into an orgy of wine sniffing, greedily sampling the aroma of each jar until Jiro is overcome and begins to sway dizzily on his feet, his bamboo pole bobbing back and forth. Taro pries off the lid of a jar with his pole, and encouraged by its heady fragrance, manages to tip some of the wine into a bowl. Jiro holds the bowl in his bound hands behind his back so that Taro can stoop and drink his fill, and after many painstaking maneuvers, they both succeed in getting roaring drunk.

Their master returns to find Taro and Jiro dancing unsteadily around the cellar, singing raucously and calling down curses on his head. Catching sight of his reflection in a wine jar, they conclude that their master has left his spirit behind to bedevil them, and curse him all the more. A sharp rap with a fan on each of their skulls recalls Taro and Jiro to their senses; terrified, they take to their heels. "You won't get away with this, you rogues!" their master blusters after them, but in fact they already have. There is a remarkably similar commedia dell'arte sketch in which two rascally servants bound hand and foot contrive to eat their way through an enormous cache of forbidden macaroni.

The Kyogen sketch called *Kusabira (Mushrooms)*, although written several hundred years ago, reveals a refreshing skepticism toward superstition and religious hocus-pocus, and a very modern mixture of terror and humor which may recall a more recent development in the popular arts, the science-fiction horror film.

A householder discovers a patch of strange-looking blue mushrooms growing in his garden. Disturbed by their sinister appearance, he tries to pluck them, but they seem to grow right back almost immediately. He decides to consult a local priest who has a reputation as a healer and exorcist.

The priest turns out to be a pompous old humbug, not above taking the credit for cures worked by nature: on the way back to the garden, he stops to ask after an invalid he has been praying for. Told that the man is doing much better, the priest remarks gravely, "I could have cured him right away, but he's better off recovering slowly." This self-assurance is slightly shaken when he arrives in the garden and confronts the mushrooms, grown even larger in the householder's absence. "They look almost human!" the priest blurts out. (Each mushroom is played by a crouching actor wearing a flat round hat.)

As the priest recites a charm to ward off blue mushrooms, yellow and green ones arrive to take their place. The priest admits that he has never encountered walking mushrooms before, and as more mushrooms infiltrate his garden, the householder begins to doubt the priest's exorcising abilities. "Nonsense," comes the reply, "can't you see my prayers are successful? In fact, they've brought every last mushroom to the surface!"

The priest refuses to acknowledge that mere mushrooms could resist his incantations; he continues chanting while the ring of mushrooms ominously draws closer. His final prayer conjures up an enormous black mushroom that lumbers up to the priest, announcing, "I'm going to eat you up!" The priest and the householder scurry off, leaving the stage to the mushrooms, who promptly throw off their caps and take out after them.

The Kabuki theater first appeared in the early seventeenth century, a lively melodramatic form that incorporated elements from dance, puppet plays, and Noh drama (to which Kabuki bears roughly the same relation as does the Peking Opera to the classical Chinese drama). And like the Peking Opera, Kabuki involves music, dancing, and an exaggerated, almost ritualized, style of acting. The rigid separation of comedy and tragedy is not observed in Kabuki; clowns provide welcome comic relief in these melancholy dramas of romantic intrigue, vengeance, and suicide, of fierce samurai and virtuous noblewomen (both played by men; women were banned from the Kabuki stage in 1652). The feudal magnates who patronized the original Kabuki plays presumably did not relish seeing themselves satirized onstage; comic characters in Kabuki usually represent lower-class or underworld types: thieves, rogues, gamblers, garbage pickers, servants (of many varieties), sometimes horses and dogs.

There are only a few comedies in the vast Kabuki repertory. *Three Odd Ones,* apparently an adaptation of *Tied to a Pole,* concerns a man about to leave on a journey who hires three servants—one mute, one deaf, one crippled—thinking that they, at least, will be incapable of pilfering his wine cellar. As soon as he leaves, they set about doing just that. The three odd ones turn out to be a pack of perfectly able-bodied confidence tricksters, as the master himself discovers when he returns home unexpectedly and interrupts their riotous drinking party. This play is primarily a showcase for the talents of the actors playing the three odd ones, and the humor is more in the performance than in any cleverness of plot or dialogue.

Kabuki plays are still performed by the Japanese National Theater, which makes frequent American and European tours, and today Japanese traditional drama in all its forms coexists happily with a thriving contemporary theater presenting works by modern Japanese playwrights and a standard Western repertory of Shakespeare, Shaw, Ibsen, and O'Neill, in translation. Japanese theatergoers may have acquired a taste for avant-garde experiments and Broadway-style musical comedies, but they continue to revere and heartily enjoy their "Intangible Cultural Treasures," the clowns of the Kyogen.

§ SOUTHEAST ASIA §

Throughout Southeast Asia—in Burma, Thailand, Laos, Cambodia, and Indonesia—popular drama derives from ancient Indian models. Scenes from the great Sanskrit epics are enacted on open-air bamboo platforms; performances usually begin at dusk and last until dawn. The plot line of the twelve-hour spectacle, impossibly complicated as it might seem to us, is a mythological story (or sequence of stories) that every member of the audience has been lovingly familiar with since childhood. They have come to admire the ornate magnificence of the costumes of the gods and heroes, comment critically on the actors' and dancers' mastery of the graceful conventions of their craft, and savor the satirical improvisations, comic songs, and bantering digressions of the clowns.

A clown in Burma, for example, might take inspiration from the roar of an airplane passing overhead, drowning out the hero's poetic declamations to comment cynically on the many annoyances of modern life which the ancient gods and first ancestors never had to contend with. Or perhaps the clown might explain in a conversational aside how, in his opinion, even the posturings and ravings of the demon king seem preferable to the villainies of the present government, and go on to sing a topical ballad or tell a string of the latest jokes from the capital. The clown engages in a running dialogue with the audience and steps in and out of the drama with perfect freedom, to deliver a fanciful commentary on the latest turn of the plot or simply to oblige an admirer who has tossed a note onto the stage weighted with a coin or some small gift, or perhaps including an invitation to dinner, with his request for a favorite song or comic monologue.

In Thailand this tradition of clowning is at least a thousand years old. The original Thai dramatic troupes, called *lakon jatri,* consisted of only three actors, one who took all the male roles, a second (also male) who took all the female roles, and a third who played the clowns. Their influence may still be felt in the folk drama of southern Thailand. In sixteenth-century Burma "spirit dances" and "spirit plays" performed by traveling players presented a similarly cheerful blend of clowning with religious and mythological drama.

On the Indonesian island of Java, the clown character is not only applauded and admired as a social satirist and political pundit but even revered as a minor god. These clown divinities are portrayed by puppets rather than actors, however. The puppets are made of leather, carved full-length in profile, sometimes with the torso turned slightly forward (like the figures in Egyptian paintings) to create a suggestion of three-dimensionality when their silhouettes are projected onto an opaque screen by the light of an oil lamp. The arms of the figures are jointed at shoulder, elbow, and wrist, with the leather delicately scalloped and shaped in intricate lattices and cutouts to represent the traditional costumes and symbolic attributes of mythological gods and heroes dating back to the fifteenth century. The puppets are supported by rods made of buffalo horn which are manipulated by a single puppeteer called the *dalang.* These shadow plays are called *Wayang Kulit* (literally, "shadow leather"), and the dalang not only controls all the characters but also supplies narration and sound effects and directs the orchestra that accompanies the performance (which customarily begins in the evening and lasts until early morning).

The shadow plays, like the traditional plays of Thailand and Burma, present episodes from the *Ramayana* and *Mahabharata* distinctly adapted to Javanese tastes, notably by the addition of the clown characters or *punakawan*—the roly-poly, grotesque Semar and his three sons, Bagong, Petruk, and Sareng. These robust peasant personalities are cast as advisers, servants, and companions to the epic heroes, but like their flesh-and-blood colleagues elsewhere in Southeast Asia, they freely step out of their roles to express themselves pointedly and pungently on local problems and topical events or whatever might particularly concern the audience (or particularly annoy the puppeteer).

The shadow plays present a sort of unwritten encyclopedia of traditional Javanese culture, communicating the mythological stories and moral teachings of the Hindu epics and including a comic supplement on contemporary affairs provided by that most ungodlike divinity, the punakawan. Like Yu Sze, Madhavya, and many of the other clowns of Asia, the punakawan is the supreme commoner in a world of princes and aristocrats, sensible and good-hearted (if slightly irreverent), with the opinions of a poor man and the freedom of a god: a figure made all the more popular in the theater by his rarity in the world outside.

Today in Indonesia the ordinary man has the stage all to himself in a form of popular comedy called *Ludruk.* Using actors rather than puppets, these gently satirical plays portray the struggles of a comic malcontent with the complexities of modern life. Favorite themes are the peasant's first baffling encounters with the big city, or the city dweller, more sophisticated but equally set in his ways, who is forced to contend with unemployment, the high cost of living, and other difficulties the puppet heroes of the Wayang Kulit never had to face. These comedies are sponsored by the Indonesian government; the Ludruk clowns rail tirelessly against the powers that be, but the new society which they have so much trouble adjusting to is presented sympathetically. The malcontent's acceptance of the comforts and complexities of the new society is the invariable happy end of the Ludruk comedy. Although the traditional agrarian society that produced the shadow play is slowly disappearing, the traditional drama is generously subsidized, carefully preserved, and still very much alive in present-day Java.

The clowns of Asia have shown themselves extremely capable of coping with the sweeping social changes that have transformed their traditional cultures over the last three decades. In the popular epics of India and Southeast Asia, clowns have accepted the mixed blessings of modernity with good-natured satirical resignation. In Japan and Java the ancient forms have not lost their vitality, and throughout Indonesia and in China the clown himself has become an agent of social change, and the popular theater an important force in the shaping of a new society.

· 9 ·
CLOWNS IN THE LIVING THEATER

Dan Leno, Will Rogers, George M. Cohan, Fanny Brice, the Great Teams, Modern-Day Zanies, the Sophisticated Clowns, and Marcel Marceau's "Bip"

Marcel
Marceau

Weber and Fields

Carol Channing

Dan Leno

In the last decades of the nineteenth century, America had become a complex industrial society; migrants from Europe and rural areas of the United States poured into the large cities, acquiring new tastes and customs, without wholly abandoning the old ones they had left behind. The American theater reflected this cultural diversity, offering a remarkably varied bill of fare. The operettas of Gilbert and Sullivan and imported confections by Strauss, Offenbach, and other European composers inspired a rich musical theater in America, first in the light operas of Sigmund Romberg and Victor Herbert, later in the musical comedies of Irving Berlin and Jerome Kern. (Although all these except Kern were born in Europe, the Broadway musical was America's most distinguished contribution to the theater in the twentieth century.) The legitimate theater concentrated on scenic realism (or what the nineteenth century thought of as realism: onstage simulations of train wrecks, Indian attacks, Civil War battlefields, and gold-rush mining camps—generally the same kind of escapist fare provided by today's movie spectaculars). The traveling minstrel shows were beginning to lose momentum after fifty years of popularity. Except in the smallest communities they were no longer the only show in town; they faced serious competition from the new music halls and variety theaters. The term "variety" is hardly an exaggeration; a single bill might easily include acrobats, animal acts, comedians, singers, and dancers of all sorts, perhaps even a one-act play starring one of the great ladies of the legitimate stage such as Ethel Barrymore or Sarah Bernhardt. The price of admission was a quarter at most, and the bill changed every week.

The variety show was the creation of a clown turned acrobat turned singer turned producer, named Tony Pastor (1837–1908). Beginning in 1881 Pastor's Theatre on New York's 14th Street presented comedy and musical acts—family entertainment "suitable for ladies and gentlemen" of all classes of New York society. By the beginning of the new century, enterprising theater managers across the country, particularly in the East, had developed Pastor's successful formula into a thriving network of variety theaters. Vaudeville was the next step—continuous entertainment, afternoon and evening, alternating comic and "straight" performers. Vaudeville comedians leaned heavily on dialect comedy and broad ethnic stereotypes. Benjamin Franklin Keith, owner of the largest circuit of vaudeville theaters, rigidly enforced the ban on "blue" material and Keith was not a man to be trifled with. A performer booked by Keith (or one of his competitors) could spend a profitable season, four or five performances a day, or even a career "on the circuit."

New York City was the center of the vaudeville circuit, supplying most of the country with new performers and fresh routines, musicians, managers, and entire companies. But the clowns' and comedians' training schools were still the traveling circuses, medicine shows, and "Tom shows" (tent productions of *Uncle Tom's Cabin*, often heavily rewritten to include comedy and song-and-dance routines, along with patriotic displays and animal acts). After a few instructive seasons on the road, a talented performer might graduate to musical reviews or variety shows or return to the touring life on the vaudeville circuit; in turn, the star of vaudeville or variety theaters might hope for a role in a Broadway musical comedy, and perhaps eventually an appearance in the *Follies*.

The producer of the *Follies*, Florenz Ziegfeld (1869–1932), assembled the most extravagant sets, the gaudiest costumes, the most beautiful girls, and the funniest comics on Broadway for these annual variety spectaculars. From 1907 to 1932 Ziegfeld's comic headliners included Will Rogers, W. C. Fields, Fanny Brice, Ed Wynn, Leon Errol, and Eddie Cantor—all still remembered from radio and film appearances—and many others almost as popular who are virtually forgotten today, such as Willie Howard, Bert Wheeler, Marilyn Miller, and Ann Pennington. The leading black vaudevillian, Bert Williams, was a singer, dancer, storyteller, and mime, and above all, an accomplished clown who ridiculed the conventions of blackface comedy by blackening his own face with burnt cork. People who had never seen Ed Gallagher and Al Shean's vaudeville act recognized their famous tagline—"Positively, Mr. Gallagher?" "Absolutely, Mr. Shean!"—which became a popular catchphrase of the 1920s.

Apart from the *Follies* New York's Palace Theatre was vaudeville's most prestigious showcase. The Palace opened in 1913 with Ed Wynn heading the bill; the "divine Sarah" Bernhardt, aging but still captivating, appeared there shortly afterward, and "playing the Palace" quickly became synonymous with stardom in the legitimate theater. But by 1930 the movie industry had come of age, and Hollywood offered a brand of fantasy and excitement that vaudeville could not match. Theater managers discovered that renting and projecting two-reel comedies was cheaper than hiring live comedians. Consequently, ticket prices in movie theaters were lower. After a few years short vaudeville acts largely survived as a diversion while the projectionist changed reels. Many of the great vaudeville headliners migrated to Hollywood; those who remained in New York found work in revues, musicals, and straight plays, or went back on the road, playing nightclubs and cabarets, traveling shows and summer stock. The demise of vaudeville coincided with the Great Depression of the 1930s, and many show people hung up their baggy pants and tap shoes to find less glamorous jobs, if they were lucky, or to join millions of their fellow Americans in the unemployment line. The outbreak of World War II brought many vaudevillians out of retirement and back on tour with the USO and other wartime troupes entertaining defense workers on the homefront and the armed forces overseas.

The British equivalent of variety and vaudeville was the music hall. Informal programs originally put on in the music rooms of pubs and taverns moved into the "halls" around the middle of the nineteenth century. The music halls gradually lived down their early associations with the barroom, and their lively and varied program of singing, dancing, and comedy became the favorite amusement of the respectable middle classes. As in America, leading actors and concert artists lent their prestige to the music-hall stage, while the jugglers and ballad singers and other variety performers competed for bookings on a grueling circuit that might take them to fifty different cities in a single year.

The most popular of these artists began to make appearances on the legitimate stage, and particularly in pantomime, where the elastic story lines could easily be stretched to accommodate favorite songs and specialty turns from the music halls. The biggest parts in the Victorian panto—the comic "dame" (played by a man) and the principal boy (starting around 1880, always played by a girl)—often went to variety artists who were more concerned with promoting their own careers than providing fresh interpretations of the stock characters of pantomime. Clown, the most difficult of the earlier roles, disappeared from pantomime altogether; even the formidable Harlequin was regularly upstaged by the new arrivals and dwindled into a minor figure. In London and a few large cities the Christmas panto still survives in a corrupt and rather colorless form, often with pop stars and television personalities taking the leading parts.

§ DAN LENO §

In the 1880s and 1890s, while the lively art of pantomime was still almost as lively as in the days of Joe Grimaldi, the liveliest of pantomime artists was Grimaldi's greatest successor, Dan Leno. Born George Wild Galvin in 1860, Leno made his debut in the halls in 1885. At first his specialty was clog dancing, a vigorous, rhythmic folk dance performed in heavy wooden shoes. Dan opened his act dressed as a fussy, half-hysterical, and remarkably agile old woman in a song-and-dance called "Going to Buy Milk for the Twins," followed by a comic Irish number, "When Rafferty Raffled His Watch." Clog dancing was a popular attraction at country fairs and seaside resorts, but Londoners thought of it as rather a rustic pastime and were not impressed by Dan's virtuoso clogging. Dan sensibly kicked off his clogs and began to build a new act around "patter" songs (something like comic monologues set to music) and character sketches "founded in fact." Leno was a tireless worker and quite a perfectionist; many of his sketches ended up in the fireplace, after countless revisions, and never reached the stage. To get the timing of a sketch exactly right, Dan would walk for miles, running through his "patter" and trying out motions and gestures until he could match his new character's every footstep to the music.

Leno played his first season in pantomime at Drury Lane in

1886–1887. For many years he took women's parts exclusively—queens, princesses, washerwomen, and housewives. All these haughty leading ladies and comic "dames" were composite portraits, part unerring mimicry, part inspired exaggeration, both necessary to create an essentially realistic character on the vast Drury Lane stage in the larger-than-life context of the pantomime spectacle. His most famous dame role, Mother Goose, required a series of transformations. Leno began the sketch as a ragged farmwife sleepily driving her donkey cart to market; suddenly an automobile (already a favorite target of turn-of-the-century humorists) appeared from nowhere, plowed into the cart, and overturned it, scattering the widow and her livestock. The car disappeared and another commotion erupted all over the stage—as Leno, skirts flying, scurried after frightened geese, pulled two live donkeys to their feet, furiously untangled the harness, and uprighted the cart, all the while hurling a stream of most unladylike invective after the fugitive motorist. After this frantic excursion Leno transformed himself into a wealthy, arrogant Mother Goose, a beautiful, coy Mother Goose, and finally, the original Mother Goose, old, with aching feet, but happy to be herself again.

Each of Leno's characters was a definite original, with a distinctive walk and gestures, expressions and mannerisms all her own. Leno's subtlety and sensitivity as an actor did not by any means slow him down on stage. He remained essentially a dancer in all his roles, and the plots of many of his pantomimes give at least an indication of his "electrical" performing style. A scene from *Jack and the Beanstalk* (borrowed from Goldoni's commedia dell'arte play *A Servant of Two Masters*) has Leno as Jack's widowed mother accepting marriage proposals from two different suitors and then managing, though only just, to serve two different wedding banquets at the same time, in two different rooms of the same house.

After Leno had played female leads in dozens of pantomimes, the manager of Drury Lane asked him how he thought he might do in a male role. "Well, I don't know," Dan replied modestly, "but I *ought* to be all right because, you see, I was born that way."

Dan brought his new series of comic heroes to America in 1897. He opened at Hammerstein's Olympia Music Hall in New York, billed as "The World's Funniest Man" (this was none of his doing and Leno was understandably nervous about making his first appearance in a strange country with so much fanfare). But New York received Dan warmly; the press reported that four enormous bouquets were passed to him over the footlights, at which Leno explained wryly that this was the customary tribute paid to great beauty, while screwing up his face as grotesquely as he could (the newspaper account described him as a "hatchet-faced" little man who could make his eyes large or small at will, with a rubbery mouth that roamed freely over the lower half of his face in an amazing variety of expressions). Sir Max Beerbohm has supplied us with a more detailed portrait of Dan Leno (remarkably flattering from the pen of so acid a caricaturist as Sir Max) intended for the edification of his grandchildren, that they might have some appreciation of Leno's comic genius. And genius it was, Sir Max maintained, although he had done little to change classic styles of comedy (except to rely more on the patter song than anyone before him). Beerbohm believed that Leno's art involved the total communication of his personality through voice, expression, and gesture, and that the effect was instantaneous and completely irresistible; Leno was "sympathetic" and "lovable" at first sight. His mournful, heavily creased features, which reminded Sir Max of nothing more than a sad-faced baby monkey, relaxed immediately into a wide grin. His voice, shrill, cracked, but unfailingly cheerful, suggested a "will to live in a world not at all worth living in." All his characters were developed through close collaboration with his audience: "He selected and rejected according to how his jokes, and his expression of them 'went'; and his best things came to him always in the course of an actual performance, to be incorporated in all subsequent performances." After many performances Leno's new character was polished to comic perfection: "Not a gesture, not a grimace, not an inflection of the voice, not a wiggle of the body, but had its significance, and drove its significance sharply, grotesquely, home to us all."

Sir Max closed his tribute to Leno with the prophetic suggestion that one day the refinement of sound recording and photography would permit audiences of the future to experience and appreciate the great performances of the past. "I wish Dan Leno could have been thus immortalized! No actor of our time deserved immortality so well as he." Dan Leno lives today only through a few rare recordings of his songs, faded photographs, and the vivid recollections of Sir Max Beerbohm and other contemporary admirers. In 1903 Leno was committed to an institution. After a long rest cure he returned for another pantomime season on the Drury Lane stage, but the spirit of "desperate hopefulness" that Sir Max so much admired seemed to have deserted him; he died the following year, in 1904.

§ WILL ROGERS §

Will Rogers was born in Oklahoma, then called the Indian Territory, in 1879. He himself was one-eighth Cherokee, or as he proudly put it, "We didn't come over on the *Mayflower* but we was here to meet 'em when they landed." His formal education was sketchy; he preferred to concentrate on riding and roping and was making his living as a cowboy by the time he was seventeen. Over the next few years he worked as a gaucho in South America, traveled from there to South Africa, joined an English circus, and appeared in a Wild West show at the St. Louis Exposition of 1904. Will brought his rope-spinning act to Madison Square Garden in New York the following year.

At first the grinning, gum-chewing cowboy (who hated gum and only chewed it to hide his nervousness) performed his intricate rope tricks in silence, never speaking a word; he was afraid his twangy Oklahoma drawl would only sound ridiculous to an audience in New York. But the stories he told backstage went over so well with his fellow performers that he reluctantly tried his first ad lib. At the finish of a difficult trick he flashed his disarming grin and drawled, "Spinnin' a rope is fun—if your neck ain't in it." This drew a generous laugh, but Rogers was still unconvinced that Oklahoma humor would go over in New York. He drew up a list of subjects to improvise upon between rope-spinning routines, and before long he found that just reading the newspapers for a few hours every day provided plenty of fresh comic material. "I started reading about Congress; and, believe me, I found they are funnier three hundred and sixty five days a year than anything I ever heard of." In many years of doing his "little specialty with a Rope and telling Jokes on National Affairs," Rogers touched on almost every conceivable topic, attacking political pretense, pomposity, and humbug in all its forms. Congress remained a favorite target. "I didn't know before I got there, and they told me, that Rome had Senators. Now I know why it declined." When asked whether he had any political ambitions himself, he replied, "There's already too many comedians in Washington. Competition would be too keen for me."

Rogers professed amazement that his "ordinary little Vaudeville act" could become the hit of the *Follies* and the personal favorite of

Florenz Ziegfeld, who usually thought of comedy as something to fill up the time while his showgirls changed costumes. Rogers was also a favorite with several presidents: Woodrow Wilson liberally sprinkled his speeches with quotations from Rogers' routines (and vice versa, of course), and Franklin Delano Roosevelt frequently invited him to the White House. This prompted one critic to imagine Rogers as a modern court jester, an honored guest at the White House whose persistent satirical attacks on Congress helped popularize the President's New Deal policies. Rogers preferred to think of himself as "nothing but a very ordinary Oklahoma Cowpuncher who had learned to spin a Rope a little and who had learned to read the Daily Papers a little." Yet Will Rogers invites comparison with the frontier comedy of Dan Rice and the long tradition of the "stage Yankee" in the American theater, beginning with Royall Tyler's Jonathan in *The Contrast.*

Rogers traveled widely in Europe, speaking his mind on America's role in world affairs with the same shrewdness and sympathy that had impressed President Wilson during World War I. His observations on European politics in his daily newspaper column were just as much to the point. The trouble with the Soviet Union, as Rogers saw it, was that "They haven't got what you might call a constant critic."

America's constant critic reached his audience through his radio broadcasts, his column, which was syndicated in some five hundred newspapers nationwide, and the movies. He had made several silent films in the twenties, which necessarily emphasized riding and roping rather than satirical comedy. The talkies brought the full range of Rogers' personality to the screen, and though he might be cast as David Harum or the Connecticut Yankee in King Arthur's Court, Will Rogers always played Will Rogers. (This is not to say that Rogers couldn't act; in the same year [1934] that he became the number-one film box office attraction in the nation, he was also attracting favorable notices from the critics in a West Coast production of the O'Neill comedy *Ah, Wilderness!*) In his films he refused to wear makeup, thinking it an "actorish" affectation for his personality, which was completely natural. His relaxed conversational style created a bond with the film audience, not just of friendship but of intimacy. The simplicity, directness, and optimism that had always brightened his performances were appreciated all the more during the Depression of the thirties. One reviewer, trying to sum him up in a phrase, wrote that Rogers had "the heart of a child—*that* is his charm." But on this subject, like so many others, Rogers had the last word: "When I die my epitaph, or whatever you call those signs on gravestones, is going to read, 'I joked about every prominent man of my time, but I never met a man I didn't like.' I am proud of that. I can hardly wait to die so it can be carved. And when you come around to my grave, you'll probably find me sitting there proudly reading it."

Rogers was killed in a plane crash near Point Barrow, Alaska, in August 1935. He was buried not far from his birthplace, and his epitaph reads simply, "Will Rogers."

§ GEORGE M. COHAN §

George M. Cohan reigned as the unchallenged "King of Broadway" for almost twenty years, and, like any popular monarch, he gave the public what they wanted: exuberant showmanship, apple-pie sentimentality, and flag-waving patriotism. (According to Will Rogers, Cohan had worn out more flags than any war.) The composer of "I'm a Yankee Doodle Dandy," "Over There," and "A Grand Old Flag" was only technically exaggerating when he sang, "I'm a real-life nephew of my Uncle Sammy, born on the Fourth of July."

Actually, Cohan was born on the third of July, 1878. At the age of eight he joined his father, mother, and sister in the family song-and-dance act, and he grew up on the vaudeville circuits. In his middle twenties he made his first attempt on Broadway. *Little Johnny Jones* opened disastrously; Cohan reworked it on the road and reopened in New York. The show was the hit of the season, and Cohan, singing "Give My Regards to Broadway" and "Yankee Doodle Dandy," was the hit of the show, a star at age twenty-six. Cohan followed this success with twelve more musicals and comedies in the next seven years; he opened the George M. Cohan Theater in 1912, with a production of a new play written, produced, directed by, and starring George M. Cohan.

As a performer his secret was "perpetual motion." His manner was brash and self-confident; he more than made up for his slight stature with energetic song-and-dance routines, hat, cane, and Cohan blending into a single blur of activity. He once starred in film versions of three of his plays, *Broadway Jones, Seven Keys to Baldpate,* and *Hit-the-Trail Holiday,* which together were completed in ten weeks. "They had me running about the country like a wild man, but no one ever heard me complain of the work. No one ever heard me acknowledge that I was tired. I was always there, with the big smile and apparently making light of it all." Cohan combined this seemingly limitless energy with unabashed Yankee pride, Irish sentimentality, and a good deal of pure blarney; as a playwright he was concerned solely with pleasing an audience, which he said meant that "you must lie like the dickens."

His song "Over There," written in a little over an hour, became the unofficial theme song of the American Expeditionary Forces in World War I, and sold over two million copies at home. Cohan was awarded the Congressional Medal of Honor for "Over There" and his tireless wartime fund-raising activities, but his reign on Broadway ended soon after the war. Cohan's clean, sentimental musicals and melodramas now seemed dated, songs like "Mary's a Grand Old Name" in *Forty-Five Minutes from Broadway* hopelessly old-fashioned and corny. ("Gosh, how I hate that word!" Cohan complained.) After a string of failures Cohan made a successful comeback in the premiere of *Ah, Wilderness!*, starring, for the first time in many years, in a play he had *not* written. But in spite of rave notices and a first-night ovation, Cohan still regarded this as something of a comedown. Reportedly, when a friend offered congratulations, Cohan only shook his head. "Imagine my reciting lines by Eugene O'Neill! Why, he ought to be on the stage reciting lines by *me!*"

Today Cohan's songs are far from forgotten, having been revived and repopularized in the film biography *Yankee Doodle Dandy*, with James Cagney, and more recently in the stage and TV musical *George M.*, starring Joel Grey. Largely through the efforts of lyricist Oscar Hammerstein II, a statue of Cohan was erected on Broadway at Times Square, complete with his familiar hat and cane, smiling as he surveys his former kingdom.

Vaudeville had always been an international community, and just as George M. Cohan typified the energy and excitement of Broadway, or Will Rogers the earthiness and honesty of the American West, many other nations sent their own unaccredited but highly appreciated theatrical ambassadors. The gnomelike Scot Sir Harry Lauder proved that the music hall was not an English monopoly. Sir Harry performed in impeccable national dress of tam-o'-shanter and kilts, revealing impressively bandy legs as he tapped the stage with his corkscrew walking stick and sang "Just a Wee Deoch-an-Doris" or "I Love a Lassie" in a thick Scottish burr. Maurice Chevalier symbolized the romance of the Paris boulevards for many Americans, as a star of music halls, movies, radio, legitimate theater, and television. A more recent import, Stanley Holloway staged a one-man revival of the English music hall as the irrepressible Cockney philosopher Alfred Doolittle in the stage and film versions of *My Fair Lady,* and appeared as Bottom in *A Midsummer Night's Dream,* the gravedigger in *Hamlet,* and other Shakespearean clowns in Canada and Australia as well as Britain and the United States.

§ FANNY BRICE §

Like George M. Cohan, Fanny Brice is probably better remembered today from her Hollywood musical "biographies" than as a performer in her own right. *Funny Girl,* the original Broadway musical and film, and the film sequel, *Funny Lady,* all starring Barbra Streisand, made an entertaining retelling of Fanny Brice's eventful offstage life, but only hinted at how funny the lady herself could be.

Fanny Brice was born Fannie Borach in New York City in 1891. She began her career as a teen-ager, playing piano in a Lower East Side movie house, then followed her natural bent for comedy as a performer in burlesque and vaudeville. As a star of the *Follies* from 1910 to 1924, she became Broadway's best-loved musical comedienne. Plain and angular, with a long face, large mouth, mousy brown hair, and enormous, green eyes, Fanny Brice was by no means a "Ziegfeld girl." She capitalized on the contrast by creating a highly unprovocative fan dancer who had trouble coping with her fans or a clumsy ballerina wobbling her way through "The Dying Swan." She burlesqued the glamour queens of Hollywood and the great beauties of the past, Madame Pompadour or Marguerite Gauthier in *Camille* (to W. C. Fields's Armand), a performance much closer to Second Avenue, New York, than Second Empire Paris.

But her most popular creation was the precocious child terror "Baby Snooks," a character she first developed in her vaudeville act in 1912 and revived on radio in 1936. Much of her regular material was too topical for radio audiences outside New York to appreciate, but her weekly half-hour broadcasts made Baby Snooks a national favorite. Snooks was a seven-year-old tyrant, clever, mischievous, and all too ready to throw a tantrum in order to get her own way. Her radio trademark, a prolonged, earsplitting "WAAAH," came as the eagerly awaited climax at every broadcast.

A typical episode began with Snooks's father nervously preparing for his first public speech. He has decided to practice at home by declaiming through a mouthful of marbles, in the best tradition of the ancient orator Demosthenes, who cured his persistent stutter by filling his mouth with pebbles. Snooks, who has talked nothing but baby talk since earliest childhood, insists that her own diction could use a few marbles. Her father gives her a marble to shut her up and Snooks recites a poem in clear, ringing tones. Her father hands her a second marble, then a third and a fourth, and the flow of eloquence continues. There is really nothing to it, Snooks explains; she has simply swallowed the marbles. Father grabs Snooks, holds her upside down, and shakes her. Out come the marbles and the eagerly anticipated "WAAAH!"

Fanny Brice identified so closely with Baby Snooks that she often stayed in character for as long as an hour after her broadcasts. (In fact, many radio listeners were astonished to discover that Snooks was played by a middle-aged comedienne and not by a real child.) She took great pride in this; she said, "When I did a character I *was* that character." Offstage, her great comic talent became something of a disadvantage; the public could not accept her as a serious person: "They don't expect it and they won't take it from you. You are not entitled to be serious. You are a clown."

§ THE GREAT TEAMS §

In vaudeville two clowns could often be better than one, and the great comedy teams specialized in a kind of clowning that brought out the best in two contrasting, and even conflicting, stage personalities. Even before the dialect duets of Messrs. Harrigan and Hart, the minstrel shows had introduced the elegant master of ceremonies, "Mr. Interlocutor," the "straight man" who set up the jokes for the raffish "end man," "Mr. Bones." In their fifty-five years together on stage, from 1875 to 1930, the team of (Thomas) McIntyre and (James) Heath developed a more freewheeling style of blackface comedy, each playing straight man in their sketches by turns, topping each other's jokes and trading off the laugh lines between them. The musical-comedy team of (David) Montgomery and (Fred) Stone inspired a whole string of Broadway hits written especially for them. They played the Tin Man and the Scarecrow in the first stage version of *The Wizard of Oz* in 1903; Victor Herbert's *The Red Mill* (1906) was the greatest of their many successes. The Mutt and Jeff duo of (Joe) Weber and (Lew) Fields specialized in dialect comedy with a sideline of slapstick violence; the smaller Weber always came out the loser in his bouts with the towering Fields. Clean family entertainment was their watchword—broad parodies of popular plays, filled with easy, obvious jokes and agonizing puns. Julia Marlowe's triumph in *Barbara Friet-chie* inspired *Barbara Fidgety;* after Richard Mansfield's swashbuckling *Cyrano de Bergerac,* Weber and Fields put on their putty noses for *Cyranose de Bric-à-Brac.* After many successful seasons in their own Weber and Fields Theater, the strain of their long partnership began to tell. The breakup of the act made nationwide headlines, and popular demand for a comeback brought about a successful Weber and Fields revival on radio many years later. As far as the public was concerned, age had only improved their old material:

WEBER This dog is worth five hundred dollars.
FIELDS Nonsense, how could a dog save that much money?

Around the turn of the century Bobby Clark and his friend Paul McCullough, both aspiring acrobats, joined a circus as clowns. Clark and McCullough gradually turned from tumbling to pure clowning, and eventually moved on to Ringling Bros. Circus, and then vaudeville. During the twenties and thirties the team appeared on the Broadway stage, with a successful season in London in 1922, and in as many as thirty-six successful Hollywood films. These short two-, three-, and four-reelers displayed a kind of wild originality that made Clark and McCullough second only to the Marx Brothers in box-office popularity. By this time the team was virtually commuting between Broadway and Hollywood; the pace was too much for McCullough. He suffered a total nervous collapse and was hospitalized; upon his release he stopped for a shave on his way home. Suddenly, while joking with the barber, McCullough impulsively seized a razor and slashed his throat. Clark was shattered by his friend's suicide but determined to carry on alone, at the same incredible pace and as successfully as ever. While he was still with the circus, Clark hit upon his distinctive personal trademark. Just before a performance he realized he had misplaced his glasses, grabbed a black makeup pencil, and drew himself a new pair. The greasepaint glasses went over very well with the circus audience—and with all Clark's other audiences for the rest of his career, whether he was playing an acrobatic laundress in Victor Herbert's *Sweethearts* or Molière's Monsieur Jourdain. In one of his film performances, in 1938, United Artists insisted that Clark wear *real* glasses; the film was not a success.

Clark's appearance in a Molière play was not at all unusual; in later life he became something of an authority on the history of comedy, lectured in drama schools on seventeenth- and eighteenth-century acting styles, and played in revivals of Congreve and Sheridan, as well as Molière.

Wherever they played, (Ole) Olsen and (Chic) Johnson refused to confine their comedy to the stage and inventively exploited the unexplored resources of the theater, including the aisles and the balcony, the lobby, and even the sidewalk. One of their shows, which ran for a record 1404 performances on Broadway, required a company and crew of seventy-five, including miscellaneous relatives and friends, not just to keep the action as lively and chaotic as possible on the stage, but to bring off a whole devilish array of offstage effects, as succinctly summed up in the title of the play *Hellzapoppin.* Here are just a few: In one of the boxes a violent argument breaks out between a man and his wife. Suddenly he picks her up over his head and hurls her into the audience below. (The "wife" is of course an almost weightless, very realistically painted dummy.) A latecomer slinks down the aisle, finds a vacant seat, takes off his coat, and hangs it on a hanger that conveniently drops from the ceiling. He sits down, the hanger flies back up to the ceiling, and the coat is whisked away. At regular intervals a pageboy walks down the aisle, holding a potted plant and calling for Mrs. Jones. Each time he reappears, the plant has grown appreciably larger; by the time the audience files out after the show, the boy is perched in the branches of a large tree in the lobby, still plaintively paging Mrs. Jones. A man wearing a fright wig over a hideous false face sits down next to an unescorted woman and begins to make rather ominous advances. She steadfastly ignores him until he peels off the false face, revealing the face of Olsen (or Johnson). The woman screams with terror, runs up the aisle and out of the theater. Through the entire evening a man sits on the edge of the stage, reading the paper and taking no notice of the pandemonium that surrounds him. He was there when the audience came in; as they get up to leave, he is still there. When *Hellzapoppin* was made into a movie, Olsen and Johnson seemed to adapt quite easily to a new and challenging medium. At one point the film begins to jump. When they address a few words of admonition to the projection booth, the screen splits, they find themselves trapped in separate frames, and are only brought back together after they threaten to fire the projectionist outright.

Olsen and Johnson were both Midwesterners who began in vaudeville with a fairly conventional musical act. As this developed into a highly unconventional comedy act, they moved on to Broadway with *Hellzapoppin,* followed by *Sons o' Fun, Laffing Room Only,* and *Pardon Our French,* and finally to movies, radio, and television.

The movies they made for Warner Brothers were something of a disappointment. The studio promoted them as "America's Funniest Clowns" and made them follow story lines that seriously cramped their uninhibited comic style. They were at their best on Broadway, before a live, laughing, gasping, shrieking, and always unsuspecting audience, with no restrictions on their cheerful theatrical lunacy, except that everything that happened had to happen quickly and unexpectedly and that nothing could be what it seemed or what it ought to be.

The team of (Joe) Smith and (Charlie) Dale stayed together from their first appearance in vaudeville in 1898 until Dale's death in 1971, certainly one of the theater's most enduring partnerships. Their best-known sketch, "Dr. Kronkhite and His Only Living Patient," was a classic of malapropism, comic misunderstanding, and complete verbal confusion. Both doctor and patient speak in heavy unidentifiable accents; Dale, as the nervous patient, greets Smith, the white-coated Dr. Kronkhite, with understandable scepticism:

DALE Doctor, I'm dubious . . .

SMITH Pleased to meet you, Mr. Dubious. I would like to see you inhale.

DALE *(bristling)* I didn't come here to be insulted!

The consultation continues in this vein for some time, at least until the doctor demands his ten-dollar fee and the conversation takes an unexpectedly practical turn:

DALE (*genuinely perplexed*) What for?
SMITH My advice.
DALE Here's two dollars, Doctor. Take it. That's my advice.

This unpromising doctor-patient relationship lasted for some forty years and several thousand performances, in vaudeville, in films, and on television; the aging vaudevillians in Neil Simon's comedy *The Sunshine Boys* were reportedly inspired by Smith and Dale. Smith and Dale created other characters and starred in the Broadway comedy *Mendel Inc.,* but when Judy Garland brought vaudeville back to the Palace Theatre in 1952, Smith and Dale naturally revived the nonchalant doctor and his one-patient practice for a final extended engagement at the Palace.

Radio's most popular comedy team, Bob (Elliott) and Ray (Goulding) materialized on Broadway in *Bob and Ray, the Two and Only.* Mike Nichols and Elaine May satirized the anxieties of the fifties and early sixties in sophisticated sketches and improvisations in which easy laughter was often followed by a disconcerting twinge of self-recognition. Both Nichols and May have since followed separate careers. Nichols is now a major film director with an impressive list of stage credits as well; Elaine May has written, directed, and acted in a number of film comedies with the same deft, scalpel touch that she displayed in her work with Nichols.

It is easy to forget that, during the twenties, the Marx Brothers were a great stage team, years before they appeared in films. In fact, *The Cocoanuts* and *Animal Crackers* were almost literal film records of long-running Broadway hits, down to the painted palm trees on the backdrop in the case of *The Cocoanuts.* Onstage they were unhampered by standard Hollywood formulas, the sticky romantic subplots and lavish musical numbers that are the despair of Marx Brothers movie buffs today; or, in other words, they were best left alone. While making their funniest films for MGM, *A Night at the Opera* and *A Day at the Races,* they rehearsed before live audiences, selecting and refining their routines for their final performance on film. In their later films they lost this spontaneous contact and began to depend on scriptwriters and gag men for fresh material. On Broadway, too, they had naturally worked from a script, but they usually thought of it as merely a source of useful information on the other actors' speeches and whereabouts and their own exit and entrance cues. Their lines they revised, reworked, and refined to suit themselves; George S. Kaufman, co-author of one of their Broadway successes, liked to recall how shocked he had been when he heard one of his own lines delivered in an actual performance.

In 1951, after the Brothers had left Hollywood, Groucho began a ten-year stint (not counting endless reruns) as the host of a radio and TV quiz show. With a live studio audience, an announcer straight man, and a steady stream of contestants as comic foils, *You Bet Your Life* supplied a perfect format for Groucho's personal specialties—the instantaneous ad lib and the well-honed insult ("I never forget a face, but I'm willing to make an exception in your case").

England's answer to the Marx Brothers was *The Goon Show,* broadcast over BBC radio for almost ten years. The Goons, in reality Spike Milligan, Peter Sellers, and Harry Secombe, discovered that the most ordinary objects and the most trivial incidents of everyday life were indistinguishable from the maddest of fantasies, if you only looked at things in the right way. This Goon sketch pictures an encounter between two characters called Minnie and Crun, otherwise unidentified. The scene, we are told, is the English Channel. The year is 1941. It is raining.

MINNIE What a nice summer evening. Typically English.
CRUN Yes, the rain's lovely and warm. Here, hold my elephant gun.
MINNIE You can't shoot elephants in England.
CRUN Why not?
MINNIE They're out of season.
CRUN Does that mean we'll have to have pelican for dinner again?
MINNIE Yes, I'm afraid so.
CRUN Then I'll risk it. I'll shoot an elephant out of season.

It is easy to see from this why the Goons's particular brand of humor has been called surrealistic. Spike Milligan, who wrote the scripts for *The Goon Show,* has himself been compared to such great masters of English nonsense writing as Lewis Carroll and Edward

Lear. As a playwright, Milligan has reached even greater heights of absurdity, notably on one occasion, when the curtain rose and took Milligan along with it, clinging desperately to the fringe as he disappeared into the farthest reaches of the proscenium.

§ MODERN-DAY ZANIES §

Ed Wynn played the zany innocent for more than five decades, first in vaudeville, then on Broadway in a succession of shows such as *The Perfect Fool, The Grab Bag,* and *Hooray for What* during the twenties and thirties, as a radio personality of the forties, and finally as one of Hollywood's most beloved character actors in the fifties and sixties. He made one of his last appearances as Uncle Albert in the Disney film *Mary Poppins,* buoyantly singing "I Love to Laugh" while his laughter slowly floats him up to the ceiling like a helium balloon.

Born Isaiah Edwin Leopold, he simply tinkered with the two syllables of his middle name, and made it his stage name when he appeared in vaudeville. He remained on the circuits for several years and his career seemed to be going nowhere, at least until a season with the *Follies* and several other revues in 1914–1915. His cheerful, almost childlike personality and his lisping, bubbly way of talking combined with his outlandish wardrobe to make him seem more like a whimsical children's book character than a headliner in the *Follies.* His costumes were a show in themselves, everything oversized, from head (by the time he appeared on Broadway, years later, he had amassed a collection of eight hundred hats) to foot (his shoes, though less numerous, were enormous). As a boy he had worked in his father's millinery shop in Philadelphia, and not only the hats but much of his comic material had more than a suggestion of the ingenious fantasies and "impossible inventions" of an extremely imaginative child.

In one of his best-known sketches he demonstrated a whole battery of remarkable labor-saving devices. First he produced a pole, exactly eleven feet, four inches long, in case he wanted to touch someone he wouldn't touch with a ten-foot pole. Then he flicked the lid of a cigarette lighter, and a tiny arrow appeared, which, as Wynn explained, pointed to the nearest person with matches. Next came an ear of corn mounted on a typewriter roller; after Wynn had eaten his way to the end of a row of kernels, a bell rang, the roller sprang back, and advanced to the next row. After the mechanized corncob Wynn took out a grapefruit, attached a transparent window shade to his forehead, rolled down the shade, and fearlessly devoured the juicy sections. Next came a specially designed fork, complete with a papier-mâché nose that fit over his own as he tucked into an especially fragrant piece of cheese. A sponge bracelet slipped around his wrist soaked up the melted butter during the asparagus course, and, of course, a feedbag around his neck took care of cracker crumbs.

§ BERT LAHR §

No one who saw MGM's musical version of *The Wizard of Oz* could deny that Bert Lahr was perfect for the part of the Cowardly Lion. Lahr had long been a familiar figure on Broadway, and before that in vaudeville and burlesque, with his big pug nose and rubbery face, his indescribable laugh, falling somewhere between a snarl and a yawn, and his inveterate and outrageous mispronunciations ("Don't be naïve" came out as "Don't be knave").

On Broadway Lahr appeared in a number of musicals: opposite Ethel Merman in *Du Barry Was a Lady* (the Cole Porter show that treated the world to the spectacle of Lahr in lace ruffles and knee breeches) and with Beatrice Lillie in *The Seven Lively Arts.* In *Burlesque* Lahr played a pratfall comic, down on his luck; the critics particularly praised his sensitive handling of his character's final emotional crack-up, not to mention nostalgic re-creations of his burlesque routines. The American premiere of Samuel Beckett's absurdist classic, *Waiting for Godot,* brought Lahr an even more challenging role, and more critical acclaim (although he acknowledged with a casual shrug of his shoulders that he had no idea what the play was about). Lahr had come a long way from baggy-pants burlesque to Beckett's perplexing study of ultimate meaninglessness; finally, in his last years on stage, he came full circle, back to the broad slapstick and spirited buffoonery of the classics, starring in productions of *The Birds* and *A Midsummer Night's Dream.*

§ ZERO MOSTEL §

That very mountain of a man, Zero Mostel, was another of our versatile latter-day zanies, highly acclaimed in his serious roles on Broadway but more closely associated with comedy. Mostel created the parts of the tricky slave in *A Funny Thing Happened on the Way to the Forum,* and Tevye, the tradition-bound patriarch in *Fiddler on the Roof,* probably his best-remembered role. Mostel gave a performance in Eugene Ionesco's absurdist comedy *Rhinoceros* that bordered on the uncanny. As the main character, turning into a rhinoceros, Mostel's brow furrows, his lip protrudes, his eyes grow small and malevolent, he snorts and scuffs the floor. The transformation is complete; Mostel begins to nibble the leaves off the house plants in his living room, and if at this point he were to sprout a horn in the middle of his forehead, surely no one in the audience would be terribly surprised.

After Mostel as rhinoceros, it seems appropriate to mention the urbane charm and equally amazing grace of the rotund British actor Robert Morley, who has become familiar to American audiences through his frequent film and television appearances. He has also written and starred in several successful comedies on the London stage (one of which was fittingly entitled *Hippo Dancing*).

§ HELLO, DOLLY! §

Musical comedienne Carol Channing first delighted Broadway as Lorelei Lee, the gold-digger heroine of *Gentlemen Prefer Blondes* (1953). Tall and attractive, with abundant blond hair, enormous brown eyes, and long and amazingly expressive lashes, she instantly became the darling of theatrical cartoonists. Her voice, however, is truly distinctive, sliding up and down the octaves from a husky baritone to an almost batlike soprano squeak in the course of a sentence or two. (This remarkable range, and her slightly nasal "theatrical" drawl, is not a regional accent—she was born in Seattle and educated at Bennington College, Vermont—but simply her own unique way of talking.) During the sixties *Hello, Dolly!* opened with Carol Channing in the title role and ran for 1273 performances on Broadway (a record surpassed later by *Fiddler on the Roof*). Dolly Gallagher Levi, animated, exuberant, an incorrigible plotter and matchmaker, was a perfect part for Miss Channing; in one now-celebrated scene, Dolly managed to nibble her way through a gargantuan meal without interrupting the nonstop flow of her conversation, or even pausing to swallow. The tableful of delicacies was simulated with fluffy, low-calorie ingredients, and Miss Channing cheerfully and daintily gobbled down every morsel. Eventually she acquired quite a taste for it, and even when the scene drew an enthusiastic ovation, she went right on eating, almost without batting an eye.

The earthy and exuberant "Pearlie-May" character created by stage, film, and television comedienne Pearl Bailey might have seemed like an unlikely successor to Carol Channing's matchmaker. Still, Pearl Bailey made the part very much her own in a successful all-black Broadway production of *Hello, Dolly!*, and, as further proof of Dolly's adaptability, Barbra Streisand later starred in the Hollywood film version.

§ THE SOPHISTICATED CLOWNS §

Beatrice Lillie was born in Canada and became not only the queen of sophisticated comedy on the New York and London stages, but after her marriage to Sir Robert Peel in 1920, Lady Peel as well, one of history's few titled clowns.

Midway through her first London audition for producer André Charlot, she began to feel a polite silence descending on the darkened theater. "We're Drifting Apart, So You're Breaking My Heart" was clearly not going over as a straight romantic ballad; and so, without changing a word of the lyrics, she added an ironic commentary of exaggerated inflections and wry facial expressions that clearly told Charlot she thought that it was all rather silly herself. She went on to appear in Charlot's revues for many years, and throughout her four decades on the stage she developed this tongue-in-cheek delivery of simple or sentimental material into a minor art form. She based an entire sketch on a familiar tongue twister about "a dozen double-damask dinner napkins," and she could take an innocent children's poem beginning "There are fairies at the bottom of our garden" and turn it into a musical monologue that was little short of scandalous.

Bea Lillie was scarcely over five feet tall, with sparkling eyes, a turned-up nose, and the general air of a high-society pixie wearing a stylish pillbox hat and a long rope of pearls. These she liked to twirl around her neck like a lasso, registering complete unconcern as they slipped out of their orbit, steadily winding downward until they fell in a heap at her feet. Miss Lillie's ensemble was completed by an evening gown with a long, uncooperative train that, on making her exit, she sometimes scooped up over her ankles for convenience's sake or simply gave a spirited kick, as if to say that she, for one, was very much her own woman and hardly intended to become the slave of fashion.

The versatile Noel Coward pursued several careers in sophisticated comedy, as a playwright, lyricist, director, and performer. He was called "Noel," then a fairly unusual name, simply because he was born nine days before Christmas, in 1899. He began his stage career in the role of Slightly, one of the lost boys in *Peter Pan*, and from then on was seldom out of the public eye. He wrote and starred in such elegant comedies as *Private Lives, Design for Living,* and *Tonight at 8:30.* He was the author of many, many other theater pieces—in all, 27 plays, operettas, and musicals, and 281 songs. His best-known film was *In Which We Serve,* an uncharacteristically sober drama of the Royal Navy in wartime, which he starred in as well as directed, along with many other less serious efforts. Witty, charming, always the *bon vivant* in immaculate evening dress, Coward seemed to have stepped out of one of his own comedies; his offstage remarks are probably as often quoted as his plays and were undoubtedly delivered with the same crisp precision. Coward was knighted by Queen Elizabeth in 1970. (Her Majesty, as Coward recalled it, administered the ritual sword taps on his shoulders "very lightly, thank goodness.")

But for all Coward's hauteur and elegance, many of his most popular songs are strongly reminiscent of the music hall, "Don't Put Your Daughter on the Stage, Mrs. Worthington" and "Mad Dogs and Englishmen," for example. Songs like "Someday I'll Find You" and "I'll See You Again" drip with sentimentality, and many critics have suggested that Coward's public face, his flippancy and cynicism, concealed a shy and lonely man who had created a personality for himself as consciously and deliberately as if he were writing a part for himself in one of his drawing-room comedies.

Like Noel Coward, Clifton Webb grew up in the theater. He began as a singer and dancer in musicals, moved on to comedy of manners, and then went into the movies. As a comedian and character actor, he became Hollywood's ideal of the well-bred man of the world. Gertrude Lawrence, who often played opposite Noel Coward, combined sophistication with refreshingly earthy common sense and was equally at home in musicals, revues, and the legitimate theater. Broadway comedy in the Coward grand manner seems to have died out in recent years except in occasional revivals in which Maggie Smith or Vanessa

Redgrave proves that Coward's elegant approach to clowning is by no means a lost art.

Tallulah Bankhead was perhaps the best known, and certainly the most flamboyant, of our sophisticated comediennes, as well as an accomplished and expressive serious actress. After such brilliant characterizations as Regina Gibbons in *The Little Foxes* in 1939, she moved increasingly in the direction of self-caricature in the fifties and sixties. Her colorful career and equally colorful personal life have inspired several biographies since her death; her best-selling autobiography was less revealing than her fans had hoped, but still made lively reading. It begins, "Despite all you may have heard to the contrary, I have never had a ride in a patrol wagon."

As mistress of ceremonies on radio's *Big Show* during the early fifties, she popularized the all-purpose endearment "Dahling" in the repertory of countless impersonators. Her diction combined an exaggerated Southern drawl with affected theatrical huskiness, and even the most inept imitation was likely to be instantly recognizable, let alone the real thing. Her friend and fellow comedienne Patsy Kelly recalls that Tallulah dealt with autograph hunters by drawing herself up indignantly and demanding icily, in a voice that could not possibly belong to anyone else, "How dare you mistake me for that dreadful woman?"

§ MARCEL MARCEAU'S ''BIP'' §

Marcel Marceau, the king of modern pantomime, was born in Strasbourg, France, on March 22, 1923, though he dates the beginning of his artistic career even earlier. "In the womb of my mother," he maintains, "I was already a mime." An avid moviegoer at the age of five, he began to re-enact Keaton and Chaplin silent-comedy routines, painstakingly rehearsing in front of a mirror at home before trying them out on his fascinated young friends after school and at summer camp.

He worked for the Resistance during World War II, guiding Jewish refugees over the Alps to safety in neutral Switzerland. His older brother also survived the war, though his father, a kosher butcher by trade, was among the many who died in Auschwitz. Marceau served with the French Occupation army in Germany before coming to Paris to study acting with Charles Dullin and Etienne Decroux, the two great masters who introduced him to the art of pantomime. He created his familiar pantomime alter ego, "Bip" the Clown, in 1947, while performing with the distinguished repertory company founded by Jean-Louis Barrault and Madeleine Renaud. Marceau formed his own company and began presenting what he called mimodramas, short sketches in which Bip took on an impressive, ever-changing variety of identities.

Bip's appearance never changes; whiteface and bright red lips, striped shirt, white pants, black slippers, and a tall stovepipe hat, often adorned with a colorful flower on a long drooping stem. In the mimodramas Marceau's modern Pierrot character might become a lion tamer, wild Apache dancer, street musician, balloon hawker, pottery seller, painter, poet, sculptor, skater, or butterfly collector. "On stage I express the inner person," says Marceau, and Bip can experience all seven ages of man in the space of a few minutes, turning his body, shifting his expression, reaching out his hand, or stepping with precision into a new attitude. Standing in a spotlight on a bare stage framed by black curtains in back and at the sides, Bip invites us into his invisible pantomime universe, where life, as it turns out, is as comical, as terrifying, and as complicated as it is in our own visible world. Bip appears first as a cocktail party reveler, with one arm, and before long *both* arms, resting casually upon the mantelpiece. But after a few drinks, as his feet begin to slide out from under him and his elbows to slip from their imaginary perch, Bip leaves the party behind and proceeds on to dinner. Unable to choose among so many tempting delicacies, Bip goes after them all, fastidiously removing a shred of meat from between his front teeth, napkin at the ready to mop up the occasional mishap in a concerted yet exquisitely well-mannered attack. He washes it all down with a glass of wine, gargling lustily with the dregs of his wineglass to restore his well-exercised palate at the end of an extremely satisfactory meal.

Then, as Bip is simply staring off into space, his hand creeps out of one of his pockets, gliding and darting like a snake, makes a sinuous reptilian progress across his chest, past his neck and chin, and finally recalls Bip from his reverie by biting him squarely on the nose.

Instantly recovered from his self-inflicted snakebite, Bip appears next as a conscientious craftsman, a mask maker trying on a whole series of young, handsome, old, and grotesque faces, examining each one until he is convinced that it comes up to his fussy artistic standards. He slips on a mask with a wide, foolish grin, its cheeks puffed out with laughter. This one also passes inspection, but as he starts to try on another he finds the mask he has on refuses to come off. Tugging impatiently at his chin and forehead, then pulling with all his might, Bip ends by clawing at his face in desperate panic while the mask's foolish grin now seems to mock Bip's terrified efforts to remove it.

Bip's nightmarish struggle finally turns the smiling mask of comedy into an image as sinister as a grinning skull and as inescapable as death itself. Marceau's mimodrama mixes comedy and tragedy quite deliberately: he believes in man as a reflection of both the elusive simplicity and infinite complexity of the universe itself. As Bip explores his invisible world, Marceau magically lets us see this for ourselves. He observes that audiences all over the world laugh at exactly the same moments in a performance. This he sees as proof that silent comedy becomes, at its best, a truly universal language; we might also take this as a tribute to the universal appeal of Marceau as an artist and interpreter of the human condition.

Besides *Les Pantomimes de Bip*, Marceau has presented longer pieces, *Paris in Laughter*, *Paris in Tears* and a full-length pantomime adaptation of Gogol's fantasy *The Overcoat*. During Marceau's first American tour, in 1956, he appeared on television with Sid Caesar and Red Skelton, both gifted pantomime comedians of the "Golden Age" of television, and in the next decade, as a frequent guest on TV talk shows, putting aside Bip's top hat and frock coat in rare speaking appearances as Marcel Marceau, demonstrating and, as far as possible, explaining the elusive art of pantomime. Today Marceau operates a school for mimes in Paris and continues to perform three hundred days out of the year. In 1947 Marceau's was the only permanent pantomime company in the world, but since then Bip has performed before audiences in some sixty-five countries, and thanks largely to his silent example and the successful efforts of Marceau's pupils, pantomime is now a flourishing art form in a half-dozen countries around the world.

Marceau's early associate, Jean-Louis Barrault, has also done much to reacquaint modern film and theater audiences with the ancient art of pantomime. The film *Les Enfants du Paradis (Children of Paradise)*, made in 1944, is an inspired re-creation of the Parisian popular theater of the 1840s; Barrault plays a character modeled on the famous mime Baptiste Deburau, who was credited with being the first to bring the sad-faced clown Pierrot to the pantomime stage. Barrault in turn introduced Pierrot to the modern stage, and twentieth-century audiences in Europe and America applauded him as heartily as had the "children of paradise" of nineteenth-century Paris (these were the spectators who occupied the cheapest seats in the galleries, "closer to heaven than earth"). Pierrot's patient attempts to thread a needle became a suspenseful life-or-death battle with invisible powers of unlimited perversity. He then turned to picking pockets, and in a moment was triumphantly holding up a watch. Suddenly, a look of alarm shot across his pale face. His own watch was missing. But alarm turned to relief and then to quiet satisfaction as he restored the watch, reflecting how skillfully and imperceptibly he had picked his own pocket.

More than any other form of theater, pantomime enlists our own powers of imagination and invites our total participation in the unseen spectacle. As Bip's hand becomes a slithering serpent or Pierrot triumphantly picks his own pocket, we realize that these two French masters of pantomime have the ability to suspend the rules of ordinary reality and entice us into their invisible world, an ability that is nothing less than magical.

· 10 ·
CLOWNS
IN THE
SILENT MOVIES

The First Film Clowns, Charlie Chaplin,
Buster Keaton, Harold Lloyd,
and Harry Langdon

—————————————————————————

Starting around the turn of the century, the comedy partnership of clown and cameramen developed quickly into a new and popular art form and an increasingly lucrative industry. The clown came naturally and fearlessly into this silent, flickering world, populated by club-wielding policemen and heavily clad bathing beauties who were surrounded by the noiseless collisions of vehicles of every imaginable type, from rocketing tin lizzies to self-propelled brass beds. The air was thick with flying pies. In spite of these hazards, performers from the vaudeville and legitimate theaters, circuses, and the music halls began a mass professional migration from the stage to the silent-film studio.

A performer might reach a wider audience with a single two-reel comedy than he would face in a lifetime on the vaudeville circuits. A few—Chaplin was one of them—realized at the outset the immense commercial potential of this new medium. But many performers preferred to remain on the stage and spurned studio contracts, dismissing the movies as a penny-arcade novelty that could never compete with live actors playing to a live audience. And some, even while making films, still thought much the same of these early two- and three-reel efforts, cranked out in a matter of hours and almost as quickly forgotten. The quality of many of these early silent movies did little to discourage such opinions. Production techniques gradually improved; highly inventive performers and fiercely competitive producers began to exploit the opportunities of the new medium. These developments helped to create a distinctive film comedy style, quite independent of Broadway or vaudeville, which soon produced a remarkable number of "classic" film comedy masterpieces.

Certainly the film's greatest advantage over the stage was freedom. Performers were no longer confined by canvas walls and painted flats, and early filmmakers were naturally fascinated by exterior locations. A chaotic street scene, crowded with unpaid extras, would have been the envy of Harrigan and Hart, and a realistically dusty comic car chase disappearing down a rutted country lane could now go farther and faster than any machine that Grimaldi had ever dreamed of. And as soon as they had unrestricted access to the world outside, the silent comedians naturally started to improve on it. Using stop motion or trick photography, speeding up, slowing down, or simply reversing the film, they repealed the laws of gravity, set new, if unofficial, Olympic records, and felt free to fall up a chimney or jump into a second-story window. A film might be built around an army of extras or an extended solo performance (Chaplin's films were both), and besides playing five or six different roles, just as Grimaldi and Hart had done, an actor could now play opposite himself, if he chose to, for a single scene or an entire film. Trick photography was only one way for a comedian to be in two places at once; the other was simply superhuman whirlwind motion, forward or backward, or both, like the Keystone Kop who falls off the running board of his paddy wagon still clutching his partner's coattails. Instantly both Kop and paddy wagon fly into reverse, and the Kop is back on board again almost before his feet have touched the ground. Automobiles, trains, trucks, buses, and trolleys would serve as well for the silent comedian; anything on wheels that could hurtle off a cliff or through the wall of a house whenever life threatened to get slow was pressed into service.

The silent clown managed to survive these and many other disasters with a fortitude verging on indifference that more fragile mortals in the audience had to admire. He could pass through the grinding gears and pounding pistons of an enormous machine that finally spat him out unscratched, or simply loll in bed while an entire building collapsed around him, leaving him safely surrounded by a heap of fallen rubble. In *The Navigator* Buster Keaton and Kathryn McGuire, who share a farewell embrace before sinking under the sea for the last time, suddenly, unaccountably find themselves rising *out* of the water, perched comfortably on the conning tower of a surfacing submarine.

For Keaton and his colleagues even suicide was impossible. In *Steamboat Bill, Jr.* Buster, looking more mournful than ever, finds a likely looking precipice, takes a running start, goes into a faultless swan dive, and bounces harmlessly through a painted canvas backdrop. A lovelorn Charlie Chaplin, in *The Vagabond,* jumps off a bridge, only to be fished out by an old woman of such surpassing ugliness that he promptly throws himself back in again. The next time, however, it is the lovely Edna Purviance who pulls him out, in order to explain that she loves him after all and it has all been a terrible mistake. With such a happy ending in the offing, suicide is clearly out of the question.

The movie camera allowed the clown to overcome insurmountable obstacles. Freed of all the restrictions of the physical world and all the limitations of the human body, the clown still had to deal with all manner of everyday adversities, yet with the cameraman on his side, he realized instinctively that these too were only temporary. In 1926 the dreamy, bespectacled, and virtually indestructible Harold Lloyd starred in a film whose title, *Why Worry?,* neatly summed up the silent clown's optimistic philosophy of life. For all his ineptitude Lloyd clambered around skyscrapers with a kind of zany self-confidence that makes terror completely irrelevant, and rode runaway cross-country streetcars with the oblivious ease of a lifelong commuter. Charlie Chaplin, the most sentimental of all silent clowns, arranged a happy ending for his Little Tramp in all but three of his eighty-some films. Buster Keaton, the least sentimental, and the most resourceful, could count on his courage and ingenuity, or when these failed him, on a kind Providence or a passing submarine.

§ THE FIRST FILM CLOWNS §

André Deed produced the first film comedies in France in 1906. Acting as both cameraman and director, Deed made several short films that introduced silent comedy's guiding principle of furious motion recorded at superhuman speed, later brought to hyperactive perfection in the Keystone comedies of Mack Sennett. Max Linder was the first film comedian to be identified with a consistently developed character. "Max" was a dapper Parisian whose trim exterior concealed the heart of an incorrigible scoundrel. (Linder's friend Charlie Chaplin created his innocent, much put-upon Little Tramp a few years later, in appearance a baggy, disreputable caricature of Max. In fact, the Tramp might almost have been wearing a suit of Max's cast-offs several times removed.) Max had a roving, roguish eye and a talent for getting out of scrapes, elegantly but nonetheless energetically. Linder was the first film comedian to enjoy international celebrity, but the rapid eclipse of his popularity in the twenties was more than he could bear. In 1925 he killed himself in a double-suicide pact with his wife.

Several American comedy stars made their appearance around 1910. One, a round-faced, round-bellied stage character actor named John Bunny, starred in a number of homespun "rube" comedies. Ben Turpin, bald and very cross-eyed, with a blob of a mustache and an active Adam's apple, was widely popular as well as instantly identifiable. So was Roscoe "Fatty" Arbuckle, who looked something like a grinning, overgrown schoolboy, and even more like Tweedledum in *Through the Looking Glass,* but proved to be a surprisingly agile slapstick comedian. All three developed highly distinctive comic personalities, Bunny's based on a familiar stage type, Turpin's and Arbuckle's on physical appearance.

Mack Sennett's Keystone chase comedies emphasized fast action and elaborately worked-up sight gags (notably the classic pie fights) at the expense of character development. Such at least was the opinion of one of Sennett's better-known protégés, a promising young Englishman called Charles Spencer Chaplin.

§ CHARLIE CHAPLIN §

The character of the Little Tramp began to evolve in the London slums of Chaplin's boyhood; the life of the poor is often recalled in his films, always with deep sympathy and painstaking realism. As a boy Chaplin took up a career in the music halls, following his father's rather discouraging example, and as a young man came to America with the famous Karno variety troupe, which also included Stan Laurel at this time. Chaplin hoped to become a star of American vaudeville; instead he was signed by Mack Sennett, at $150 a week, for Keystone Studios.

Chaplin's Little Tramp was by no means a spontaneous creation. The familiar costume came along quickly enough, but the Little Tramp's personality developed more slowly, over the course of many years and many films. In *My Autobiography,* published in 1964, Chaplin admitted: ". . . even now I don't know all the things there are to be known about him."

In the Tramp's first film (Chaplin's second), which only runs for five minutes, he is attracted by a camera crew filming a children's auto race. Charlie insists on mugging for the camera, distracting the children and interrupting the race until he is finally driven off the track by cameramen, indignant parents, spectators, and the police in the obligatory chase sequence. Even this typical Keystone improvisation, shot on location in under an hour, has several prophetic Chaplin touches. Once his curiosity is aroused, the Little Tramp insists on staying very much in the center of things, even at the risk of inciting a riot. In this first appearance he is already slightly out of step with everyone else, and totally at odds with everything that smacks of order, authority, and organization.

In *The Tramp*, a two-reeler that appeared in 1915, the costume is now complete: enormous shoes pointing outward at forty-five-degree angles; billowing baggy pants tapering at the ankles; a dress coat so small that only the three top buttons will button, and even then one sleeve is slowly parting from the shoulder; an undersized derby; and finally, a bamboo cane. Shabbiness and elegance blend, a little uneasily, in the Tramp's appearance, and his personality reflects, in much the same way, both the nobility and the self-pity of the outcast. In this film the Tramp is torn between a high-minded passion for the farmer's daughter and a more practical impulse to rob the hen roost. Love wins out in the end over the humbler appetite, but he realizes that he can never hope to win the girl and decides after all to return to his life on the road.

With the appearance of *A Dog's Life* in 1918, the Tramp appears as a fully realized character. Chaplin's story lines take the Tramp through a tragicomic sequence of successes and reverses. He might gain acceptance, even adoration, by disguising his identity, or through some act of heroism or self-sacrifice, or occasionally in a wistful dream idyll. But, even if the film ends happily, the moment invariably comes when he is unmasked, rejected, turned out by his new friends (or abruptly awakened by a patrolman's nightstick). However low his fortunes, the Tramp never loses his dignity and natural grace, which he expresses physically in a highly individual pattern of rhythmic dance steps and gestures timed with the sleight-of-hand precision of a master conjurer. ("The best ballet dancer that ever lived, and if I get a chance I'll kill him with my bare hands," W. C. Fields said of Chaplin in perhaps the highest tribute he could pay a fellow artist.) The Tramp's emotional state does not always lend itself to delicacy, and often finds its best expression in a well-aimed kick where his persecutors least expect it.

Chaplin played many other characters besides the Tramp, and the Tramp was a whole impostor's repertory company in himself; his outrageous impersonations, often inspired by the timely theft of someone else's clothes, gave him a chance to assume his natural dignity in society, as a preacher or a well-heeled gentleman, if only for a reel or two. In his later films Chaplin permitted the Tramp to assume a number of new identities: a novice trapeze artist in *The Circus* (1928), a prizefighter in *City Lights* (1931), the little barber and even "der Fooey" himself, Adenoid Hynkel, dictator of Tomania, in *The Great Dictator* (1940), a scathing attack on Nazi Germany. While the character of the Tramp was still evolving, Chaplin played dozens of different characters and types: an actor masquerading as a glamorous actress, a soldier in the trenches, a woman who has misplaced her husband, an intoxicated playboy called "The Pest," and bungling apprentices and incompetent shop assistants of every imaginable description.

Chaplin played opposite Edna Purviance in most of his films. She was a talented actress with the fragile beauty of an old-fashioned melodrama heroine, and a quality of slightly daffy otherworldliness made her the ideal leading lady for the Little Tramp. Mabel Normand played the pert, flirtatious beauty who inspired and even mischievously instigated a number of memorable Keystone chase comedies. In *Tillie's Punctured Romance* (1914) Normand and Chaplin, in one of his high-society "pest" roles, joined Marie Dressler, the star of the popular Broadway comedy on which the film was based, in a lopsided love triangle that was resolved over several reels of refined mayhem. Beneath her remarkably forbidding exterior, Marie Dressler was a witty and sympathetic character actress who co-starred with the equally rough-hewn Wallace Beery in a number of films as well as appearing with Greta Garbo in *Anna Christie* and with Billie Burke and John and Lionel Barrymore, among others, in *Dinner at Eight*.

At the height of his popularity, Chaplin was commonly said to be not simply the greatest of silent film artists, but actually the world's most famous living human. When we watch his films, it is easy to understand why Chaplin's comedy touches people of all ages, all classes and kinds, and in every country. Afterward, though, we may have a little difficulty explaining exactly how he does it. Critics often describe Chaplin as the perfect twentieth-century hero, the innocent waif in a world filled with absurdity and hostility; to them he is the common man, the ordinary citizen struggling to cope with the loneliness of a society where material possessions have more value than human awareness. But no matter whether we see Chaplin as a symbol of man alone in a world he never made or as a joyous affirmation of the invincible human spirit, one thing is certain: he makes us laugh and cry, and sometimes do both at the same time.

The Gold Rush (1925) contains several of Chaplin's most inspired silent-comedy routines, as well as a famous pantomime sequence that, as it progresses gradually from humorous improvisation to lyrical pathos, records the full range of Chaplin's genius as a performer.

In one of the earlier scenes Charlie and his fellow prospector Big Jim McKay (played by Mack Swain) are trapped by a blizzard in an isolated and empty cabin in the Klondike. Their plight is indeed desperate. If they venture out into the blizzard, they will freeze (Charlie is dressed for the Alaskan winter in the customary derby, shiny suit, and baggy pants); on the other hand, if they stay in the cabin, they face an equally certain death by starvation. Smiling reassuringly, Charlie pauses to take stock of the situation, and suddenly his face lights up. He pulls off one of his shoes, puts it in a pot, and sets the stove to boil. The shoe is cooked until tender, salted to taste, and lovingly placed on a platter. Charlie whets his carving knife expectantly and sits down at the table, eyes wide and mouth watering. Charlie carves with a flourish, separating the sole from the well-worn uppers. Big Jim takes his portion with a certain reluctance, but Charlie digs in and savors every bite, delicately winding the laces on his fork like so much spaghetti. Finally, as Charlie sucks the last bit of flavor from the hobnails, he comes across a bent nail that he shares with Big Jim. They hook their fingers around it, make a wish, pull.

The next scene opens with Charlie's other shoe bubbling in the pot and both of Charlie's feet wrapped in rags, making them bigger and bulkier than ever. But the second meal is not a success; Big Jim is beginning to hallucinate. He suddenly imagines Charlie to be an enormous chicken and advances on him menacingly, preparing to wring his neck. And as Charlie darts away from Big Jim's outstretched hands, he seems to become a chicken, flapping around the cabin and finally hopping up on the table, fluttering distractedly, just out of reach. Big Jim goes for his rifle, fires, and misses. The sound of the gunshot snaps him back to reality. The chicken becomes Charlie again, waving his arms in front of Big Jim's eyes, trying frantically to bring him back to his senses as the scene shifts from horror to comedy again.

In a later sequence Charlie has returned to town and moved into another cabin. He has invited the girls from the dance hall in for a festive New Year's Eve party, for which he sets an elegant table, fashioning a lace tablecloth from old newspapers. As he waits for the guests to arrive, he imagines the entertainment he will provide. Holding a fork in each hand, he spears two dinner rolls that become dancing feet performing a spirited high-kicking nautical number called, as the title card informs us, "The Oceana Roll." Totally carried away by the cabaret atmosphere, Charlie holds up a hand to acknowledge the imaginary applause, bows appreciatively, then realizes with a start that he is alone. Charlie's admiring audience of beautiful women never materializes; the dance-hall girls have forgotten about him completely. No longer the radiant, self-confident variety star, Charlie is once again the dejected Little Tramp, sitting and staring wistfully at the table set for four.

Later, Charlie returns to the goldfields with Big Jim, who is still looking for his lost claim. After an exhausting trek up the mountain, they take shelter in still another lonely cabin as the persistent blizzard whistles outside. Buffeted by the wind, the cabin begins to slide across the icy slopes, riding out the storm and finally coming to rest on the brink of a steep cliff, neatly balanced on the edge of oblivion.

Charlie gets up the next morning and heedlessly steps into the half of the cabin that overhangs the abyss. The cabin begins to tilt, then rights itself as Charlie scrabbles back along the floor to the other side of the room. Charlie next busies himself with breakfast. Since the windows are covered with frost, Charlie is unaware of the gravity of the situation. He blithely picks up a table and moves it across the room; the floor tilts downward, then rights itself again as Charlie changes his mind and replaces the table.

Big Jim has joined him now, and the cabin starts to seesaw dizzily back and forth as they both pace across the room, the floor swinging downward as Jim steps over the abyss. They begin to think they are suffering from liver trouble, then realize that there must be some other cause for this spectacular attack of vertigo. Charlie tries the door, finds that the hinges have frozen, and puts his shoulder to it. The door stays firmly shut, so Charlie tries again, giving himself a running start from the other side of the cabin. The door gives way and Charlie hurtles out into space, saving himself only by holding to the latchstring, legs kicking the empty air. The door slowly swings shut, flinging him back inside the cabin. As Big Jim catches him, Charlie faints with relief.

Big Jim makes good his escape, tosses a rope in to Charlie, and pulls him out just as the cabin finally slips over the edge of the cliff. Happily, they find Big Jim's claim marker, and Charlie has hit pay dirt. He faints again at this second shock but revives in time to claim his sweetheart, and sails back home a wealthy man.

Chaplin returned to his native England in March 1975, at the age of eighty-five, and was created a Knight Commander of the British Empire by Queen Elizabeth II. After the ceremony Chaplin announced that he preferred to be known as "Sir Charles" and not "Sir Charlie," perhaps to dispel the suspicion that he was simply playing another one of his Little Tramp's high-society masquerades.

§ BUSTER KEATON §

Buster Keaton was born in 1895 and started his vaudeville career at the age of three, when he joined the family comedy act, billed as "The Three Keatons." Harry Houdini is said to have given him the name "Buster" after watching the six-month-old Keaton tumble down a backstage staircase without uttering a single cry. This marks the first appearance of Keaton's imperturbable silent-comedy character, but in the "Three Keatons" vaudeville act, Buster played a mischievous miniature replica of his father, complete with chin whiskers and corncob pipe. Like the Grimaldi father-and-son routines, the Keatons' act always finished with an exasperated assertion of parental authority, and on one occasion the elder Keaton hurled Buster out over the footlights to express his displeasure with an unruly audience. In spite of his peppery stage personality, Buster's father was essentially a kindly man, although a bit of a drinker, and Keaton's childhood was a happy one.

The three Keatons preferred to improvise, commedia style, rather than repeat old material. This they did as much to please themselves as the audience; as Keaton recalled, "We found it much more fun to surprise one another by pulling any crazy, wild stunt that came into our heads." And, like Grimaldi, Keaton loved to build models and invent fantastic gadgets, many of which were incorporated into the family act. His lifelong fondness for tinkering with machinery later served him well as a film director; he mastered every phase of production—camerawork, processing, and editing. His famous special effects and ingenious camera tricks are as impressive today as they were in the twenties, and his own explanations of how he worked out his scenes and set up camera shots still make fascinating reading.

Keaton made his first films for Fatty Arbuckle's Comicque Studios in 1917. Arbuckle gave him considerable freedom to work up his own gags and contribute new routines. The young Keaton, with his famous flat hat and stern, classical profile, appeared as an agreeable contrast to the almost spherical Arbuckle as a supporting player in several films before he opened his own Keaton Studio in 1920. He never worked from a script, and he believed that rehearsing for a take discouraged spontaneity. Keaton knew exactly what he wanted and exactly what he could expect from his actors—including himself—and the ten features and countless shorts released by the Keaton Studio in the next eight years contain many of the finest, funniest moments in silent comedy.

Keaton explained that he never smiled because he had other ways of expressing happiness, and besides, he was always too busy concentrating on what he was doing to tell whether he was smiling or not. His handsome Irish features expressed his shifting moods and preoccupations with great subtlety: high cheek bones, straight nose, and square jaw, with an intense faraway gaze that always seemed to be fixed on something just over the horizon. As a director and as a performer, Keaton strove for the same economy and precision; even in extreme long-distance shots, his every reaction is as crisp and sharply outlined as his memorable profile. Unlike Chaplin, Keaton was never a pathetic figure and in only one film, *Go West,* did he really play for an audience's sympathy. He was acutely suspicious of the world in general, the treachery of machines and his fellow man in particular. As we have mentioned, Keaton's brand of silent-comedy optimism involved his unshakable confidence in himself and his ability to deal firmly and inventively with catastrophe.

In *Sherlock Junior* (1924) Keaton plays a movie projectionist who falls asleep in his booth and, in an extended sequence, steps through the screen and finds himself the hero of a suspenseful comic melodrama. In *The Navigator* (1924) Keaton and Kathryn McGuire are the only passengers on a drifting ocean liner, completely alone with hundreds of doors, hallways, hatches, and other admirable props, including a sturdy diving suit. In *Go West* (1925) Keaton, as a cowboy named Lonesome, rescues a cow named Brown Eyes from the butcher by tying a set of antlers to her head and passing her off as a deer. *The General* (1926) is about a hijacked locomotive, which Keaton, the brave engineer, drives back to Confederate lines. (This film was inspired by an actual incident from the Civil War, known as "the Great Locomotive Chase.") We are already familiar with the bungled suicide attempt in *Steamboat Bill, Jr.* (1928). Suffice it to say that Keaton is also sucked up by a cyclone in the next scene and later succeeds in saving an entire town from destruction.

Keaton Studio was absorbed by Metro Goldwyn Mayer in 1928, and Keaton himself was fired after two more films, neither of them very successful. Suddenly unemployed at the age of thirty-three (for the first time in thirty years), he was one of the great silent comics whose career was tragically cut short by the coming of sound. The rest of his life was marred by financial and marital problems and ill health, in part brought on by heavy drinking, and brightened only occasionally by guest appearances and brief cameo roles in films (notably in Chaplin's *Limelight* in 1952). The revival of interest in silent films brought Keaton back to Hollywood, with no regrets, during the last ten years or so before his death in 1966, and enabled him to collect and restore many of the irreplaceable prints of his early films, which would otherwise have been lost to us.

A favorite Keaton moment, with both audiences and critics, occurs in *The General.* Buster is speeding southward on a full head of steam after rescuing the stolen locomotive, as well as the beautiful and rather vapid Annabelle Lee, from a pack of Yankee desperadoes. Buster is determined to make their dwindling fuel supply last them until they cross the Confederate lines; he begins to search for something else to burn in the firebox besides the few remaining logs. Annabelle Lee offers to help by tidying up the cab of the locomotive in her own fastidious way. She picks up one of the precious logs, notices a large knothole, frowns at its ugliness, and throws it off the train. She offers to help Buster stoke the firebox and hands him a tiny, flawless stick of kindling. Then, as Buster's eyes bulge in shocked disbelief, she continues to sort through the logs, finding some imperfection in almost all of them. Furious, Buster picks her up by the shoulders, starts to shake her violently—then kisses her lightly on the forehead. After this split-second romantic interlude Keaton turns back to the comic crisis. The impeccable technique and timing, as well as the sentiment, are the essence of Keaton's silent-comedy style, the perfect use of every moment.

§ HAROLD LLOYD §

Unlike Chaplin and Keaton, who served their apprenticeships on-stage, Harold Lloyd was a film original. In the early comedies for Mack Sennett and Hal Roach, Lloyd experimented with various characters, with names like "Willie Work" and "Lonesome Luke," the latter heavily indebted to Chaplin's Little Tramp. Today he is remembered for what he called his "glasses" character, the smiling, bespectacled, all-American (and slightly backward) boy who made his first appearance in *Over the Fence* in 1917, and was simply called "Harold" in his later feature-length films. Harold seemed inseparable from these celebrated glasses (actually a pair of heavy tortoise-shell frames with no lenses), which he wore in his "human fly" ascent to the top of a skyscraper in *Safety Last* (1923), and at the bottom of several memorable pileups on the football field in *The Freshman* (1925). Harold's shy, studious temperament belied his driving ambition, usually romantic or financial, and this combination of diffidence and determination exposed Harold to embarrassment, humiliation, and a varied sampling of near-catastrophes in the path of ultimate success.

In *Grandma's Boy* (1922) he is pitted against a mere gang of bullies and hoodlums, which hardly compares with the clock-hanging perils of *Safety Last*. In one of the best-known scenes in silent comedy, the human fly almost reaches the top of the skyscraper, city traffic moving in slow, antlike columns far below him. He slips, loses his footing, and only saves himself from falling by clutching one of the hands of a gigantic clock. In *The Freshman* Harold's gridiron triumph is preceded by a number of painful reverses, including a stint as understudy for the tackling dummy.

At the end of the silent era Harold Lloyd retired from the screen with a large fortune, which he invested quite profitably, and (except for a single, unsuccessful comeback film in 1947) lived happily in his Hollywood mansion until his death in 1971.

§ HARRY LANGDON §

Harry Langdon's unique appearance recalls nothing so much as a plump-cheeked baby, heavily and inexplicably made up for a vaudeville turn. Langdon (1884–1944) always performed in whiteface, his tiny, wistful eyes circled in black, with a smudgy mouth, heavily traced eyebrows, and a single lock of hair curling out from under his turned-up hat brim. Langdon's was a child's personality as well— innocent, mischievous, and a bit greedy. In the adult world things happened too quickly, and Langdon generally reacted either with bewilderment or with a dreamy, abstracted indifference. He lived by daydreaming and survived more by good luck than perseverance or wit. Langdon's whiteface makeup owes something to Pierrot, but in his films *Picking Peaches* (1924), *The Strong Man* (1926), and *Long Pants* (1927), he emerges as a silent-comedy descendant of the dwarfs and innocent fools of the distant past.

Chaplin and Keaton had always put their point across through pantomime. Even today, in an age somewhat unfamiliar with the conventions of silent comedy, we not only understand what they are saying but also find it a little hard to believe that we have not actually heard them say it.

The arrival of sound in the late twenties meant more than voices and music on film; it witnessed the disappearance of several great silent clowns. Early sound-recording equipment was cumbersome, and performers had to stay close to the microphone if they wanted their lines to register; for a year or two, shooting was almost impossible outside the studio, and in general the freedom enjoyed by the silent clown was now sadly and severely restricted.

As the clown was denied, at least for a while, many of the richest resources of his medium, and as studio and audiences began to think of physical comedy as somehow dated and old-fashioned, the sight gag increasingly gave way to verbal jokes and dialogue. The traditional clown was becoming a comedian, in the modern sense of the word, often still as funny as his predecessors but rarely as touching, and no longer capable of Keaton's or Chaplin's instantaneous shifts from comedy into tragedy and back again.

·11·
CLOWNS
IN "TALKIES"
AND TELEVISION

Laurel and Hardy, the Marx Brothers,
W. C. Fields, Mae West, Jimmy Durante,
Joe E. Brown, Dizzy Dames and Dumb Blondes,
Margaret Rutherford, Jerry Lewis,
Lucille Ball, Flip Wilson, Jacques Tati,
Woody Allen, and Others

Chaplin was the only silent clown to resist the coming of sound with much success. In two films made during the thirties, Chaplin introduced background music that he had composed himself and lavish sound effects, but speech was still presented through title cards (and highly evocative but unintelligible bursts of gibberish). The Little Tramp, of course, steadfastly refused to adjust to modern times and never spoke a word on the screen.

Several popular silent clowns definitely profited by the introduction of sound. The screen personalities of Will Rogers, Laurel and Hardy, and W. C. Fields took on new and unsuspected dimensions: Rogers' accent was pure Oklahoma, Hardy's Georgia genteel, Laurel's clipped Lancashire, and Fields of course spoke a dialect entirely his own, perhaps most accurately likened to the mumbling and croaking of a large, intoxicated toad.

§ LAUREL AND HARDY §

Stan Laurel and Oliver Hardy had already appeared in films, even in some of the same films, when Hal Roach had the inspiration of teaming them up in a short called *Putting Pants on Philip* (1927). Laurel and Hardy together were much more successful than Laurel and Hardy separately, and their best films of the thirties were in the highest tradition of the old thick-and-thin comedy teams of vaudeville.

Stan Laurel (1890–1965) was Chaplin's understudy in Fred Karno's variety program, *A Night in an English Music Hall.* Laurel also did several pantomime routines, and after two tours with Karno crossed over to vaudeville. Chaplin was already starring in Keystone comedies, and Laurel became one of the most popular, and easily the best qualified, of his early impersonators. After seeing a preview of Laurel's first film, *Nuts in May,* in 1927, Chaplin toyed for a while with the idea of hiring him for his own studio. Certainly it is just as well that he did not. Under contract to Hal Roach, Laurel was completely at liberty to develop his own style and work up his routines on his own, instead of serving out his time as a supporting player in Chaplin's company and almost certainly in Chaplin's shadow.

Laurel also began to supply other Hal Roach comics with material, and throughout the thirties worked closely with the director, writers, and cameramen on his own films, exercising almost complete artistic control. He followed the common silent-era practice of using the reactions of a "sneak preview" audience as a film's final test before the release of the commercial print. Admittedly, Laurel's appearance on the screen did not immediately suggest the great director, the cutting-room wizard, or the inspired idea man: short, slight, with a child's eyes looking out of a comic masklike face and close-cropped hair that seemed to feel some kind of electric repulsion for his high-domed forehead. Perhaps his best known comic mannerism was the sudden shift from childish self-satisfaction to abject and equally childish self-pity, usually prompted by a caustic word or a stinging glance from Hardy, and culminating in the familiar high-pitched, sobbing whimper.

Oliver Hardy (1892–1957) came from Harlem, Georgia. As a boy he had run away from home for a brief tour with a minstrel show and later operated his hometown's first movie house. Hardy watched a great many of the primitive film comedies that were being cranked out by the dozens and decided he could do as well. But, anticipating *Sherlock Junior,* he stepped out of the projection booth and ended up in melodrama. Because of his impressive size—he stood six feet two and weighed two hundred, and later three hundred and twenty, pounds—he was cast at first as the "heavy" or villain. (A hint of the sneering, sardonic blackguard of melodrama was still present in his later comic personality.) As a comedian, though, Ollie gave the impression of weightlessness, like an inflated balloon man. His torso, face, and dimpled chin-within-a-chin described decreasing circles, touched up with a black dot of a mustache. The carefully combed hair, black bowler, and black suit reflected Ollie's image of himself as a bit of a dude (as well as a persistent suggestion of the slicked-down melodrama heavy).

Ollie is essentially a natural clown trying to pass himself off as a straight man. His elaborate cavalier manners and Deep South gentility, both slightly bogus, almost never deceive anyone but the gullible Laurel, which accounts for the attitude of pained superiority that Ollie adopts toward him. Stan is friendly, rather simple, always eager to be of help (which invariably spells disaster), and incapable of deceiving *anyone*. Both were bunglers, and their incompetence was not just complementary but actually competitive. Typically, Ollie chides his partner for botching some simple task; a demonstration of the correct technique only makes things a little worse. Unimpressed, Stan tries again, Ollie corrects him, and destruction, Laurel and Hardy's highest calling, begins to spread in an ever-widening spiral. Buildings are reduced to rubble, automobiles to heaps of scrap; almost anything smaller ends up as either an unrecognizable powder or an indescribable paste. And when Stan and Ollie finally pause to survey the wreckage, they usually burst out laughing. After all, they have overcome frustration, humiliation, and rage. The artful simplicity of their approach, perhaps a little violent but certainly not painful, evokes laughter, sympathy, and finally, envy; by temperament they both prefer chaos to complexity, and they usually convince us that they are entirely right. And finally, by striking a blow against materialism, they uplift as well as amuse, clearing away a little of the clutter of civilization that oppresses us all so much.

Laurel's favorite of all their films was *The Music Box,* which won an Academy Award in 1932. Essentially, *The Music Box* is one long sight gag, based on a characteristic premise. Stan and Ollie are trying to deliver a piano to a house set on a high cement terrace, approachable only by means of several dozen formidably steep steps. Laurel and Hardy's determination to get the piano up to the porch is more than matched by the piano's apparent determination to stay on the sidewalk, a classic Laurel and Hardy triumph of matter over mind.

After their best films in the thirties, *Our Relations* (1936), *Way Out West* (1937), *Blockheads* (1938), plus *Saps at Sea* (1940), changes of studio and management deprived Laurel of the creative supervision he had exercised over every phase of production. The team went on to make nine more features, most of them predictable parodies of Hollywood costume epics. Working in this plot-bound format, they had little opportunity to develop the intricate sight gags and sustained feats of demolition that they showed such a genius for in all their earlier work. These films were widely seen, a source of considerable embarrassment to Laurel and Hardy themselves. Only when they began an extended personal-appearance tour of Europe in the early fifties did they finally appreciate the extent of their popularity all over the world, even though their best pictures had been made more than a dozen years before. Arriving in Ireland, they were puzzled by the hundreds of boat whistles blowing in the harbor and the cheering crowds gathered on the shore. When all the church bells in the city began to play the familiar Laurel and Hardy theme, "The Cuckoo Song," they just looked at each other and burst into tears.

§ THE MARX BROTHERS §

Minnie Marx was determined to see her sons, Leonard, Adolph, Milton, Julius, and Herbert, succeed in show business. In 1908 she organized her motley teen-agers into an act and propelled them onto the vaudeville stage. By the end of World War I the brothers had changed their names to Chico, Harpo, Gummo, Groucho, and Zeppo—and Zeppo, who had been too young to play the circuit, replaced Gummo. Their break came in 1924, when (following in the footsteps of their famous uncle, Al Shean, half of the team of Gallagher and Shean) they left the circuit to open in their own Broadway musical, *I'll Say She Is.* Its success led to even greater acclaim in the stage comedies *The Cocoanuts* and *Animal Crackers* and, when these productions were filmed by Paramount Pictures, to the Marx Brothers' debut in movies.

Sound was essential to an appreciation of the Marx Brothers' fast-paced mixture of verbal and visual gags (even the mute Harpo's honking horns and harp solos required a sound track). The Brothers' contrapuntal verbal styles relied for humor on puns ("Will you join me?" a young woman asks Groucho. "Why?" he replies. "Are you coming apart?"), aphorisms ("How much better it would be for the children if the parents had to eat the spinach"), malapropisms (Chico claims he knows what an auction is: after all, didn't he sail the Atlantic

Auction to get to America?), wisecracks ("I'm Beatrice Rheimer," a woman says to Groucho. "I stop at the hotel." "I'm Ronald Cornblow," Groucho replies. "I stop at nothing"), threats ("I'd horsewhip you—if I had a horse"), gags (Groucho, describing Chico, says: "Gentlemen, he may look like an idiot, he may speak like an idiot, but don't let that fool you—he really is an idiot!"), insults ("Marry me," Groucho beseeches Margaret Dumont in *A Day at the Races*, "and I'll never look at any other horse"), and sheer nonsense (about to sign a contract, Chico confesses, "I can't write," to which Groucho responds, "That's all right. There's no ink in the pen anyway"). This sort of wit, every line of it delivered with split-second timing, made the Marx Brothers' films, from *The Cocoanuts* in 1929 to *Love Happy* in 1950, as popular as any ever shown in America, and the best of them—*Monkey Business, Horse Feathers, Duck Soup, A Night at the Opera,* and *A Day at the Races*—unforgettable classics.

Many comic teams before the Marx Brothers had exploited the comic value of obvious contrasts, such as differences in height or weight. Diverse as the Marx Brothers were in personality and style, their relationships with one another, as we shall see, were complex and intricate. As these relationships developed, it became clear that Zeppo was a misfit—a sane man among lunatics—and by 1936 his name had disappeared from the bill. It was no wonder the Brothers had no need for a "straight man"; they had the perfect foil in Margaret Dumont, whose statuesque, impeccably bred matron suffered the jibes, overtures, and insults of Groucho in particular with stoic dignity. Though Miss Dumont later confessed that her first three weeks of exposure to Groucho had brought her to the brink of a nervous collapse, she managed to make seven movies with the Brothers and somehow survive the experience.

Chico's outrageous caricature of an Italian immigrant found himself in a world that was totally incomprehensible to him—which was only fair, since he was totally incomprehensible to it. His limited if literal understanding of the English language created a communication gap that Chico eagerly widened with every word. Slow to grasp an idea, he was just as loath to let it go once he'd got it. In *The Cocoanuts* Groucho plants Chico as a shill at an auction, instructing him to make false bids to force the legitimate bidders higher; but Chico, who has understood little but the words "bid" and "higher," not only outbids everyone at the auction, he tenaciously outbids himself, raising his own last offer every time Groucho calls for a new one. This is not to say that Chico was incapable of a little swindling of his own. In *A Day at the Races* he sells betting tips on horses under the cover of peddling "tootsie-fruitsie" ice cream. Groucho bites, only to discover that the tip is in code, and to decipher it he must buy, first a code book, then a master code book, then a Breeder's Guide, and so on, until he realizes—too late, for the race is already over—that he has been had. Whether he was conning or being conned, chasing women or playing the piano (which he did by jabbing his index finger at the keys as though firing a pistol), Chico's supreme confidence never deserted him, least of all when he had next to nothing to be confident about.

Groucho was as sharp as Chico was slow (though Chico's skirmishes with the language were more than enough to bring the quick-thinking, fast-talking Groucho up short, dumfounded). With a smear of greasepaint mustache and a cigar protruding impudently from his mouth, Groucho scuttled about in his swallowtail coat, his bushy-browed eyes shifting about in search of a sucker to hustle. When his ingenious schemes backfired, Groucho saved himself with a piece of double-talk so confusing that his victims had forgot their objections before they'd had a chance to voice them ("Be free, my friends," he tells the bellboys demanding two weeks back wages in *The Cocoanuts,* "one for all and all for me and three for five and six for a quarter"). Margaret Dumont, in *A Night at the Opera,* is indignant when she discovers Groucho—an hour late for their dinner date—seated at the table next to her with another woman. "It's now eight o'clock," she complains, "and no dinner." "What do you mean, no dinner?" Groucho barks. "I just had one of the biggest meals I ever ate in my life, and no thanks to you either." Befuddled, Dumont replies: "I've been sitting right here since seven o'clock." "Yes, with your back to me," Groucho says, uncannily turning the tables. "When I invite a woman to dinner, I expect her to look at my face. That's the price she has to pay." And his ready explanation for his attractive blond companion undoes Dumont completely: "Do you know why I sat with her? . . . Because she reminded me of you. . . . That's why I'm sitting here with you, because *you* remind me of you. Your eyes, your throat, your lips, everything about you reminds me of you, except you. How do you account for that?" In Groucho's masterful hands the lady never has a chance. Nor do the victims of any of Groucho's con-artist characters, for no matter what role he played, Groucho was always Groucho—smooth, slick, and one step ahead of his opponents all the way.

Harpo, with his floppy loose-fitting wig, high hat, long baggy coat, and bulb horn, was a brilliant pantomime artist. There was little he could not express, with his vast vocabulary of gestures and astonishing reservoir of properties, which he plucked from the lining of his overcoat. Though he sometimes resorted to whistling, his very silences could convey the essence of his mood. Like Joe Grimaldi, he had an enormous appetite and catholic taste—he would eat flowers, cigars, thermometers, telephones, ink bottles, and neckties with aplomb. In *The Cocoanuts* he plucks the buttons off a stony-faced pageboy's vest and pops them into his mouth, while Chico explains, "He's hungry." Harpo was as enthusiastic about women as he was about eating and could not pass an attractive one without giving frantic chase, eyes winking, heart throbbing, horn honking. Despite his adult appetites, however, Harpo was very much the perpetual child, mischievous, playful, often distracted, constantly baffling his keeper-interpreter Chico or infuriating the hustler Groucho, whose ambitious schemes he naïvely spoiled. Most at home in the company of children (in *Monkey Business* he insinuates himself into a Punch-and-Judy show), Harpo took nothing so seriously he could not turn it into a game: as a dogcatcher, for example, he entices one victim into his wagon by goading it into chasing him, and lures the rest in with an elaborate collection of street posts. Harpo's has accurately been called the most complex of the Marx Brothers' characters. In his autobiography, *Harpo Speaks!,* the silent partner analyzes the character that won for him a lasting place in the world of pantomime—devoting pages to an art that never required him to utter a word.

In the following scene from *The Cocoanuts* Groucho and Chico huddle over a map of the Cocoanut section of Florida as Groucho does his best to give Chico directions to the auction grounds:

GROUCHO Now here is a little peninsula and here is a viaduct leading over to the mainland.
CHICO Why a duck?
GROUCHO I'm all right. How are you? I say here is a little peninsula, and here is a viaduct leading over to the mainland.

CHICO All right. Why a duck?

GROUCHO I'm not playing Ask-Me-Another. I say, that's a viaduct.

CHICO All right. Why a duck? Why a—why a duck? Why-a-no-chicken?

GROUCHO I don't know why-a-no-chicken. I'm a stranger here myself. All I know is that it's a viaduct. You try to cross over there a chicken and you'll find out vy-a-duck. It's deep water, that's viaduct.

CHICO That's why-a-duck?

GROUCHO Look . . . suppose you were out horseback riding and you came to that stream and you wanted to ford over there. You couldn't make it. Too deep.

CHICO What-a you want with a Ford if you gotta horse?

GROUCHO Well, I'm sorry the matter ever came up. All I know is that it's a viaduct.

CHICO Now look . . . all right-a . . . I catch-a on to why-a-horse, why-a-chicken, why-a-this, why-a-that. I no catch-a on to why-a-duck.

GROUCHO I was only fooling. I was only fooling. They're going to build a tunnel in the morning. Now, is that clear to you?

CHICO Yes. Everything except-a why-a-duck.

GROUCHO Well, that's fine. Now I can go ahead. Now, look, I'm going to take you down and show you our cemetery. I've got a waiting list of fifty people at that cemetery just dying to get in. But I like you—

CHICO Ah—you're-a my friend.

GROUCHO I like you and I'm going—

CHICO I know you like-a . . .

GROUCHO To shove you in ahead of all of them. I'm going to see that you get a steady position.

CHICO That's good.

GROUCHO And if I can arrange it, it will be horizontal.

CHICO Yeah, I see—

GROUCHO . . . Now, you know how to get down [to the auction]?

CHICO No, I no understand.

GROUCHO Now, look. Listen. You go down there, down to that narrow path there. . . . And then, there's a little clearing there, a little clearing with a wire fence around it. You see that wire fence there?

CHICO All right. Why-a-fence?
GROUCHO Oh, no, we're not going to go all through that again!

The Marx Brothers' humor may defy description, but the term "surrealistic nonsense" is not inaccurate. As in a dream, new meanings emerged as their comedy supplanted the order that generally governs the relations between thoughts, words, things, and acts with an order all its own. But their humor went deeper than that: during the Depression these court jesters, attacking the Establishment in all its weaknesses, spoke to and for the frustrated, embattled American, reminding him that his survival depended on independence of mind, defiant enterprise, and above all, irreverence of spirit.

Well into his eighties, Groucho continued to admonish us not to take ourselves too seriously. When he visited New York in 1974 to promote the revival of *Animal Crackers,* he was informed by the maître d' of a well-known restaurant that he would not be seated until he put on a tie—which would be supplied by the house. In retaliation Groucho created a scene the restaurant management is not likely to forget. He stopped waiter after waiter to ask, "Do you have frog's legs?" forcing each of them to lift his trousers so that he could verify the answer for himself. After finally ordering braised celery and coffee, Groucho removed the borrowed tie and went from table to table, and waiter to waiter, exhorting the men to follow suit. "Anyone who doesn't take his tie off is chicken," he shouted—not one whit more tolerant of petty convention or smug authority than he had ever been. Groucho died in 1977.

The Marx Brothers were not the only film team with tremendous appeal. The Three Stooges brought to the screen a lunatic sort of physical comedy that threatened to overwhelm the spectator with its very violence. Abbott and Costello, whose beginnings were in burlesque, are best known for their first and perhaps finest film, *Buck Privates,* and for a pun-filled routine about a baseball game entitled "Who's on First?" Their slapstick humor—which leaned heavily on physical contrasts (Abbott was tall and thin, Costello short and fat)—lacked dignity, however, and they often substituted vulgar silliness for genuine comedy. The team of Bob Hope and Bing Crosby played itinerant entertainers in a seemingly endless string of movies known as the Road series (*The Road to Singapore, The Road to Zanzibar, The Road to Morocco,* and so on).

§ W. C. FIELDS §

W. C. Fields (1879–1946) began his career as a "tramp juggler" in vaudeville, a comic pantomime act in which, incredibly, he never spoke a word. Fields played the famous Orpheum circuit, which took him all over Europe, unhindered by the language barrier, and even to Australia, New Zealand, South Africa, and the Orient. Fields's juggling was expert, and his deliberate mistakes were even more inspired, so that an act scheduled for twenty-one minutes took twenty-seven, with the extra six taken up by the audience's applause and laughter. In the midst of juggling six cigar boxes, or whatever it might be, he would drop his hat, do a double take, and casually pick it up, without relaxing his expression of furious concentration or taking his eyes away for a moment from the spinning cigar boxes. A foresighted newspaper reviewer of 1912 remarked that Fields would be "supremely funny" in himself, even if he were not a first-rate juggler. On his return to Europe in the following year, he appeared along with Sarah Bernhardt in a command performance for the Royal Family of England.

Fields joined the *Follies* in 1915, breaking his long onstage silence at the age of thirty-five, after almost twenty years in vaudeville, and at the same time made excellent use of his pantomime talents in a number of silent films. The first, made in 1916, was based on his popular vaudeville skit "Pool Sharks"; in 1925, the year after he left the *Follies,* Fields starred in *Sally of the Sawdust,* directed by D. W. Griffith, which included several virtuoso juggling sequences and was remade as a sound film with the new title *Poppy* in 1936.

The four comedy shorts Fields made for Mack Sennett, all based on familiar stage material, became runaway box-office successes in the early thirties. *The Pharmacist* cast Fields as a cut-rate druggist who bends over backward to accommodate his fussy clientele, even offering "a free Ming china vaahze, four feet high and four thousand years old" with every purchase. His first customer makes Fields an offer on a three-cent stamp; Fields agrees to knock two cents off the price. The customer inquires if he has the same thing in black instead of purple. Fields promises to dye the stamp black, and when the customer picks out the center stamp in a sheet of a hundred, Fields obligingly cuts the entire sheet to shreds in order to extract the chosen stamp. Refusing the offer of a bag, the customer orders Fields to wrap it up instead and proposes to pay with a hundred-dollar bill, which Fields of course cannot change. The customer airily asks Fields to send him a bill, adding that he will take the stamp, and the Ming vase, with him.

A favorite set piece for Fields impersonators is the running gag in *The Fatal Glass of Beer,* which has Fields, costumed as a mustachioed melodrama heavy, repeatedly opening the door of his log cabin, each time turning to the audience and declaiming, "'Tain't a fit night out for man nor beast!" Whereupon Fields peers back into the outer darkness and impassively receives a faceful of paper snow from a bucket propelled by an unseen backstage hand.

Fields's cantankerous screen character was only a natural extension of his offstage personality, with a well-known weakness for strong drink ("Don't say you can't swear off drinking! It's easy. I've done it a thousand times!"), a fondness for the elegantly turned phrase ("He referred to my proboscis as an adsatious excrescence!"), and a long list of private grudges and pet hatreds ("How do you like children, Mr. Fields?" "Parboiled"). In his films Fields came up against a number of pesky, precocious, scene-stealing juveniles, notably the gifted child actor Baby Leroy. In his frequent guest appearances on ventriloquist Edgar Bergen's popular Sunday-night radio program, Fields carried on a long-running verbal feud with the dapper, wisecracking dummy, Charlie McCarthy. The battle of insults between Fields ("the original half-man, half-nose") and Charlie ("the woodpecker's pinup boy") amused millions of radio listeners throughout the late thirties and early forties, and was brought to the screen in Fields's 1939 feature, *You Can't Cheat an Honest Man.*

On radio a typical clash began with Fields cooing sweetly, "And where is that lovable little nipper, Master Charles McCarthy?"

CHARLIE *(innocently)* Here I am, Mr. Fields, right under your nose! [Fields affected a certain sensitivity about his nose, which was said to have more than once stopped traffic on Hollywood Boulevard.]

FIELDS *(drawing out the words menacingly)* Right . . . under . . .

my . . . nose. I'll ignore that, Charles, because tonight I'm imbued with the spirit of friendship.

CHARLIE *(brightly)* You're really loaded, eh?

From here, the dialogue grew heated, with Fields and Charlie exchanging pointed threats ("Quiet, you termite's flophouse!") and ingenious speculations on each other's ancestry ("Is it true, Charles, that your father was a gate-leg table?" "If it is, your father was under it!").

For his best films Fields wrote his own screenplays, usually on scraps of paper and the backs of envelopes, fleshed out with extensive ad libs and improvisations on the set; the final product was often credited to one of Fields's stable of imaginary screenwriters: *The Old Fashioned Way* and *It's a Gift* (1934) to Charles Bogle, *The Bank Dick* (1941) to Mahatma Kane Jeeves, *Never Give a Sucker an Even Break* (1941) to Otis Cublecoblis. For *My Little Chickadee* (1940) Fields's co-author and co-star was Mae West; the film was an outrageous burlesque of the Hollywood Western which brought out the best in both of them:

CUTHBERT TWILLIE [Fields] *(kissing her hand)* What symmetrical digits! . . . May I?

FLOWER BELLE [West] Help yourself!

TWILLIE Would you object if I availed myself of a second helping?

Fields died on Christmas Day 1946, but his films are, if anything, more popular today than in his lifetime. He added an extra dimension to the classical figure of the curmudgeon by making his misanthropy, shabby confidence tricks, and easily bruised dignity seem not only justified, but sympathetic, and even admirable. Hen-pecked, put-upon, and routinely victimized, Fields struck back at petty injustice and everyday banality by giving the world what he elegantly referred to as the "raahsberry."

§ MAE WEST §

Mae West has not always been recognized for the consummate comedienne she was. With her voluptuous hour-glass figure, sexy nasal drawl, impudently flirtatious eyes and fluttering lashes, bump and grind swagger, and suggestive double entendres, Mae was considered by many—including Hollywood censors—to be an "evil" woman. In fact, Mae's was a superbly comic caricature, a walking parody of the woman who uses sex to accomplish her purposes. Not that the character was a simple one: calculated as her manipulation of men might be, she was nonetheless a liberated woman—in sequins; though it may have meant exploiting her role as a "sex object" to the hilt, she knew what she wanted and precisely how to get it, and she was no man's woman. Like her character, Mae West herself was a thoroughly independent woman: throughout her long career she called the shots, writing many of the stage and screen plays in which she starred—*I'm No Angel, Diamond Lil,* and half of *My Little Chickadee,* to name but a few.

§ FUNNY FACES §

The movie close-up made it possible for actors to exploit physical idiosyncrasies to unprecedented comic effect, and many built a comic identity around a striking and distinctive facial attribute.

The feature that earned Jimmy Durante the nickname "the Schnozzola" figured so prominently in his sixty-year career in movies and on radio and television that Durante had it insured for $100,000. "The nose knows," he was fond of saying; and he was not above inviting audiences up to autograph his famous proboscis, assuring them, "It ain't gonna bite you." A song-and-dance man whose distinctive speech impersonators found irresistible ("I never mispernounce poipoisely!"), Durante immortalized the nonsensical lyrics of songs like "You Gotta Start Off Each Day with a Song," "Inka Dinka Doo," and "Umbriago," which to this day are associated with him. Just as whimsical was the closing line that became the trademark of his performances: "Good night, Mrs. Calabash, wherever you are." The identity and whereabouts of Mrs. Calabash remained forever a mystery—the remark was presumably the inspiration of a moment, but it so intrigued the public that Durante repeated it religiously for the rest of his life.

Joe E. Brown was fondly known as The Great Open Space, or The Grand Canyon—and as descriptions of his uncannily large mouth, the nicknames were only barely exaggerations. Brown was an accomplished acrobat and he had a keen sense of timing and of teamwork (instilled by years of playing professional baseball), but it was the famous mouth that his public remembered, whether wide open in a traffic-stopping howl or settled in a grin that made Brown look something like an alligator in repose. After his early movies, such as *Wide Open Faces, You Said a Mouthful,* and *Chatterbox,* Brown played character roles in *The Tender Years* (1949) and *Showboat* (1951). He triumphed in 1959 in *Some Like It Hot,* as a millionaire in romantic pursuit of Jack Lemmon, who had disguised himself as a member of an all-girl orchestra. When he is informed that his fiancée is a man, Brown, in a now-famous last line, quips, "Well, nobody's perfect," and rockets off in his motorboat to his waiting yacht.

Joe E. Brown sometimes appeared with Martha Raye, who, like him, had a distinctively large mouth. A singer and comedienne with an awkward walk and a raucous voice, Martha endeared herself to nightclub, stage, movie, and TV audiences alike. (In the 1970s she appeared as the witch on the Saturday morning series for young people, *H. M. Puffinstuff.*) During World War II and the Vietnam war, Raye donned Army fatigues and field boots and tramped to front-line hospitals and jungle outposts to entertain the fighting men from makeshift stages—smiling her famous smile no matter how extreme the discomfort or great the danger.

With enormous "banjo eyes" that rolled in their sockets like figures in a slot machine, tiny, vivacious Eddie Cantor won an affectionate following as a singer, dancer, comic—sometimes in blackface—and Broadway trouper; he brought his considerable talents to the Hollywood screen in the 1930s. France's Fernandel exhibits the impressive emotional range of his expressive "horse face" nowhere better than in *The Sheep Has Five Legs,* playing, as he does, several quite different characters. Hollywood's Billy Gilbert will be remembered for having turned the act of sneezing into a one-man art, delighting audiences with his agonized facial contortions and explosive "ah-choos."

§ DIZZY DAMES AND DUMB BLONDES §

Both Billie Burke and Zasu Pitts were capable of creating serious character roles; Billie was a great stage beauty in her youth and Zasu played Anne Rutledge in D. W. Griffith's *Abraham Lincoln* and the Bride in Erich von Stroheim's *Greed.* But both women were best known as "flutterers"—dizzy, a little vague, and always at sixes and sevens. In her delightfully cockeyed manner, Billie, for example, would walk up to a perfectly level painting and tilt it preposterously. Giddy Zasu's trademark was the constant fidgety dancing of her long slim fingers.

An unforgettable "dumb blonde" was created by Judy Holliday in the role of Billie Dawn, first in the stage version of *Born Yesterday,* then in the film. Miss Holliday won an Academy Award for her performance as the wide-eyed innocent—more naïve than dumb, as she proves when her protector-boyfriend hires a professor to "improve her mind"—whose ingenuous charm endeared her to the American public. Other comediennes have exploited the character of the dumb blonde, among them Marie Wilson, Penny Singleton, and Jayne Mansfield. Perhaps the most successful was Marilyn Monroe, whose sex-kitten appeal was increasingly enhanced by her very real comic talents, nowhere better utilized than in *Some Like It Hot.*

§ DAME MARGARET RUTHERFORD §

Dame Margaret Rutherford was perhaps the foremost comedienne of the distinguished school of eccentric elderly actresses that included Dame May Whitty, Edna May Oliver, Dame Edith Evans, Mildred Natwick, and Elizabeth Patterson. From the beginning of her long acting career, Dame Margaret, with her ample figure and impressive vocal command, played the bombastic, whimsical, crochety, or simply daft elderly characters with whom she is associated. Her film characterizations of Miss Prism, the governess in Oscar Wilde's *The Importance of Being Earnest,* and Madame Arcati, the bicycling spiritualist in Noel Coward's *Blithe Spirit,* demonstrate her unusual versatility and sensitivity as a comic character actress. It was not until late in her life, however, that she achieved film stardom, winning an Oscar for her performance as the Duchess of Brighton in *The VIPs* (1963) and gaining international recognition in the 1960s as Miss Jane Marple in four films based on Agatha Christie mysteries, *Murder, She Said; Murder at the Gallop; Murder Most Foul;* and *Murder Ahoy.*

§ DANNY KAYE §

Danny Kaye created an original comic character with a remarkable split personality—part dreamy, awkward innocent, part sophisticated cavalier. He specialized in energetic song-and-dance numbers, particularly nonsensical patter songs rattled off at superhuman speed. Kaye was baffled by the complexities of ordinary life, bullied mercilessly by machines, but was very much at home in swashbuckling fantasy; appropriately, *The Secret Life of Walter Mitty* is one of his funniest early films. Kaye is an extremely gifted musician—he did a hilarious burlesque of a heroic grand-opera tenor—but his later films overworked his original formula in a series of predictable spy and gangster capers.

Kaye brought his uniquely childlike sophistication to television in the sixties, and today he is thought of primarily as a children's entertainer, the star of a film biography of Hans Christian Andersen. He is closely associated with UNICEF, on behalf of which he has toured extensively around the world.

§ JERRY LEWIS §

An acrobat of extraordinary agility and grace, Jerry Lewis nonetheless created a screen character—"The Kid," as he calls it—that embodies in painful caricature all the clumsiness of the gawky fourteen-year-old "ugly duckling"—body convulsing uncontrollably as though released from a long stretch in a strait jacket, face contorting grotesquely, voice wailing, shrieking, bellowing, or whooping in shrill hysterical laughter. Lewis developed this character in greatest depth in *That's My Boy*, playing a misfit son whose father (Eddie Mayehoff) is determined to make a college sports hero of him. Some American critics think that Lewis has not lived up to that early performance; in their opinion, the zany buck-toothed caricatures of later films such as *The Bellboy, Ladies' Man, The Nutty Professor,* and *The Disorderly Orderly* are all but interchangeable, and Lewis has replaced character development with slapstick. Other critics—notably French and Latin American ones—believe, to the contrary, that Lewis's characters are informed by a comic vision that can be compared with those of Chaplin, Keaton, and Laurel and Hardy, and, with many European filmgoers, see Lewis as the last of the great Hollywood clowns. But after more than two decades as a performer, Jerry Lewis remains, in the eyes of most of his countrymen, a clown still in search of a sustaining image.

§ THE GOLDEN AGE OF TELEVISION §

Many of the great comedians of the 1950s came to the new medium from the stage, films, and radio. The team of George Burns and Gracie Allen (veterans of vaudeville and films), Milton Berle, Arthur Godfrey, Bob Hope, and Jack Benny all were popular radio personalities who made the transition to television with little change in comic style or format. Bob Hope, whose comedy relies more on rapid-fire delivery and impeccable timing than on the quality of his material, is known for his screen performances—the best of them in *The Paleface, Son of Paleface,* and *The Seven Little Foys*—as well as his wisecracking stand-up routines before live TV audiences. Jack Benny's situation-comedy skits, which featured Benny's wife, Mary Livingstone; the gravel-voiced Eddie "Rochester" Anderson; Benny's announcer, Don Wilson; and Irish tenor Dennis Day, turned invariably on the miserliness of Benny's exasperatingly tight-fisted comic character. (When a stick-up man demanded, "Your money or your life!" Benny, after an unnerving pause, muttered "I'm thinking, I'm thinking.") Benny's humor depended as much on exquisitely timed silences as on the predictable punch lines that followed them. His mastery of gesture went unappreciated until the advent of television, which, unlike radio, let audiences in, for example, on the "slow burns" that punctuated those silences—Benny turning toward the camera with the deadpan smile of a man pushed beyond his limits, and prolonging the pause excruciatingly before delivering the one-word line that never failed to bring the house down—a "Well!" that plumbed the depths of indignant injury.

The fifties brought both Sid Caesar and Imogene Coca to television from the legitimate theater. The stars of the immensely popular Saturday night *Your Show of Shows* created many memorable comic characters in sketches satirizing domestic life, current movies and books, and other TV shows. They are perhaps best remembered for their pantomime skits, one a mimicry of the stiff-legged movements of the mechanized figures of a Swiss clock in which they began by striking the hours and ended up striking each other in a routine that amounted to total bedlam.

Vaudeville and film veteran Red Skelton brought a durable brand of baggy-pants, pratfall clowning to 1950s television. His diverse comic characters were all sublimely joyous creations that communicated the intense pleasure Skelton took in performing. A master of the physical gag who was thoroughly at home in the pantomime tradition, Skelton appealed particularly to children, who perhaps saw in him the essence of the true clown. "I take a comic view of life," he said in 1975. "That's all there is. We're not going to get out of it alive. So why not?"

"How sweet it is!" "You're dan-dan-dandy!" "Away we go!" These expressions identify only one television performer, the oversized and many-faced personality of Jackie Gleason with his company of characters. Jackie grew up in a tough neighborhood in Brooklyn, his father suddenly disappearing, his mother dying when he was sixteen. Soon thereafter he dropped out of school to take up a life of hanging around poolrooms and appearing as a comic at local amateur-night contests. In addition to his Irish charm, he made the most of being fat in the belief that his avoirdupois added humor to his act. In 1949 he entered television in the title role in *The Life of Riley,* a family situation comedy previously made popular on radio by William Bendix. After twenty-six episodes he starred in *Cavalcade of Stars,* a variety show in which he introduced the popular *The Honeymooners,* weekly sketches involving Ralph Kramden, a Brooklyn bus driver, and his friend Ed Norton, a sewer worker (memorably played by Art Carney), and their tenement wives. Out of the comic tradition of Harrigan and Hart of a century before, *The Honeymooners* concentrated on a bickering couple who had been married ten years and fighting for "nine years and twelve months." When Ralph's frantic schemes to get rich quick failed, he pounded out his frustrations on the kitchen table.

Gleason soon added other characters to his shows, several based on types he had known or observed in Brooklyn. Joe the Bartender, the three-cent philosopher, gossiped about his customers Crazy Googenheim, Bookshelf Robinson, and Tin Horn Schwartz. Fenwick Babbitt, befuddled by the simplest job, created elaborate chaos with whipped cream while working in a bakery. Reggie Van Gleason III, the billionaire playboy in stovepipe hat and opera cape, when not drunk and chasing women, attempted to buy the Atlantic Ocean for his exclusive use. Later these were joined by Fatso Fogarty, Charlie Bratton, the Loudmouth, and Rudy the Repairman. "All my characters are psychologically constructed," Gleason has claimed, "each is consistent, and I give each a saving grace and touch of sympathy." This comic formula resulted in high ratings that made Gleason known as "Mr. Saturday Night" to millions of viewers in the 1950s and as "The Great One" in the 1960s. To Gleason it brought a personal fortune and extravagant style of living that labeled him "The Maharajah of Miami": here when entertaining past Presidents of the United States he drove along Jackie Gleason Drive, past the Jackie Gleason Theatre, and off to play in the Jackie Gleason golf tournaments.

Lucille Ball is perhaps the single most popular comic performer television has ever known. She is certainly one of the most durable. A favorite of audiences outside the United States as well as in, the pert red-headed star of the *I Love Lucy* show survived almost a generation of shifting trends in TV situation comedy, consistently delighting viewers with the zany schemes that inevitably embroiled her family or neighbors, and the native wit that just as inevitably extricated them in the nick of time.

§ TELEVISION COMEDIANS OF THE 1960S §

One of the first of the "ugly duckling" caricatures was created by the film actress Louise Fazenda in the 1920s. This now stock comic character has been adroitly exploited by television's attractive comedienne Carol Burnett, whose awkward, woebegone creatures often verge on pathos. Phyllis Diller, drawing on her own experiences as a frazzled wife and mother, has given the character a particularly outrageous expression in the bedraggled housewife who throws up her hands in the face of the ravages of time and gravity, and gleefully succumbs to them.

Redd Foxx and Bill Cosby both came to television as stand-up comics whose monologues—Foxx's heavily "blue," Cosby's drawn from his childhood memories of life in North Philadelphia—reflected the inner-city black experience. Foxx, in an overnight TV success, won an enormous following as the salty junk dealer in the *Sanford and Son* series. Cosby, who played opposite Robert Culp in the long-time favorite *I Spy* series, and more recently, in his own series, *The Bill Cosby Show,* is probably best known for his TV "special" routines, which are as biting as they are funny.

The prominence of the black comedian on television today can be traced in large part to the self-consciously black humor of Flip Wilson. And Wilson's hip-swishing, pocketbook-swinging, falsetto-voiced Geraldine Jones repopularized the nearly defunct art of female impersonation, which had languished since the days of the nineteenth-century impersonator Julian Eltinge. Widely accepted as performers "in drag" are in Great Britain (where Danny LaRue, for instance, has long been a major entertainer), this particular form of comedy has often been considered to be in bad taste in the United States—with the few exceptions of T. C. Jones and Jim Bailey, and of course the highly original Flip Wilson.

§ JACQUES TATI §

Mr. Hulot, the bedeviled pantomime clown created by French actor-director Jacques Tati, made his first film appearance in *Jour de Fête* in 1949. With the release of the critically acclaimed *Mr. Hulot's Holiday* in 1953, Tati became a most unlikely international celebrity, looking for all the world like an apprehensive kangaroo in an outgrown mackintosh, his trousers hitched up well over a pouchlike paunch and separated by a long stretch of striped socks from his well-worn pair of tennis shoes. Hulot carries his umbrella like the lance of a modern-day Quixote and cocks his head at a deceptively alert angle, but his faraway gaze definitely implies a mind preoccupied with higher things. Somehow we never quite discover what these might be, as Hulot steps helplessly into one mechanical pitfall after another, at a holiday resort, in an airport, at a Paris trade fair, in a nightclub, or in the middle of a truly epic traffic jam. In *My Uncle* (1958) a visit to his brother-in-law's ultra-modern all-automatic household involves Hulot in all-out pushbutton warfare with an aggressive collection of robot appliances and futuristic conveniences. In Tati's most recent films, *Playtime* (1967) and *Traffic* (1971), Hulot still contributes to but no longer clearly dominates the pervading chaos. In fact, Hulot's gawky presence seems to divide and multiply repeatedly, finally filling the screen with Hulots, in *Playtime*, thinly disguised first as an excursion party of American tourists, and later as the whole city of Paris. The masterful gadgets and awesome science-fiction architecture of *My Uncle* seem to have spread alarmingly over the city, so it is no wonder that Tati sees Hulot's absent-minded rebelliousness infecting all of us, creating cities, even an entire planet populated by Hulots. In these two films Tati avoids close-ups to create a panoramic comic landscape, impossible for the eye to take in all at once, crowded with small-scale Hulot replicas, engaged in unequal pantomime combat with flat tires, malfunctioning air conditioners, and all the other mechanical perils of Hulot's brave new world.

§ WOODY ALLEN §

In the middle sixties Woody Allen emerged from the nightclubs and improvisational cabarets of New York City's Greenwich Village. Slight and scrawny, with unruly red hair, large sad eyes behind tortoise-shell glasses, and a large sad nose, Allen made other people's inferiority complexes seem like delusions of grandeur; or as he ruefully summed it up himself, "My only regret is that I am not someone else." In his nightclub act he specialized in wistful, self-mocking reminiscences of neglected childhood, awkward adolescence, and maladjusted adulthood, delivered in the high-pitched nasal accents of his native Brooklyn. Years of psychoanalysis only caused his many neuroses to flourish and multiply. Seeking to console himself with philosophy, Allen discovered additional reasons for despair: "Not only is there no God, but try getting a plumber on weekends."

Over the past ten years Allen has developed from a stand-up comic of striking originality into a versatile and amazingly prolific satirist, with several recordings, two collections of essays and parodies, two plays, and the screenplays for over half a dozen films to his credit. Allen starred in both the Broadway and movie versions of *Play It Again, Sam,* as well as the films *Take the Money and Run, Bananas, Sleeper,* and *Love and Death,* all of which he wrote and directed. As a performer, Allen still makes excellent use of his own fixations, tics, and phobias; as a writer and filmmaker, he has taken on the symptoms of an entire society, exploring the greater and lesser problems of our civilization with the same probing, relentless illogic: philosophy, religion, sex, literary criticism, revolution, organized crime, Russian novels, movie cults from Bogart to Bond, utopian science fiction, automation, and the history of the sandwich. With the same humility that characterizes all great thinkers, Allen is the first to admit that his conclusions are only tentative: "I don't believe in an afterlife, although I am bringing a change of underwear."

Today, when a new talent like Woody Allen or Mel Brooks appears on the scene, the highest critical praise he can aspire to is to be compared with "the great tradition of Chaplin and Keaton." After decades of relative neglect, the great masters of silent comedy, revered in their own time as "geniuses" and "true philosophers," can be seen again today in frequent revivals and retrospectives. Eight mm. prints of silent comedies are now widely available from public libraries for home projection. Chaplin's films are still playing in commercial theaters and college film festivals; a theater in London annually devotes the entire month of August to its Buster Keaton Festival. And, of course, the influence of the old masters is very much visible in the slapstick "blackouts" on Carol Burnett's and other television variety shows, in such recent tributes as Mel Brooks's *Silent Movie,* and in the visual styles of filmmakers like Allen and Jacques Tati, ardent disciples of Chaplin, Keaton, and Harold Lloyd, who seem to perceive the whole course of modern civilization as a continuous sequence of mechanized pratfalls and scientifically calibrated sight gags.

The sound films of Laurel and Hardy, the Marx Brothers, and W. C. Fields are also staples of the revival houses and college film societies, as well as the late-night television movie repertory. The publication of books of stills from their movies, biographies, film histories, and critical studies of their work became a minor industry in the sixties, as Groucho and Fields, at least, attained the status of cult figures. When the Marx Brothers' classic *Animal Crackers,* which because of copyright restrictions had not been shown for sixteen years, reopened in New York in 1974, it quickly became the acknowledged comedy hit of the season. All-pervading influences and heirs to great traditions are all very well, of course, but sometimes there is nothing like the real thing: in this case, Groucho belting out the upbeat musical number "Hooray for Captain Spaulding" before reminiscing about his adventures as an African explorer, "When I was in Africa, I shot an elephant in my pajamas. How he got in my pajamas I'll never know."

· *12* ·

CLOWNS IN THE CIRCUS

The Whiteface, the Auguste, the Grotesque,
Grock, the Fratellini, Coco, Emmett Kelly,
Felix Adler, Otto Griebling, Lou Jacobs,
Popov, Los Muchachos, and the Clowns of Tomorrow

Popov

Grock

Coco

Whiteface

Auguste

P. T. Barnum, the founder of "The Greatest Show on Earth" and the creator of the modern circus, once remarked that clowns are the pegs on which circuses are hung. From the time they make their first flamboyant appearance in the opening parade until they wave farewell in the grand finale, the clowns always seem to steal the show, upstaging the "breathtaking," "death defying," or merely "amazing" attractions of their fellow performers with their own energetic specialty numbers, filling in between acts while the ring is being cleared, mimicking the jugglers and acrobats, and bickering cheerfully with the ringmaster. Only the clown is allowed to remain in the ring while the other artists are performing; he comes and goes as he pleases, freely interrupting the other acts or wandering into the audience to watch the show from the lap of a pretty female spectator.

The mimics, jesters, minstrels, simpletons, and baggy-pants buffoons of earlier ages all have many descendants in the clowns of the modern circus. The raffish equestrian who slides drunkenly out of his saddle, then vaults back up to show off his trick-riding skills recalls the earliest circus clowns in Philip Astley's arena. Grimaldi's Joey has many descendants, all with a prodigious craving for hot dogs. The proud pig fancier walking his pet on a leash recalls "Parmenon's pig." Circus historians have discovered over fifty varieties of clown in the modern circus.

The clowns themselves speak of three basic types. We have already come across several examples of each of these three: the Whiteface, the Auguste, and the Grotesque. The Whiteface clown originated with Pierrot of the commedia and Gros Guillaume in seventeenth-century France. Instead of flour, modern Whitefaces wear commercial "clown white" makeup or a preparation of zinc oxide, like the white sunburn cream used by lifeguards. After applying this basic white background, the Whiteface accentuates his other features, giving himself wide eyes, a big nose, and a broad grin, since he is essentially a happy, even a slaphappy character. He bears a strong resemblance to Harlequin, spiritually if not physically, with his love of mischief and his ingenious ability to get in and out of trouble. The Whiteface also has a distinct preference for bright colors, mild vulgarity, and slapstick; he feeds on applause and will often keep on improvising show-stopping encores until the ringmaster or another performer impatient to go on drags him from the ring.

The Auguste, as we have seen, was the accidental creation of Tom Belling in Berlin, although an English clown named Chadwick, who introduced the Auguste in France at around the same time (1864), is sometimes credited with this happy honor. The Auguste is a simple, well-meaning character, everyone's friend and his own worst enemy. He spends much of his time in the ring either flat on his face or flat on his backside, and seems naturally to attract buckets of water. His makeup is pink or flesh-colored with eyebrows drooping and mouth turned downward in a pathetic inverted smile. This poor but honest fellow is usually dressed in a collection of dirty rags and patches (the fastidious Whitefaces often hold their noses and screw up their faces in pantomime distaste when he approaches), but he is not always so careless of his appearance. He may be dressed in a neatly pressed and spotless tuxedo, always several sizes too big or too small for him, or an enormous overcoat that envelops him completely, dragging on the ground and making him look all the more forlorn and inconsequential. He may even appear in blackface, or in a well-fitting business suit, custom tailored in a sporty pattern of garish stripes or screechingly loud plaid. The squirting flower in the buttonhole is a favorite accessory of the Auguste's, even though it generally misfires and leaves him dripping wet, and his Whiteface adversaries spotless and supercilious as ever. His ensemble is completed by a stylish wide tie that glows in the dark or an animated handkerchief that leaps out of his pocket like a tiny flying carpet.

The life of the Auguste is for the most part a series of small disasters, but fortunately for him he enjoys his rare and accidental small pleasures to the hilt. As the partner of the Whitefaces, he routinely misses his cues, mixes up his instructions, and ruins their complicated gags. They in turn console themselves by making the Auguste the butt of most of their jokes, mercilessly exploiting his gullibility and exposing his stupidity.

The Auguste is a likable simpleton in the medieval German tradition of Hans Sachs, Hans Wurst, and Pickle Herring. Like them, the great interpreters of the Auguste character make his simplicity, his very insignificance, seem sympathetic, especially in contrast to the grinning professionalism of the Whiteface. The Auguste's broad character permits him to be both satirical and sentimental, to introduce touches of bittersweet irony and genuine subtlety which can still be felt instantly and personally by every member of the audience.

The Grotesque clown may be a dwarf or a midget or any performer who bases his character on a physical distortion of size or shape, in the manner of the dwarf jesters of the medieval court. Clowns who specialize in bizarre female caricatures, "monsters," or freakish creatures of their own invention are also called Grotesques. Dwarf or midget clowns, however, usually portray the same characters as their fellow clowns and accordingly are classified either as Grotesque-Whiteface or Grotesque-Auguste.

These categories are based on character rather than appearance, and of course are subject to endless variation by individual performers. An Auguste, for example, may appear in Whiteface (though a Whiteface almost never dresses in rags), but he shows his true identity as he takes his first pratfall or walks straight into a bucket of water. There are other categories as well—musical clowns, entrée clowns, reprise clowns, and so-called carpet clowns, who fill in while the ring is being cleared between acts. And as we have noted, clowns perform their own versions of almost every circus act as equestrians, jugglers, musicians, acrobats, animal handlers, magicians, sword swallowers, fire eaters, marksmen, singers, dancers, and (although rarely in the modern American circus) storytellers and comedians. Frequently the clowns begin their acts awkwardly, like clumsy novices imitating the real artistes, and then in a matter of seconds, seem to pick up the knack and display a real mastery of the slack wire or the spinning plates. A whole troupe of clowns erupting into the ring (or rings), all performing their comic or specialty routines at once, is called a charivari, which means an "uproar" of clowns. Most of the favorite clowns of the twentieth century have been "character clowns," permanently identified with a single highly individualized comic personality, usually based on the Auguste. Nearly everyone has a favorite clown, as do the clowns themselves, who will instantly reel off a long string of names, representing an entire charivari of great clowns of the modern circus: Grock, the Fratellini, Coco, Emmett Kelly, Felix Adler, Otto Griebling, Lou Jacobs, and Popov.

§ GROCK §

Like his father before him, Adrien Wettach (1880–1959) narrowly escaped the comfortable life of a watchmaker in the small Swiss village where he was born. The elder Wettach had trained himself as an acrobat and taken to the road. Adrien, of like temperament, joined his father at an early age, and together they toured with small provincial companies, sleeping in open fields and raiding farmers' gardens. Equipped with the acrobatic skills his father had taught him, Adrien quickly picked up more complicated stunts from his fellow performers—and in addition taught himself to play the musical instruments that would figure so prominently in his performances in days to come. But despite his obvious talents, he found that engagements were hard to come by and too far apart to sustain him through the summers (winters presented no problems, for Adrien spent them at home, attending school). Adrien took whatever jobs came his way—sometimes tuning pianos, once tutoring the children of a noble Hungarian family—but he never gave up his dream of returning to the circus.

Wettach was the ideal circus performer—equally adept as acrobat, contortionist, tumbler, musician, or any combination of these (he was able, for instance, to turn somersaults while playing the violin). But he discovered that whatever he did, he was at his best when he followed his natural bent for clowning; and how better to combine his talents than in the identity of a clown? His memory of the first clown he had ever seen—a street performer in his home village square—suggested the makeup that would be his trademark for the next fifty years: a touch of red on the tip of his nose, arching brows (painted well above his own) framing his expressive eyes, paint that extended his already expansive smile to almost the width of his face—all against the chalk-white background that covered an exaggerated forehead, with forlorn tufts of hair at his temples and atop his bald pate. Unlike most clowns' makeup, Wettach's was simple, and he relied on it very little, using it only to enhance the comic expressiveness of his own features. This was fitting enough, for simplicity was the essence of Wettach's clown—a helpless, perpetually bewildered creature, as baffled by his own props as he was by the presence of the audience itself.

Wettach came by the name Grock purely by chance. It was the custom in Europe in the early 1900s for clowns to work in pairs, so when Wettach learned that military service had separated the team of Brick and Brock, he introduced himself to Brick in Marseilles. The two men soon discovered that their clowning styles were compatible and formed a partnership that won them an engagement with the Swiss National Circus. The billing "Brick and Wettach" seemed to suggest an accounting firm rather than a circus act, so Wettach adopted the name "Grock"—which in time would appear alone on the bill and posters throughout Europe.

Grock acknowledged his debt to the great clowns of the past in his autobiography. "Just as much as any other artist," he wrote, the clown "is the product of tradition." Of those who had influenced him, he gave the greatest credit to his one-time partner Antonet, an Italian clown who starred in the Cirque de Paris. And the credit must go to Grock and Antonet together for the new respect they brought the profession of clowning. "A good clown these days," Grock was able to claim in 1931, "can occupy every bit as high a position as a good actor. He is practicing an art."

And clowning was indeed an art whenever Grock stepped into the ring—seemingly as astonished to find himself before an audience as he was to learn, from his impatient partner, that he had kept the crowd waiting for some time. Utterly baffled as to what was expected of him, he would follow his partner's pointing finger to the gigantic violin case he was carrying under his arm, then smile as though realizing for the first time what it was. After fumbling unsuccessfully with the violin case, he would catch a sharp blow in the face as the lid flew open of its own accord. From the case he would produce a violin so tiny one would think it incapable of making a sound, then proceed to play it like a virtuoso, despite the instrument's seeming determination to leap from his hands. Warming to the audience's applause, he would nonchalantly toss the violin into the air, but not quite so nonchalantly fail to catch it, again and again clutching at thin air as the instrument thudded to the stage. Determined to master the trick, he would withdraw behind a screen to practice, his arduous efforts resulting in nothing more than further damage to the violin. Returning with an apologetic shrug, resigned to the straightforward business of playing the instrument, he would discover that the violin was gone: he had left it behind the screen. He would run to fetch it and emerge smiling, ready to perform—except that now there was no bow. Once more to the screen and back again, and he would stand poised to play—but he could not. Something was wrong—and slowly it would dawn on him: he had reversed the violin and bow, holding each in the wrong hand. In an attempt to remedy the situation, he would turn around, hoping that the new position would do the trick. When this failed, he would throw both the instrument and the bow to the ground in disgust. When he picked them up again, he would discover, to his utter astonishment, that they had reverted to the proper hands as though by magic. In sheer joy he would toss violin and bow into the air, this time juggling them expertly, inadvertently mastering the trick that earlier had defeated him so miserably. Despite the audience's uproarious applause, it would not be until he was midway through the next solo that he would realize what he had accomplished, and as he chortled in delight, he would express the triumph of the man who had succeeded in spite of himself.

§ THE FRATELLINI §

The sons of a second-generation nomadic circus family, the Fratellini brothers were born on the road—Paul in Sicily, François in Paris, and Albert in Moscow. As adults, the team continued to tour the capitals of Europe, but for many circusgoers their act represented French clowning at its best, and indeed for long periods of time they made Paris their home. Paris, in return, bestowed on the Fratellini brothers perhaps the highest honor France can accord a performer—an invitation to appear in the hallowed House of Molière under the auspices of the French national theater, the Comédie Française, marking France's recognition of the clown as an artist in his own right.

And like the performances of Grock, those of the Fratellini were sheer artistry from beginning to end: François in whiteface and elegant attire, Paul as a traditional Auguste, and Albert in rags and outsized, floppy shoes would enter the ring toting musical instruments of nearly every kind imaginable. Soon after they had begun to play, Albert would light a match, edge up to François, and set his hat afire. François would continue to play, oblivious to the conflagration that raged atop his head, but Paul terrified by the flames would race out of the ring and tear back in at the wheel of a miniature fire engine. Whipping out the truck's ladder, he would prop it up against his blazing brother, and scurry to the top, wielding an enormous fire ax. Then, to the horror of the audience, he would raise the ax and bring it crashing down through his brother's head (or actually, through a false head, constructed atop the real one, but the effect was stunning). Surviving the blow as though by a miracle, the still smoldering "human torch" played on, as unaware of the hatchet buried in his skull as of his other misfortunes. And when Albert turned the full force of a fire hose on him, François would blithely open an umbrella and amble off—presumably in search of drier quarters—the ax protruding from his smoking head, both brothers in hot pursuit, one driving the fire engine, the other aiming the hose. Moments later all three would reappear with their instruments and play their musical number through to the end in perfect, uninterrupted brotherly harmony.

§ COCO §

A star of the English circus for over forty years, Coco (1900–1970) was a Russian by birth; his real name was Nikolai Poliakoff. Both his parents were actors, and he was born in a theater in the provincial town of Besinowiz. He recalls in his autobiography his decision, at the age of five, to become a circus "artiste." On his first visit to the circus, the sight of the acrobats filled his head with fantasies of performing on the high wire and trapeze; he changed his mind when he saw the tumblers, then again when the jugglers came on. He was seven when he first saw the great clown Lazerenko, famous for his daredevil acrobatic stunts. Shortly afterward young Nikolai began his apprenticeship as a circus clown, and four years later, at the age of eleven, he was already a full-fledged performer.

Coco's autobiography gives a vivid picture of the dangers and discomforts of the traveling life in those years in Russia. He moved from one small circus to the next, sharing with his fellow artistes the rigors of the climate—drenched by summer cloudbursts, snowbound and faced with starvation in winter. The upheavals of war and revolution made travel even more difficult and often dangerous. Coco was even arrested and exiled to Siberia at one time, and he seems to have suffered more than his share of professional misfortunes as well. On one occasion, as he was performing a balancing act with a samovar—a heavy Russian tea urn—on top of a table, the samovar cracked and showered Coco with boiling water. He was disabled for several months and forced to give up his ownership interest in the circus and make a new career for himself, starting all over with virtually nothing.

Coco eventually made his way to England and became a familiar figure in the Bertram Mills Circus, dressed in an oversized checked suit with enormous Russian boots, a round red nose, permanently raised bushy eyebrows, and an outrageous red wig of yarnlike hair that stood straight on end when its wearer was startled or frightened. Even in England Coco's troubles were not entirely over; injuries sustained in an auto accident kept him out of the ring for many years. Looking back on it all years later, Coco philosophically observed, "I would still be a clown if I had it to do over again. You have to be clever to make a fool of yourself."

§ EMMETT KELLY §

The best known of the modern American clowns, Emmett Kelly (1898–   ), created his mournful hobo character, "Weary Willie," while working as an advertising cartoonist in Kansas City. Kelly took Weary Willie off the drawing board and brought him to life in a nightclub act; at the same time Kelly was performing as a circus trapeze artist, but circus managers showed little interest in Weary Willie, complaining that he looked "too dirty."

Kelly later recalled that he first began to understand and actually enter into the character of Weary Willie during a long bout of depression following the breakup of his marriage. He realized that Willie was a clown unlike any other and should be allowed to develop along his own highly individual lines. The Whiteface wore a spotless white suit with a neatly starched collar; even the Auguste's ragbag wardrobe was natty and extremely colorful compared to Willie's drab tramp costume. And more important, while the other clowns were always animated and frantically active, Willie was passive, withdrawn, and seemingly paralyzed by bad luck and trouble. Willie was not by any means the first hobo clown, however. The hobo had been a familiar figure in folklore and comic art, as well as in vaudeville (remember W. C. Fields's "tramp juggler" routine in the early years of the century). In the thirties, when Kelly and Willie were starting out with the circus, the Depression had sent a new mass migration of tramps and hoboes hitchhiking and hopping freights across the country, and few circuses were without a hobo clown of one kind or another.

By 1937, when Kelly appeared in the Hippodrome in New York with the Cole Brothers and the Clyde Beatty Circus, Willie's unique character was fully developed, the hobo who would come to stand for all hoboes in the popular imagination; and indeed, the clown who would come to stand for all modern clowns. Shortly afterward, Kelly toured in England for a season with the Bertram Mills Circus; there the melancholy hobo clown was even more of a novelty and just as much of a favorite as in America. Kelly returned to New York and appeared briefly in a Broadway musical revue called *Keep Off the Grass*. Kelly drew rave notices from the critics and even managed to upstage the real stars of the show, Ray Bolger, Jimmy Durante, and Jackie Gleason. In one musical number, "The Horse with the Hansom Behind," Kelly just sat sadly and silently while the others sang, at least until the audience's delighted laughter at Kelly drowned them out completely. Another sketch began with Weary Willie awakening from a restful sleep on a bench in Central Park. He ate a hearty breakfast out of a paper bag and, after devouring the last crumb, finally produced a toothbrush and began to brush his teeth with an expression of virtuous self-satisfaction.

Kelly joined the Ringling Bros. and Barnum & Bailey Circus in 1942, and Willie's whiskery face, appearing frequently in advertisements and publicity, became the unofficial trademark of The Greatest Show on Earth for many years to come. In his most famous routine Kelly made a slow circuit of the ring, nibbling on a large cabbage, stopping occasionally to fix a woman in the audience with his unblinking melancholy stare. Kelly seemed to know instinctively which members of the audience he would get the best reaction from, and in a few moments his chosen victim and the small sector of the audience surrounding her would be shaking with laughter, blissfully unaware of the spectacles going on in any of the three rings. During the thousands of times he repeated this routine over the years, often in spite of the all-out efforts of onlookers to distract him, Kelly never once smiled or spoke a word, remaining as impassive as a Buckingham Palace guard.

Willie approached everything he did with the same high seriousness. He would use a sledgehammer to shell a peanut, or hover protectively under the high wire with a tiny pocket handkerchief unfolded in case he might be called to catch a falling aerialist. No task was too big for Willie to attempt or too small for him to bungle. Since the easy and the impossible were just as much out of reach for him, he set at both with the same painstaking determination.

In one famous routine Willie brought a broom into the center ring and solemnly began to sweep up the beam from the spotlight. Willie followed the glowing patch of light all over the ring as it moved tantalizingly out of reach of his broom. Finally, after a long pursuit, Willie simply shrugged and walked slowly out of the ring, bewildered and defeated, leaving the mystifying spot for someone else to sweep up. Even Willie, though, was not entirely untouched by the glamour of the circus. When a beautiful aerial artiste came on, it was clearly love at first sight for Willie. He ran up to her, eagerly offered to hold her cape, and stood anxiously at the foot of the ladder, eyes wide with alarm and riveted on the high wire for every moment of her act. In a few minutes Willie's beloved was back on the ground, graciously acknowledging the applause of the crowd and snatching the cape from his trembling fingers without so much as a word or a backward glance as Willie watched her vanish from his life, looking, as always, crushed, stunned, but somehow not particularly surprised.

§ FELIX ADLER §

After his first visit to the circus, at the age of nine, Felix Adler decided that he wanted to be a tightrope walker. But his practice sessions on the clothesline in his backyard in Clinton, Iowa, were discouraging; Felix spent more time sprawled on the ground than he did in the air, and in the end had to agree with amused neighbors and passersby that his act was not so much breathtaking as it was funny. Turning defeat to victory, Felix gave up the "high wire" and became a clown—in fact, more than just a clown: for fifty years he was "the King of Clowns," the star performer in the Ringling Bros. and Barnum & Bailey Circus's Clown Alley.

Adler's appearance in the ring always brought a chuckle of recognition from the crowd, and indeed he was unmistakable in his tiny pointed hat and inflated clown suit—which gave him the look of an enormous, bouncing balloon—his face and bald pate chalk-white, with outsized, festively painted laughing eyes and smiling mouth, brows over an inch high, and a large round nose that lit up bright red on cue. Adler's special trademark was the small pig that he led on a leash in the circus parade. Adler estimated that during his fifty years of clowning he had had to train hundreds of piglets to stand on their hind legs and dance—for no matter how well a pig performed its tricks, its career was invariably short-lived; once it had lost its babyish appeal (which in the case of a pig lasts only for a matter of weeks), Adler had to give it away to an appreciative fan and start over with a new ingenue.

The circus was Adler's life; for a time his wife even joined him in the ring, becoming one of the first woman clowns ever featured by the Ringling Bros. and Barnum & Bailey Circus. And for Adler, the business of clowning—like the character he created—was a happy one. Unlike many clowns he did not believe that tragedy was an essential ingredient of comedy or that the clown's life was necessarily a sad and lonely one. Though he readily admitted that he'd seen a lot of clowns who were broke, he maintained that in all his years in the ring he'd never known a clown with a broken heart.

§ OTTO GRIEBLING §

A skilled bareback rider, fourteen-year-old Otto Griebling (1896–1972) arrived in the United States from his native Germany in 1910 and quickly landed a job as an apprentice with the Ringling Bros. and Barnum & Bailey Circus. Otto was terrified of the trainer to whom he had been assigned, and the longer he stayed, the greater his terror became. One day, in Madison, Wisconsin, Otto's trainer handed him a five-dollar bill and ordered him to go and buy two quarts of milk and two loaves of bread. Once off the circus grounds, Otto panicked and hopped a freight train, which took him into the Wisconsin countryside, far from the dreaded trainer.

For two years the boy worked as a dairy hand, living in barns and stables, blissfully free of his oppressor. But his longing for the circus life gnawed at him, and when he heard that the Circus was once again in Madison, he returned to the city as impulsively as he had left it. On his way to the circus tents he stopped at a store and bought two quarts of milk and two loaves of bread, which he presented tremblingly to his former trainer. The man took the boy and his offering in with a long silent stare and wordlessly counted his change. Otto was back in the Circus—this time to stay.

After a decade of bareback riding, he took up clowning with such success that he remained in the ring for over half a century, a star performer until the Circus played Madison Square Garden in 1972. During this engagement he died at the age of seventy-five.

With his flattened hat, loose-fitting coat, baggy pants, ragged shirt, string of a tie, and well-ventilated socks and shoes, Otto's clown was the picture of the tramp. His sad, downcast eyes and "O" of a mouth—surrounded by a shadowy stubble that would have undermined anyone's self-respect—conspired to express a combination of anxiety, puzzlement, and desperation, in a silent plea for help that seemed destined to go unheeded. Otto, for his part, was willing to help any and all. Again and again throughout the show he would offer to assist the other performers as they made their entrances, but hard as he tried, no one (except the audience) appreciated his fumbling efforts.

It was characteristic of his clown that no matter how painfully he was rejected or how abysmally he failed, he never gave up. He might, for instance, appear just before a performance was about to begin with an enormous block of ice and roam the aisles in an eager but more and more desperate search for the person in the crowd who had ordered its delivery. Dismayed at his failure to locate the elusive customer, he would retire, his burden still in tow—only to reappear later on in the show, doggedly trying once again to deliver what by this time would be a much smaller block of ice. The show's end would find him still at it, the original chunk of ice now ludicrously reduced to a single cube—which would melt before his very eyes, leaving him crestfallen and utterly baffled as to what his next step might be. Or, in a similar routine, Otto would wander among the audience dressed as a messenger boy, paging a Mrs. Jones, for whom he had a telegram. Unable to locate the woman, he would give up at long last, but return, again and again throughout the show, each time visibly older, his uniform more frazzled, until, in his final appearance, he is white-haired and stooped, barely able to move, but still clutching the undelivered telegram in his shaking hand.

§ LOU JACOBS §

Born in Germany, like Otto Griebling, Lou Jacobs too has been a Ringling Bros. and Barnum & Bailey Circus clown for more than half a century. Originally an acrobat and contortionist, Jacobs—like so many other clowns—more and more frequently incorporated comic routines into his acts, until his performances amounted to pure clowning. He is best known to several generations of fans for his fanciful costumes and broad sight gags. Though his famous face—white-painted eyes extending high onto the forehead of his bald, egg-shaped head, enormous upturned mouth, and rubber-ball nose—always remained the same, he might appear one night in a satin gown complete with a fashionable wide-brimmed hat and ostrich-feather fan, and the next in a long plaid coat with wildly exaggerated lapels, and a scraggly necktie. As a contortionist, Jacobs was particularly adept at cramming himself into a tiny, already crowded car, to emerge along with an impossible number of his fellow clowns in the standard but mind-boggling opening routine. Or he would tear around the ring in his mobile bathtub, which allowed him to take a leisurely bath while he was driving to work. Jacobs' pet dachshund was his frequent companion in the ring and inspired a number of outrageous visual puns, as when he made his entrance with the dog sandwiched between two giant hot-dog rolls, which Jacobs nibbled at with obvious glee.

Now well into his seventies, Jacobs continues to perform regularly and to teach at Clown College in Venice, Florida, where he also serves as Headmaster.

§ POPOV §

The comic star of the Moscow Circus, the largest in the world, is a one-man show in himself, Oleg Popov. Dressed in a black velvet jacket, tight-fitting vest, baggy trousers, and a floppy checked cap, Popov wears a shaggy red wig, but no makeup. His smiling, snub-

nosed clown's face is entirely his own. Popov might begin a performance by jumping onto a slack wire, twirling rings around his wrists
and his other foot, while spinning a large washtub on top of his head
and flourishing in one hand an umbrella that suddenly snaps and
turns into a flag. While all this is going on, Popov hops up and down at
a faster and faster tempo until the sagging wire starts to crack like a
whip. But in spite of his prowess as a juggler and an acrobat, it is as a
clown that Popov has achieved international popularity. In his own
country he was designated a People's Artist of the Russian Soviet
Federated Socialist Republic at the age of twenty-eight, the youngest
performer ever to be awarded this coveted title.

Popov was born in Moscow in 1930. After his father was killed in
the war, Popov left school and worked at a number of jobs for three
years until he won a scholarship to the Moscow Circus School. Here
students attended classes six days a week in a rigorous course of study
that included dancing, juggling, acrobatics, gymnastics, music, history of Russian and Western theater, and history of the circus. As a child
Popov had demonstrated a talent for mimicry, entertaining his friends
with imitations of Charlie Chaplin (still acknowledged by Popov to be
the most important influence on him). While attending the Circus
School, however, Popov had decided on a career as a trapeze artist,
and immediately after his graduation in 1950, he went on tour, which
took him to every large city and gave him the chance to attend every
circus and see every clown in the Soviet Union.

Popov's own debut as a clown came about as the result of one of
those fortunate accidents that seem to abound in the history of
comedy. The regular clown was injured and Popov was sent on in his
place, completely unrehearsed and unprepared. Popov decided that
the best tactic on the spur of the moment, in someone else's spotlight,
would be an exact imitation of the absent performer, down to the last
comic grimace. The audience seemed to enjoy the deception, and he
finished his act to an appreciative round of applause and the backstage
congratulations of his fellow performers. He was encouraged to
improvise a routine of his own and came back into the ring after the
intermission dressed in an apron and tall chef's hat, his arms full of
pots and pans, all borrowed from the circus kitchen. He began by
juggling the pots and pans, then became a gourmet chef, fussily
preparing a sumptuous pantomime banquet and rewarding himself at
the end with a humble carrot, which Popov happened to discover in

the pocket of his apron. With the success of that impromptu performance, Popov became a clown, and the juggling chef is still part of his
repertory of comic characters.

Like many contemporary European clowns, Popov sees himself as a
realist, and the characters he creates are as full of enthusiasm and zest
for living as he is himself. He tries to deal sympathetically with human
frailty, since, as he says, "The high dignity of man must be shown in
the ring of any modern circus." Popov frequently appears between
acts to offer a humorous commentary on the previous performance or
engage in a bantering dialogue with the audience and the other
performers. Like most European clowns, Popov does not restrict
himself to pantomime and is always ready to speak up when he has
something to say. In this way he turns every performance of the
Moscow Circus into a comedy based on a dramatic conflict that is
presented, developed, and ultimately resolved, all according to a
unifying conception supplied by Popov as narrator, director, and
principal actor.

In one sketch Popov might appear as a proud consumer, wheeling a
large washing machine into the ring to show it off to the audience.
Offering to give a demonstration of this extraordinary labor-saving
device, he will produce a black hen, put it inside the machine, close the
lid, press a number of buttons, and stand back expectantly. The
machine hums, whirs, vibrates, and rocks back and forth for a few
moments; Popov reaches in, and with a ceremonious flourish, takes
out a white chicken. A spectator may call out for another demonstration, but Popov will explain that the warranty has just expired and the
machine may no longer be reliable. Indeed, at that very moment
Popov sneezes energetically, and the remarkable washing machine
flies into a dozen small fragments, which Popov hastily scoops up as
he rushes out of the ring.

Now Popov is a snake charmer, sitting cross-legged before a large
wicker backet. He begins to play his flute, but nothing happens. When
he plays a little louder, a brightly colored snake appears, nodding and
swaying in time with the music. Another clown walks by with a tray of
sausages. Several links are dangling over the edge of the tray; Popov
makes a few passes over them with his flute, and the trailing sausages
lift themselves up and drop back on the tray. Popov is enchanted. A
second clown happens by, whose baggy pants, to his obvious embarrassment, suddenly drop to his ankles, revealing a pair of bony knees

and extremely gaudy shorts. Popov plays a seductive melody, "The Sheik of Araby," and the pants climb dutifully back up to their owner's waist. Popov bows gravely, happy to be of service, and dances out of the ring, still playing his magic flute.

Popov often uses live chickens in his routines and seems to identify very closely with them, although never so much as in one sketch that begins with him shooing a hen off a chair and out of the ring. Popov sits down with a sigh of contentment, unaware that the previous occupant has left a large egg on the seat of the chair. Popov's assistant, who has been watching all this, mischievously asks Popov how he feels. "Marvelous!" Popov replies, blowing him a kiss and grinning at the audience. The assistant suggests that he carefully examine the spot where he is sitting and see if he still feels so marvelous. Popov obligingly stands up and reveals a newly hatched chick on the seat of the chair. Popov tenderly picks it up and bears it triumphantly out of the ring, leaving his assistant scratching his head in bewilderment.

§ LOS MUCHACHOS §

Los Muchachos, the International Boys Circus, has its home base in a remarkable town in northwestern Spain called The City of Boys. Founded in 1957 by a priest, Father Jesus Silva, as a refuge for homeless and runaway boys, the town now has over two thousand inhabitants, ranging in age from four to the late teens. The community is governed by an elected mayor, town council, and a small police force; its citizens devote four hours each day to academic subjects, as well as work at a trade in the city's bakery, grocery store, souvenir and pottery shops, printing press, or shoemaker's workshop.

Since the Circus Training School was opened in 1964, the boys' city has received applications from youths in fifteen countries to attend the classes in circus technique taught by professional performers from all over Europe. If an applicant is judged to be strong enough to endure the strenuous five-year course, and if he agrees to abide by the laws of this entirely self-governing community, he may study to be a gymnast, aerialist, acrobat, juggler, magician, equestrian, or clown, and eventually perhaps be among the hundred or so most accomplished students who are selected to tour with Los Muchachos in France, Germany, Great Britain, and more recently, the United States.

When Los Muchachos first came to Madison Square Garden in 1973, their performance opened with a vivid pantomime dramatization of the birth of a clown: A teenager named Pancracito, dressed in his ordinary clothes, stepped into the spotlight in the center ring. Noticing a hand mirror and a makeup tray, he immediately gave in to the natural impulse and began to make up his own face, drawing black circles around his eyes, filling them in with clown white, and adding a pair of high, inquisitively arched eyebrows. Next he touched a dab of brilliant red greasepaint to his nose and painted on a wide curving grin. Then a handsome clown costume with red, green, and blue stripes caught his eye, hanging beside a full-length mirror. He quickly slipped into the clown suit, donned the soft black hat hanging next to it, and stepped in front of the mirror to admire himself. To his surprise, he saw a full-fledged Harlequin staring back at him; he began to make a few tentative gestures and experimental funny faces, almost as if he were imitating the image in the mirror. Then he seemed to notice for the first time the laughter and applause coming from the darkness that surrounded the ring. He stepped away from the mirror and began to explore this new circus world, hesitantly at first, then skipping boldly around the edge of the ring. At once, almost a hundred Harlequins appeared, filling all three rings; the smaller ones leaped onto the shoulders of the larger boys, forming human pyramids, pillars, and shifting, symmetrical formations, all revolving and merging together like the brightly colored patterns in a kaleidoscope. The audience watched this spectacle as if for the first time, through the wondering, delighted eyes of the newborn clown.

The youthful energy and the sense of discovery that fill the arena in the opening parade later overflow into the stands as the young performers circulate through the crowd, shaking hands and personally welcoming everyone to their newly created world. In their version of the traditional Spanish bullfight, the hero is the two-man bull, equipped with a formidable set of papier-mâché horns. He immediately takes out after the guests of honor, Señor el Presidente and his wife, and tosses them out of their seats. He rampages right through the picadors, pauses to lift his leg and terrorize the matador with a well-aimed stream of water. The bull paws the ground, shoots real steam from his nostrils, and charges, leaving a small army of exhausted bullfighters strewn around the ring in heaps of spangles and crushed velvet. Finally, the president's lady steps forward, brandishing her fan, and subdues the monster with a delicate tap on the nose. The bull sinks to his knees, and the two Muchachos clowns who have served as his forequarters and hindquarters emerge to take their bows before scurrying off to change for the next routine.

§ THE CLOWNS OF TOMORROW §

Whimsical Walker was an eminent Victorian clown who began in Drury Lane pantomime in London, personally negotiated the American purchase of Jumbo the elephant for P. T. Barnum, and came to the United States to appear with The Greatest Show on Earth. A memorable royal-command performance for Queen Victoria herself, which opened with one of Walker's performing donkies braying out the melody "See the Conquering Hero Comes," suggested the title for his autobiography, *From Sawdust to Windsor Castle.* Writing in the early 1920s, Walker asked his readers, "Where are the clowns to come from?" The last few decades of Whimsical Walker's career had seen the decline of pantomime, the harlequinade, and the great tradition of Joe Grimaldi; with circuses, carnivals, and traveling shows fast disappearing in America, Walker's question seems even more pertinent today.

Circusgoers of only thirty years ago could remember real charivaris of one hundred or more clowns swarming into the ring. By the early seventies there were estimated to be fewer than two hundred professional circus clowns performing in the entire country. At one point, the population of Ringling Bros. and Barnum & Bailey Circus's Clown Alley had dwindled to a mere thirteen (although their number has since been increasing steadily every season); smaller circuses tried to make do with one clown, and even the most exuberant performer may find himself hard pressed to be an uproar of one. Emmett Kelly, Jr., still carries on in his father's oversized footsteps, as the star of his own circus, but many of the great personalities have died or retired from the ring: Felix Adler in 1960, Coco in 1970, and Otto Griebling in 1972.

Fortunately, when the clown seemed to have become very much of an endangered species in America, the Clown College was established in 1967 at the winter home of Ringling Bros. and Barnum & Bailey in Venice, Florida. The college was founded by the circus's present owner, Irvin Feld, and is currently run by Dean Bill Ballantine, assisted by Headmaster Lou Jacobs and a staff of veteran circus professionals. The college receives about four thousand applications annually, but only forty students are selected for the demanding two-month course, at the end of which each graduate performs his act for a jury that makes the final ruling on which of the apprentice clowns will be offered a contract with one of Ringling Bros.' traveling shows. The turn-of-the-century childhood dream of running away to join the circus has been modernized and systematized at the Clown College, but the translation of a dream into a career is as difficult and chancy as ever. Few contracts are offered; many Clown College alumni must find jobs with other circuses or content themselves with part-time appearances at shopping centers and street fairs, or entertaining children in hospitals, schools, and community playgrounds. Happily, new clowns appear every year.

The students in Clown College learn all the traditional techniques—acrobatics, juggling, stilt-walking, falling and tumbling, and of course slapstick—but the emphasis is on the creation of an original clown personality, partly through makeup, costumes, and props, but primarily through a real understanding of what it means to be a clown. This may be the accidental inspiration of a moment, but, as we have seen, generally the moment comes after many difficult years of experimentation, practice, and development.

Elizabeth Sylvester, an Englishwoman who performed over a century ago, is believed to have been the first woman clown, and an American named Lulu Craston, herself the daughter of a clown, performed for a while during the 1930s. But these two were rare exceptions in a profession overwhelmingly dominated by men. Since 1970, when Clown College became coeducational, an average of two new women clowns have appeared in Clown Alley every season, and many have chosen to renew their first one-year contracts. Some of the women clowns who have appeared in the last few years contend that the clown character has no real gender and can be played equally well by performers of either sex. Others, though, take pride in creating their own distinctively female characters and believe that the portrayal of women in the ring by Grotesques and shrill female impersonators is one long-standing circus tradition that *should* be allowed to die out quietly.

The Clown College is the best-known but not the only formal training school for clowns in America. At New York University a course in circus technique is offered to drama students. In Pennsylvania a geography professor named Charles Boas organized the Circus Kirk, a nonprofit enterprise that makes an annual summer tour of some eighty-five cities in eight different states. All fifty performers who make up the Circus Kirk are amateurs, high-school and college students who rig their own tents before sunrise and load their own equipment in a ten-truck caravan before moving on at night. In spite of persistent financial difficulties, Professor Boas is determined to keep the Circus Kirk in operation, providing a unique opportunity for his amateur troupe and for young audiences who might otherwise never see a circus or a clown except in a movie or on a television screen.

In England Coco's hand-picked successor is a young clown named Tombo Roberts who began his circus apprenticeship in the traditional way, first appearing in the ring when he was two years old. The son of a circus owner and operator, Tombo grew up on the road, sometimes attending as many as thirty-two different schools in a single year, as well as devoting himself to a more demanding course of study after school and during vacations as a pupil of the great clown Coco. Shortly before Coco's death, when Tombo was fourteen, the old clown announced to the boys' parents that their son was talented enough to become a truly great clown. Today his parents are concerned that Tombo, for all his training, may not be able to find a place with a circus at all. In Britain, as in America, the costs of outfitting and maintaining a traveling show have become prohibitive; a tour in Hungary acquainted the Roberts family with the Eastern European system of handsome government subsidies for circuses and scholarships for young performers attending state-run training schools like the Moscow Circus School. Tombo and his parents, like many other performers, wish that Western governments would show a similar willingness to keep the circus and its traditions from disappearing forever.

The future of the circus may be uncertain, but after all, clowns have always been able to survive greater and lesser tragedies in the past, from the fall of Rome to the death of vaudeville. Our attempt to answer the original question, "What is a clown?", has shown us that there can really be no final answer. New performing styles, new forms of comedy, and, especially, new and original comic personalities are continually evolving. Today this process of change seems to be more rapid than ever. Contemporary clowns can now command a global audience, traditional forms have survived and adapted to a series of technological revolutions, and the appetite of these new media for new performers and fresh material seems almost inexhaustible.

Fans of the circus, the silent film, the great comedians of the thirties or "The Golden Age of Television" may be convinced that the performers of today can never repeat the triumphs of the past, and of course they are perfectly correct. Comedy remembers the past but continues to exist and reflect the present, just as we do ourselves. A thoughtful observer of the current scene might easily conclude that we are more in need of the clown than ever, and that the clown's unique way of looking at the world is our best hope for survival. In any event, the elusive secret of the art of clowning, the creation of a real comic identity, still offers the promise of a rewarding life's work to the Emmett Kellys and Charlie Chaplins of the future, as well as the prospect of a lifetime of enjoyment for all of us in the audience.

For, as their story through the ages has testified, clowns are pegs not only on which to hang circuses but also part of ourselves.

FURTHER READING

Armin, Robert. *Fools and Jesters: With a Reprint of Robert Armin's Nest of Ninnies.* Edited by J. P. Collier. London: Shakespeare Society, 1842.

Bergson, Henri. *Laughter.* New York: Macmillan, 1913.

Bishop, George. *The World of Clowns.* Los Angeles: Brooke House, 1976.

Burgess, Hovey. *Circus Techniques.* New York: Drama Book Specialists, 1976.

Chambers, E. K. *The Medieval Stage.* 2 vols. London: Oxford, 1903.

————. *The Elizabethan Stage.* 4 vols. London: Oxford, 1923.

Chaplin, Charles. *My Autobiography.* New York: Simon and Schuster, 1964.

Crichton, Kyle. *The Marx Brothers.* New York: Doubleday, 1950.

Dickens, Charles. Ed. *The Memoirs of Joseph Grimaldi.* 1838. Reprint. London: MacGibbon & Kee, 1968.

Disher, M. Wilson. *Clowns and Pantomimes.* 1925. Reprint. New York: Benjamin Blom, 1968.

Duchartre, Pierre Louis. *The Italian Comedy.* 1929. Reprint. New York: Dover, 1966.

Durgnat, Raymond. *The Crazy Mirror: Hollywood Comedy and the American Image.* New York: Horizon Press, 1970.

Feibleman, James K. *In Praise of Comedy.* New York: Horizon Press, 1970.

Fernandez, Ramon. *Molière: The Man Seen Through the Plays.* New York: Hill and Wang, 1958.

Fox, Charles Philip, and Tom Parkinson. *The Circus in America.* Waukesha, Wisconsin: Country Beautiful, 1969.

Gazeau, M. A. *Les Bouffons.* Paris: Libraire Hachette, 1882.

Grock. *Grock: Life's a Lark.* 1931. Reprint. New York: Benjamin Blom, 1969.

Hodges, C. Walter. *Shakespeare's Theater.* New York: Coward-McCann, 1964.

————. *Shakespeare and the Players.* London: G. Bell and Sons, 1973.

————. *Playhouse Tales.* London: G. Bell and Sons, 1974.

Hornby, John. *Clowns Through the Ages.* London: Oliver & Boyd, 1962.

Jenkins, Alan C. *Circuses Through the Ages.* London: Chatto, Boyd & Oliver, 1972.

Kahn, E. J., Jr. *The Merry Partners: The Age and Stage of Harrigan and Hart.* New York: Random House, 1955.

Keaton, Buster. *My Wonderful World of Slapstick.* New York: Doubleday, 1960.

Kelly, Emmett, with F. Beverly Kelley. *Clown.* New York: Prentice-Hall, 1954.

Kerr, Walter. *Tragedy and Comedy.* New York: Simon and Schuster, 1967.

———. *The Silent Clowns.* New York: Knopf, 1975.

Kronenberger, Louis. *The Thread of Laughter.* New York: Knopf, 1952.

Lahue, Kalton C., and Samuel Gill. *Clown Princes and Court Jesters.* London: Thomas Yoseloff, 1970.

McCabe, John. *Mr. Laurel and Mr. Hardy.* New York: Grosset and Dunlap, 1966.

McKechnie, Samuel. *Popular Entertainments Through the Ages.* New York: Benjamin Blom, 1969.

McNamara, Brooks. *Step Right Up.* Garden City, N.Y.: Doubleday, 1976.

Maltin, Leonard. *Movie Comedy Teams.* New York: Signet, 1970.

Mander, Raymond, and Joe Mitchenson. *Pantomime.* London: Peter Davies, 1973.

Mast, Gerald. *The Comic Mind.* Indianapolis: Bobbs-Merrill, 1973.

Mayer, David. *Harlequin in His Element: The English Pantomime, 1806–1836.* Cambridge, Massachusetts: Harvard University, 1969.

Meredith, George. *An Essay on Comedy.* New York: Scribners, 1897.

Nagler, A. M. *A Source Book in Theatrical History.* New York: Dover Publications, 1952.

Nicoll, Allardyce. *Masks, Mimes and Miracles.* 1931. Reprint. New York: Cooper Square, 1963.

———. *The World of Harlequin: A Critical Study of the Commedia dell'Arte.* Cambridge: University Press, 1963.

Niklaus, Thelma. *Harlequin, or The Rise and Fall of a Bergamask Rogue.* New York: George Braziller, 1956.

Poliakoff, Nicolai. *Coco the Clown: By Himself.* London: Dent and Sons, 1940.

Popov, Oleg. *Russian Clown.* London: McDonald, 1970.

Quigley, Isabel. *Charlie Chaplin: Early Comedies.* New York: Dutton, 1968.

Robinson, David. *Buster Keaton.* Bloomington: Indiana University Press, 1969.

Smith, Cecil. *Musical Comedy in America.* New York: Theatre Arts, 1950.

Taylor, Robert Lewis. *W. C. Fields: His Follies and Fortunes.* New York: Doubleday, 1949.

Towsen, John H. *Clowns.* New York: Hawthorn, 1976.

Walker, "Whimsical." *From Sawdust to Windsor Castle.* London: Stanley Paul, 1922.

Welsford, Enid. *The Fool: His Social and Literary History.* 1935. Reprint. London: Faber and Faber, 1968.

Wood, J. Hickory. *Dan Leno.* London: Methuen, 1905.

INDEX